TECHNOCRACY VERSUS DEMOCRACY

TECHNOCRACY VERSUS DEMOCRACY

The Comparative Politics of International Airports

ELLIOT J. FELDMAN
Brandeis University

JEROME MILCH
University of Pittsburgh

with a foreword by
THEODORE J. LOWI

Auburn House Publishing Company
Boston, Massachusetts

Written under the auspices of the Center for International Affairs, Harvard University, and the University Consortium for Research on North America, a partnership of Brandeis, Harvard, and Tufts Universities, and The Fletcher School of Law and Diplomacy.

Library of Congress Cataloging in Publication Data

Feldman, Elliot J.
    Technocracy versus democracy.

    Includes index.
    1. International airports.   I. Milch, Jerome E.,
1945–   .   II. Title.
TL726.15.F44 387.7′362   81-17671
ISBN 0-86569-063-4   AACR2

Printed in the United States of America

To Anita and Lily

Foreword

PUBLIC WORKS AND
THE PUBLIC'S WORK

The island of St. Martin is almost certainly unique in the world. This tiny postage-stamp paradise in the Caribbean is an international territory, half Dutch and half French, with two official governments, two official languages, and two official currencies. There is even an international border, marked by official road signs. The one thing it lacks to make it two completely separate states is customs barriers. Consequently, citizens and tourists live, travel, and work without hindrance, and the island has become a single economy.

However, there are some differences in the level of economic development, the important manifestation of which is the international Queen Juliana Airport, which was built by the Dutch on their side of the island. It was the pride of Queen Juliana herself, who often vacationed in St. Maarten (the Dutch spelling). The French side of the island is just as dependent upon Queen Juliana as is the Dutch side, and the French are not unaware of the nationality of the airport. Charles de Gaulle refused to visit St. Martin because his flight from Guadeloupe would have depended upon the Dutch airport in the entirely different political principality of St. Maarten. President Valéry Giscard d'Estaing was only slightly less nationalistic. Although he enjoyed visiting the neighboring Martinique and Guadeloupe, he, too, refused to visit St. Martin. On a rare visit by one of his ministers in the early 1970s, it was necessary for the French to arrange the visit by a flight on a very small one-engine plane into a tiny landing strip on the French side of the island. The military contingent accompanying the minister (as part of a 14th of July ceremony) had to be flown in by helicopters.

Although the French are probably hyperpatriotic (*chauvinism* is a French word), they are certainly not unique in seeing an international airport as a symbol of power and status for a nation and for the city in whose metropolitan fringe the airport is located. An international airport is a symbol of accomplishment and of ability to plan large projects. But it is not an empty symbol. Its location has a profound influence on the metropolis, the region, and—through that—the national economy. It influences the level of economic activity as well as the direction of development. Planners assume a 5:1 ratio between direct investment in an airport and the secondary and tertiary investment following therefrom.

It is no wonder, therefore, that the public—even in a highly capitalist society—asserts an interest in its airports. There are ample incentives for free, private enterprise to build airports, yet there are no free enterprise international airports. An investment of $100 million to $200 million is not beyond development syndicates, and an airport is not a public good, since its services and benefits are quite divisible through user charges and real estate value improvements. Nevertheless, they are *public* works.

There is no mystery about any of this. International airports simply fit into a long tradition of public enterprise. The public, in some form or another, has always intervened where important land-use decisions are made. Disposition of royal domain is not far removed from the modern use of eminent domain, a power considered inherent in all modern governments, including those that are distinctly non-royal. There is a public claim on all private property, most likely to be exercised when a strategic decision is going to have a large and long-standing influence on the use of land. An airport is modern only in the technology that made the airport necessary; otherwise, it is indistinguishable from roads, bridges, canals and harbors, chateau-forts and cathedrals, universities and marketplaces. As a public work, each was intended to have an influence on civic virtue as well as economic incentive.

However, countries do differ in their approach to public works and land-use decisions, and these differences are very meaningful. Given their importance for the polity and the economy, these decisions, when appropriately analyzed, can reveal a great deal about the character of government and politics in a country. Study of such decisions in several countries at comparable moments of economic development is an appropriate method for teasing out political and economic patterns that are universal, in contrast to those that are bound by culture.

Doing the Public's Work: Three Case Histories

Three personalized sketches of famous public works exploits will provide a historical backdrop for the contemporaneous cases analyzed systematically in the pages to come. The first two are from the Paris and New York of the 1850s. They begin with the Bois de Boulogne and Central Park and the two men (Georges Haussmann and Frederick Law Olmsted) who through their public works did so much to shape permanently these two cities. The third is a sketch of one man whose special place in New York City for thirty years is an institutional and conceptual link between the 1950s and the present.

Georges Haussmann—Servant of the State. Haussmann, an Alsatian Protestant, descendant of moderately successful textile manufacturers, was diverted to public service by the Revolution. Young Haussmann studied law because it was the most exciting profession in a new republic, but his sights were on the army or public service. Eventually he chose the prefectorial corps because it came under the Ministry of the Interior, where his family had some influence. Haussmann spent twenty years in prefectorial service in cities all over France before attaining the top post, Prefect of the Seine, in 1853.

Because of its long record of violence, Paris had a unique form of government. Its municipal council was not elected but was nominated by the Minister of the Interior on recommendation of the Prefect. There was no mayor; the executive powers of the mayoralty (and far more than that) were held by the Prefect of the Seine, a département of which Paris was the major component. To keep the Prefect of the Seine from equaling the head of state himself, Napoleon I split the powers over the city into two parts: Control of *things* went to the Prefect of the Seine; control over *people* went to an equal, the Prefect of Police.

In Paris the Prefect worked directly with the head of State, who in 1853 was Louis Napoleon. Elected President following the Revolution of 1848, he took absolute power in 1851 by *coup d'état* and had himself proclaimed Emperor Napoleon III in 1852. Louis Napoleon governed to a great extent by plebiscite and sought

popular recognition by posing as something of a "sentimental socialist." He had well defined and energetic ideas about the rebuilding of Paris, and he had the commitment necessary to see
them through. Haussmann was his choice. The perfect servant
of the State, Haussmann had no independent taste but a strong
sense of order and form. Sometimes his decisions were contrived
and artificial, but the results were substantial because he was able
to balance the aesthetic preferences of Napoleon III with the
technical requisites of his excellent engineers and architects. He
was also able to balance the military requirements of the defense
of Paris, through arterials and plazas, with the political requisites
of mob control, through slum clearance and deconcentration of
the poor.

Haussmann, drawing directly from Napoleon III, rebuilt Paris
by making decisions in the name of France and imposing them
on the government of the city of Paris. The rebuilding began with
the Bois de Boulogne, within days of Haussmann's appointment
in 1853. But that was a mere beginning. Haussmann proceeded
with the construction of les Halles, the central market with great
iron and glass pavilions inspired by French railway construction
(which had also inspired the Impressionist painters). Haussmann
went on from there to an even more ambitious success, the completion of the first *grande croissée*, an uninterrupted "highway"
east-west from Boulogne to Vincennes (rue de Rivoli) and north-
south (Sebastopol–St. Michel), and in the process removed the
ugly and politically dangerous slums around the Louvre and on
the Ile de la Cité which had defied even the great Napoleon I.
Haussmann designed and built the Boulevard St. Germain, which
completed a task that Napoleon I had been unable to complete.
He rebuilt and vastly extended the famous sewers of Paris (obsolete at the time of their sanctification by Victor Hugo), and he
freed most of Paris from dependence on the Seine for drinking
water. Finally, Haussmann designed and built most of the Etoile,
one of whose seven spokes bears the famous Prefect's name, Boulevard Haussmann. The Etoile set the pattern which dominated
Paris's subsequent physical development.

For seventeen years Haussmann governed one great central
city as perhaps no other regime—monarch or planning commission—has ever governed any Western democracy. He was a person
of uncommon administrative talent, extraordinary dedication and
incorruptible character who enjoyed the confidence of an almost

unassailable chief of state during a political era which, especially in France, combined great sentiments about democracy with great fear of people in the mass. Haussmann's power rested upon the power of the state, the power of an emperor who sought centralization, and the power of a national bureaucracy—not just any bureaucracy, but the bureaucracy of the Interior Ministry with its prefectorial corps. Haussmann's own self-designation captures as well as any the base of power for the public's land-use policy decisions of that period: "A democrat, and very liberal, but nonetheless authoritarian."

Frederick Law Olmsted—Aristocratic Amateur. The 1850s were also the beginning of an era of important public land-use decisions in New York City. In 1853, the year of Haussmann's appointment, the New York State Legislature authorized the City of New York (which until 1898 was little more than Manhattan Island) to acquire land for a large, centrally located park. Until less than twenty years earlier, much of the land in question had been in the public domain; but important land-use decisions by the political parties controlling City Hall at that time provided for the subdivision and sale of these lands to private interests, at great short-run profit to the land speculators with inside information. Out of these very sales arose the concept of "honest graft"—profit that comes not from illegal transactions such as bribery but from the advantage of knowing something a few days or a few hours before everyone else. The reacquisition of these properties in the 1850s meant that still another group at City Hall would realize another round of profit-taking. By 1857 there was no progress toward park development except the land acquisition itself, because no provision had been made for park management. Discovery of the scandalous waste of at least five million dollars led the State Legislature (with its heavy Republican majority) to impose on the city a new board of commissioners for the park, composed of eleven members chosen from the three great factions, Tammany Democrats, Reform Democrats, and Republicans. Two upper-class Reform Democrats served respectively as President and Treasurer.

This board selected Frederick Law Olmsted to be Superintendent of Central Park. Olmsted was a literary man with many acquaintances and modest fame but no direct experience managing large enterprises or planning and building parks. As his biographer put it, "Nothing in his record—a farmer who had not made his farm pay, a writer who had made nothing but reputation, a publisher who had gone bankrupt—suggested his capacities." Scion of a reasonably wealthy Mayflower family, Olmsted was basically self-educated. He tried his hand at the family farm and business before striking out on a career in journalism and publishing. Although his travels around Europe had made him a great admirer of parks, especially those of London, and although he knew and loved the land, he probably wrote more about the sea or about movement across land than about stationary developments of land itself. Nevertheless, support and sponsorship of his candidacy for Superintendent of Central Park came from such luminaries as Asa Gray, Peter Cooper, Washington Irving, Horace Greeley, William Cullen Bryant, and August Belmont.

The original plan for Central Park, having languished so long, was almost immediately terminated in favor of open, public competition for what was to be New York's largest public works project. Olmsted, already installed as Superintendent, himself entered the competition for the new design with a collaborator, London-born architect Calvert Vaux. Their plan was chosen over thirty-two others and was the beginning of a collaboration between the two men which literally provided the leadership for the parks movement in the United States.

Upon Olmsted's accession as Superintendent, more than five hundred employees of the city were already working on Central Park. They were organized in some fifteen work gangs, each with a foreman, or "boss laborer." It is from just such work gangs and boss laborers that the concept of political boss originates in the United States. The political parties had a profound interest in the construction of public works and were even willing to permit an upper-class reformer to build a central park because what went in was less important to them than what came out. But Central Park was a great Tammany haven. Tammany leaders and their capitalist fellow travelers were the chief beneficiaries of honest graft, and Tammany followers got the jobs. The city at large was a beneficiary also, because public works made the city an employer of last resort. Unlike Paris, New York City never has had an experience with revolution. But it has been a city of violence, fed by the unrest of unemployment. In the decade preceding the Olmsted appointment, between one and two million immigrants flowed into New York, and most of them remained. The machines were built on this flotsam and jetsam and performed a service as a kind of employment agency. But the parties could not have flourished unless the rest of the citizens saw parks and other such developments as a contribution to city spirit. As Robert Moses was to say frequently during his long reign over the public works in New York City in the twentieth century, "As long as you are on the side of parks, you are on the side of the angels."

Thus New York City provided boldly for public works, because such projects were an important basis for cooperation between political parties that controlled the city government and corporate factions that controlled the city economy. Central Park was one great achievement of architecture and politics, for which much credit in both respects goes to Olmsted, who was able to provide and maintain a stable linkage between machines and economic leaders. Yet, by his own choice, Olmsted did not move on from Central Park to other public works in New York City. Instead, he formed the partnership of Olmsted, Vaux and Company to practice the new profession of landscape architecture on a national scale. Theirs was a national clientèle, including private corporations and wealthy private individuals as well as city, state and federal governments.

Olmsted left a tremendously important mark on the face of the United States, but very little of it in New York City, as can be seen from a listing of his most famous accomplishments: Prospect Park in Brooklyn, Fairmont Park in Philadelphia, Riverside and Morningside Parks in New York City, Mount Royal Park in Montreal, the capitol grounds of Washington, D.C., Stanford University campus, the Chicago World's Fair and South Park in Chicago, the University of California in Berkeley, and Yosemite National Park. His clientèle in the private sector included Mariposa Mining Estates in California and the Boston and Albany Railroad Company.

Olmsted's New York is more than just an ocean and a culture apart from Haussmann's Paris. Olmsted's authority was based exclusively upon the convenience of the political parties and the strength of their coalition with local capitalists. Haussmann's authority was the authority of the state, and his strength was that of a political dictatorship and a strong national bureaucracy, dealing with a city made vulnerable by its participation in a communal, violent uprising. Yet, in a peculiar way, Haussmann has more in common than Olmsted with contemporary experience in the United States, as well as France and elsewhere. This is not to say that Olmsted has been forgotten or rejected. But although Olmsted has many admirers, Haussmann is the hero among planners and designers of public works. For example, historian John Reps reports that the index to Daniel Burnham's plan for the City of Chicago at the beginning of the twentieth century contains more references to Haussmann than to any other subject except the City of Chicago itself. Up to a point, Haussmann is the more modern of the two because his Paris is, up to a point, a triumph of technology and administration. But only up to a point, because little of Haussman's Paris would have come to pass without the underlying support of the dictatorship. Could technology and administration have done it alone? An upper-class reformer like Olmsted went very far with civic spirit; all over the United States there is evidence of its effectiveness. But civic spirit alone could not rebuild a single city.

Robert Moses—Power Broker. Robert Moses is probably the only figure in American history who can compare even distantly with Georges Haussmann. Moses, the son of a Jewish business family from New Haven, was educated at Yale, took a Master's degree at Oxford and completed a Ph.D. in political science at Columbia. Though he had literary tastes and wrote occasionally for literary magazines, his specialty—and his passion—was public administration.

Moses's first job was as a municipal investigator for the privately financed Bureau of Municipal Research, 1913–1918. He worked for a year for the New York State Association, a reform-oriented, privately endowed group concerned with state government. He attracted the attention of soon-to-be governor Al Smith and rose to be his Chief of Staff. Smith later appointed him President of the Long Island State Park Commission in 1924, a job he held until 1963, with a brief diversion in 1927–1928 as secretary of state (of New York) and as Republican candidate for governor in 1934 (beaten badly by Herbert Lehman). His success with project after project drew other jobs his way, until his curriculum vitae equaled that of the Mikado's Grand Pooh Bah.

The following is a list of important public positions to which Robert Moses was appointed as the sole or most important official (with the dates of appointment and retirement). Note well that he held most of these jobs simultaneously: Jones Beach State Parkway Authority (1933–1963); Bethpage Park Authority (1933–1963); Henry Hudson Parkway Authority (1934–1938);

Marine Parkway Authority (1934–1938); Chairman and Chief Executive of the Triborough Bridge and Tunnel Authority (1934–1968); Park Commissioner of the City of New York (1934–1960); Member, New York City Planning Commission (1942–1960); New York City Construction Coordinator (1946–1960); Member, Long Island Railroad Commission (1950); Chairman, Power Authority of the State of New York (1954–1963); President, New York World's Fair (1964–1965). He also served as Chairman of many other commissions, temporary commissions, and a number of important honorary and civic groups.

The list of public works accomplishments attributable to Robert Moses in New York City alone is as impressive as Haussmann's list in Paris: nine major bridges, including Henry Hudson, Throg's Neck, Bronx-Whitestone, Brooklyn-Battery, Triborough, and Verrazano-Narrows; scores of miles of expressways and parkways, including Harlem River Drive, Deegan and Cross Bronx Expressways, Grand Central, Bronx River, and Northern State Boulevard Parkways; most of the important modern parks in the city and on Long Island; an impressive assortment of public works structures, including Jones Beach, Coop City, Shea Stadium, United Nations headquarters, the Coliseum, and Lincoln Center; several of New York's most important public, semi-public, and private housing developments; and a number of major New York dams that provide the city and state with their electrical power.

Robert Moses was in effect Prefect of the State of New York— or at least of Long Island and New York City. Yet, if anything is more striking than the individual accomplishments of Robert Moses himself, it was the number of separate organizations and offices involved. There was essentially one agency for each major accomplishment or sector or region where public works were to be built. It was of course remarkable that one person chaired so many organizations, but the fact is that each organization had its own separate bureaucracy, its own separate constituency, its own legal authority, its own relationship to higher governmental authority, and its own set of financial resources. Each project or cluster of related projects seems to have been a government in itself.

Governors and mayors were drawn to Robert Moses because he had talent for bringing public officials and party leaders together with banks and other large financial interests to build strategic public works—works that influence regions. Beginning with parks, it was not a large step to park*ways* (limited-access arterial highways in less dense populations that facilitate escape from cities). From there it was not very far to step toward bridges and other access roads, and then to the expressways that require for their construction the removal of large numbers of persons and the displacement of enormous and costly amounts of urban property. In the 1920s Moses had the support of a strong government and a strong political party system. But that would only explain, if anything, his initial success on Long Island. By the time Moses became involved in New York City, Jimmy Walker had been forced out as mayor, Tammany Hall was in a shambles, and the anti-Tammany Republican reformer Fiorello La Guardia had been elected. Yet, it was La Guardia who started Moses on his life as the Prefect of New York City; Moses never had nor sought a party base for his political power. Mayors and governors reappointed Moses to the positions he held and offered additional positions to him because they needed him, not the other way around. As Robert Caro, the author of the great biographical study of Robert Moses, put the case, "What Moses had succeeded in doing, really, was to replace graft with benefits that could be derived with legality from a public works project. He had succeeded in centralizing in his projects—and to a remarkable extent in his own person—all those forces which are not in theory supposed to, but which in practice do, play a decisive role in political decisions." (*The Power Broker*, p. 18). The only thing wrong with Caro's observation is that he makes it appear to be new to the twentieth century or unique to Robert Moses. Graft was never the important magnet, it was "honest graft." And what were those forces that Moses centralized around himself?

There is no mystery about these forces, even though specific agents are often extremely difficult to identify. First, there is an extremely strong interest in what are called the primary economic benefits: direct capital gains, sought in particular by banks, realty companies, insurance companies, and investment houses. Secondary benefits include underwriting fees, building and sales contracts, specialty service contracts, and associated jobs. Tertiary benefits include long-range investment opportunities, new business and new populations—in sum, growth.

But the forces are not only economic. Economic forces are necessary, but they are insufficient without the political. Political forces can never build a bridge or an airport, but they can keep all these things from being built, no matter how much economic incentive there may be. Political interest in public works includes distribution of opportunities to share in the economic interests, especially the secondary and tertiary benefits. Political interest includes credit with constituents for growth. Political incentive includes pride in that growth and in having improved the quality of life in the area affected by the public work—in short, immortality, which motivates many political people far more than economic access. One can understand a person like Moses only from these multiple perspectives.

Nothing was new about the talents of Robert Moses or the forces he was able to harness for public works. What was new was the pattern. Each project was an autonomous whole. Its design or siting may have been part of some larger plan, but each project was itself the result of a coalition of economic and political interests through and around Robert Moses, in his capacity as head of the agency, commission or authority. His power was their need for him to serve as conduit or linchpin, catalyst or middleman, contract agent or coat-holder. For purposes of the particular project, each coalition was then a syndicate of mixed interests and incentives, and each was solemnized by legislative authorization in a formal office and agency, a matter on which Moses was particularly meticulous.

Replacing the Emperor

This last point is of immense importance. The legislature was as important to Moses as the emperor was to Haussmann. A legislative mandate is more legitimate than an emperor's command, and in the right hands a legislative authorization is just as efficient. Each Moses agency was given explicit jurisdiction, and each was given a general grant of eminent domain: to seize private property for a public purpose. For Moses, the legislature went beyond the norm by giving his agencies "quick-take" or "appropriation" powers. In a normal eminent domain proceeding, the agency condemns a piece of property, offers the owner a price, and then bargains with the owner for a "fair price," after which the owner vacates the premises. Under an "appropriation" authorization, the agency can seize the property first, clear it, incorporate it into the public works, then bargain after the fact with the *former* owner. The legislature also provided each Moses agency with a certain amount of autonomy by permitting it to finance itself through the sale of bonds. Moses had very few of the problems of getting neighborhood consent that so plague contemporary agencies, because for him consent came from the legislature, not from the people. Rarely was there a need to hold elaborate hearings or a referendum to approve bond issues. In the great era of public works, especially in the 1950s and 1960s, the implicit assumption appears to have been that there was a Paretean calculus at work, whereby as long as public works were seen to contribute to the general welfare and growth of the regional product, almost everybody was gaining something, albeit different amounts, while nobody could be shown to be losing anything.

If the legislative mandate helps to explain Moses, the changing place of the legislature helps explain his decline, and why he is a transition into, rather than the beginning of, the modern era of public works. Moses is not the tragic story of the man who planted the seeds of his own destruction. In fact, Moses had great power to the very end. Moses helped create the institutional pattern that will last long after him and has already spread far beyond his theater of operations.

The most extreme and stable expression of that pattern is probably the Port Authority of New York and New Jersey, a perennial competitor of Moses. Founded in 1921 as the Port of New York Authority, it foundered for years over a narrow interpretation of its legislative mandate, which was to integrate the Port of New York with existing and new transportation facilities, presumably railroads. The Port Authority began to prosper only when it discovered its true constituency: highway users. From that discovery, it moved from one success to another, based upon the very broad and indeterminate legislative mandate it received from the New York and New Jersey legislatures and Congress (because of the need for an interstate compact). It successes were no longer based upon specific legislative authorization but rather upon the support of the *users* and the consent of the bondholders. Responsibility therefore went to the bondholders, rather than the legislature, the citizens *or* the users. This transfer of responsibility is especially true of revenue bonds that finance particular revenue-producing public works; and it is all the more true of state-related public works projects because of the provision in the U.S. Constitution, Article I, Section 10, explicitly forbidding states or agents of the state from impairing the obligations of contracts. In other words, once a state or local authority sells bonds to finance a new project, accountability passes to the bondholders. The authority is under obligation to be profitable and, because of Article I, Section 9, it was forbidden from taking on any project, such as mass transit, if the probability of a deficit were high.

Consent, therefore, came to be based upon a favorable ratio of costs to benefits for each and every public works project. The ratio could be demonstrated more systematically and credibly for those public works based on user charges, but cost-benefit ratios nevertheless were also the basis for consent for other public works. Thus, without a dictator, without a capitalist upper class, without political machines, without specific legislative consent, and without a great Bureaucratic Entrepreneur like Moses, consent could nevertheless be generated—and it was. It was generated by research and careful documentation by experts on the relationship between the costs and the benefits of each project. This calculus takes a thousand different forms, but in each instance it is generated out of the research, the formulas, and the assumptions of experts—identified not as personalities but by credentials.

Some of these experts are in the agencies set up to make public works. They are career bureaucrats, or technocrats. Some of the experts are in the public and private agencies set up to invest in public works. Some of the experts are in large and small corporations who intend to use the facilities. A few of these experts are free-floating professionals in universities and non-profit organizations available to all contending parties on a fee-for-service basis. Some experts are available on a non-paying basis for civic spirited groups, usually those which rise to oppose the coming of a large project.

Although experts use similar methods, they can differ in the extreme on their conclusions because of different assumptions, different weightings, different formulas and different values, even if the data available to all sides are identical. Some differences among experts are honest. Some differences are distinctly not honest but are motivated by the outcomes desired by their employers. Experts are, alas, for hire. But this can be a blessing in disguise, because conflicting conclusions and recommendations give citizens more direct opportunities to enter into the process of decision making on public works. Moreover, since it is rare for officials to be as confident as Robert Moses about the popularity of the project they favor, they often (much more often now than in the past) seek a public constituency. Never mind that this public will not remain the constituency after the project is built, consent and accountability will still focus on the relationship between the agency and the financing community. But increasingly the public does count at the time when the most crucial decisions are made about justifying the project, justifying the upfront financing, and especially justifying the forcible removal of hundreds (sometimes thousands) of property owners.

The relationship between the expert and the public is becoming more crucial, more intimate, and more complex than anything that the theory of democratic government could possibly have anticipated. Ironically, at the same time, great personalities are disappearing. There is no Georges Haussmann or Robert Moses, but only a cadre of faceless technocrats. There is no plebiscite for a bonapartist dictator or a dramatic grant of authority from him to a prominent public official. There is no dramatic legislative grant to a prominent bureaucrat/politician. There is instead a broad legislative delegation of authority to a type of role player and a methodology, and to a procedure involving a modified plebiscite project by project.

From Parkways to Airways

The construction of a large international airport is one of the great modern public works in which this relationship developed and can best be seen for all of its dramatic interplay. In such a complex public project, there are many role players other than the expert and concerned citizen. All the traditional economic and political forces identified earlier around Robert Moses and still earlier around Georges Haussmann or Frederick Law Olmsted are still at work in their own way. But the new element—the element which puts all the traditional forces into special context—is the expert and the relationship between the expert and the immediate public. We neglect this relationship, in theory or practice, only to our peril.

By such a long and circuitous route have we reached this marvelous book by Elliot Feldman and Jerome Milch. In these pages I have written mainly about a rich but dead past. They are writing about the future. But, alas, we are living our future now. Their work is governed by the assumption that the building of large public works is the most important deliberate governmental act shaping cities and that a single public work can shape a city permanently. Where options narrow in the central cities, the focus of public action turns to the metropolitan fringe. Recognizing that, the authors focused on the single largest type of public work in the metropolitan fringe, the international airport. Here is a public decision large enough to deserve careful study for its own sake, yet by that very fact is an opening to the very core of a nation's political process—how that nation sets its priorities and how it distributes its costs and its benefits. This study of the politics, economics, and technology of eight international airports in five countries is probably the most ambitious cross-national policy analysis ever undertaken. Many books have studied institutions and policies across several countries. The best example for policy analysts is probably Andrew Shonfield's *Modern Capitalism*. But leaving aside the fact that Shonfield's book is now woefully out-of-date, it does not go too deeply into specific cases of policy or policy making. Other cross-cutting books, such as Harold Wilensky's *The Welfare State and Equality*, stay at the aggregate level and do not get very far into the politics or the political economy of modern nation-states. For that, real actors, real decisions and real relationships have to be carefully observed in several countries within the context of comparable cases. Other studies have looked at the interaction of technology and politics, the most effective probably being Nelson's *The Moon and the Ghetto*. But with all his insight, Nelson looks briefly at only three cases, all in the United States.

Feldman and Milch have maintained their discourse at the level of Shonfield and Nelson and have added flesh-and-blood case studies in five industrial states. Since the policy-making case study is not a form of political science preferred by Europeans or Canadians, Feldman and Milch would be serving all of us well if they had published their accounts of the decisions in Italy, France, Britain, Canada, and the United States without attempting anything theoretical at all. But they have. They present fundamental, and occasionally controversial, theoretical insights in several substantive areas of great relevance to all students of modern industrial states.

One such area of especially important insights is the politics of land use in each of the separate countries. The political analysis of land-use decisions is very scanty in the United States and virtually nonexistent elsewhere. Another area where they have developed important insights is that of the interaction among various types of modern role players in policy making. Their analysis of the interactions between economists, other technicians, bureaucrats and politicians equals any work that has been done up to now, and they have the added advantage of data from several countries. Their five-country critique of the use and abuse of outside consultants alone makes the book worth reading.

Still another area in which they have made an important contribution is that of the involvement of citizen participation in public works decisions. A great deal of research on citizen participation has been done during the last ten or twelve years, but Feldman and Milch have brought new insights to existing work and have opened up some entirely new avenues of inquiry. Close field studies of support groups and opposition groups surrounding eight airports in five countries provide a unique data base for the evaluation of the interaction of technology with politics.

This leads to still another important dimension of the book: evaluation of the influence of culture versus institutions in shaping policy choices. This theme cuts through the entire book, giving continuity to the many discrete case studies and at the same time confirming the importance of the case study method in comparative politics.

One final area of concern tends to tie together all the rest. This is the question of planning and the prospects of democratic planning. Feldman and Milch have quite properly entitled their work *Technocracy versus Democracy.* That is the future we are living. We simply don't know the outcome of the struggle.

If we are living our future now, are we also living the future of the next generation? Is it possible that our bold choices are taking up their options as well as ours? How much future does one generation have a right to live? It was the conservative Edmund Burke who argued that generations yet unborn have rights. The time may already be late for balancing the rights of our descendants against the conceits of contemporary democracy and science.

To call big plans, big projects, and big technologies "conceits" is not to denounce them but to raise questions about them, questions that politicians, engineers, economists, and other technocrats are least likely to ask. They are questions also not being asked of or by the softer social sciences and philosophy, but should be. The bigger the public project, the closer it encounters fundamental questions about the nature of a good society and how it might be attained by good government.

Technocracy versus Democracy is not a book of social or political philosophy; it is a careful and responsible account of facts about technocrats and politicians that attempts to lift these facts to the level where discourse about basic values can begin. The authors boldly attempt to answer all the empirical questions with fresh data, a multi-country context, and some concluding propositions that at last bring political factors into play with economic and technical ones. For the still larger issues of technocracy versus democracy the book does not hold out solutions, because there are no solutions as such. Fundamental political problems, such as the adjustment of democracy to technocracy, are not like puzzles. What Feldman and Milch have done at this level is to contribute to the proper posing of the question. As one seventeenth century thinker put it, ". . . in the Solution of Questions, the Maine Matter was the well-stating of them; which requires mother-witt, & Logick . . . ; for let the question be but well-stated, it will worke almost of itselfe."

THEODORE J. LOWI
John L. Senior Professor of
American Government, Cornell University

ACKNOWLEDGMENTS

We are grateful to more than 300 interview respondents who gave of their time and knowledge, often more than once and usually with exceptional generosity. They are not listed here because we have chosen to protect confidentiality. They include spokesmen, attorneys, and members from more than a score of citizen groups; they include citizens whose property was expropriated and public officials responsible for expropriation. Professional appraisers and private consultants spent hours explaining their procedures to us. The presidents and vice-presidents of eight airlines, the chief executive officers of airport authorities, and many people from the staffs of civil aviation agencies and the industry answered our questions. So did ministers, deputy ministers, and directors-general of ministries and government agencies. Although our text rarely cites them, they are the basis of this study. Without their cooperation this book would not exist. We may sound more sympathetic to some than to others in our assessment of their positions and views, but we found justice on all sides.

A study of this scope and duration requires many types of help. We enjoyed the hospitality of friends and relatives in different cities, and they often provided contacts that directly furthered our work. In London we benefitted especially from the kindness of Alison Brimelow, Tom and Jean Gardner, Phoebe Lambert, Scott Russell, and Elizabeth and Richard Simon. At various times they housed us, took our phone calls, scheduled appointments, and led us to the doorstep of central political officials.

The Italian portion of the study involved a team of extraordinarily able and devoted graduate research assistants. Essential contributions were made by Lynne Bantle, Scott Dennis, Tom Eshelman, Kevin Kramer, Per-Henrik Mansson, and Dominique Prat. They worked together so effectively that two of them met on this project and married. They also produced data at which Italian social scientists have marveled.

Maxine Ramirez de Arellano provided invaluable help with this study in Rome, and Guiseppe Fassina and Riccardo Pirola of the Società Esercizi Aeroportuali were particularly generous with knowledge and guidance. Most of all, we want to thank Elda Stifani and her family, for they provided the whole Italian team with hospitality and Elda proved herself a tenacious and irreplaceable resource.

Key help in Montreal came from Kevin O'Shea and Michael Stein. Our kind hosts in New York were Irwin and Lea Polk, and we are particularly grateful to Don Stevenson for contributions to the study in Toronto that well exceeded any obligations of his public position.

In Paris we benefited from a combination of friends and active helpers. Jean-Louis and Angeline Bourlanges were wonderful hosts, developed contacts for us, made appointments, and helped with correspondence. Sabine Arrighi served as an invaluable coordinating secretary. We enjoyed hospitality and wise counsel also from Jean-Paul and Michelle Bailly, Sylvia Duchacek, and Violette Delhaye. Jean-Yves Delhaye was of vital help, and Annick Percheron was especially resourceful when we encountered particular problems in data-gathering. Robert Espérou was unfailingly kind and wise.

Mike and Rhoda Goldberg, and Gordon and Lucy Stead have been wonderful friends and keen contributors to this effort in Vancouver. We are also grateful to Maurice Levi for long and thoughtful discussions there, and to Cheri Nataros who served us with a fine seriousness of purpose as a research assistant.

We also have had considerable help in preparing the manuscript. Paul Rulison has proved himself an excellent research assistant and a promising scholar in his own right. He has helped us with the final details, often from questions raised by astute and critical readers. Portions of the manuscript have been read by Ronald Brickman, Richard de Neufville, Mark Hulliung, Peter Katzenstein, Bert Rockman, David Rosenbloom, and Fred Whelan. Dorothy Nelkin and Douglas Ashford read most of the manuscript in draft while providing us steady encouragement over the years. The whole manuscript was read by Seyom Brown, Tom Ilgen, Otto Keck, Christopher Leman, Theodore J. Lowi, and Gordon Stead. Each has provided us with criticisms and comments, and although mistakes surely remain they have saved us from many. In addition, we want to thank Alan Altshuler, Ezra

Suleiman, and Sidney Tarrow, who have followed this project from the early stages and have been generous with their ideas and counsel.

Portions of the manuscript have been presented at various times, and in various forms, over the years of this project. We are grateful to forums at the American Political Science Association, the University of Massachusetts (Amherst), MIT, The Centre for Transportation Studies at the University of British Columbia, the Canadian Political Science Association, the Institute of Air Transport (Paris), the Abbotsford International Air Show in British Columbia, Cornell University, the University of Bari, the University of Naples, Milan's Politecnico, Harvard University's Seminar in Comparative Politics at the Center for International Affairs, and the Northeast Political Science Association for invitations that have made it possible to present our ideas to different audiences.

The Fondazione Luigi Einaudi in Torino provided the study a home in Italy, and the Harvard University Center for International Affairs has provided a home for the preparation of the book for several years. During that time Sally Cox, David Maxson, Grant Hammond, Ben Brown, Peter Jacobsohn, Ray Vernon, and Sam Huntington have helped us in many different ways. The Center is an exceptionally good place to pursue scholarly work.

The Center for International Affairs is a member of, and the administrative center for, the University Consortium for Research on North America. The Consortium has provided support services for the preparation of this volume, and its scholars have provided constant insight into the problems of central concern to us. The Consortium's coordinator, Leonie Gordon, faithfully typed much of the manuscript and supervised its dissemination to various readers. Stephanie Newburgh completed the manuscript preparation.

No single scholar has been more generous to both of us than Ted Lowi. His constant encouragement is an important reason why this research was done and this book was written.

This study cost far less than most efforts of this scale, but it still was expensive. We had to travel to each of the sites, and we had to spend quantities of time in each place. Separated during most of the writing of the book, we probably helped Ma Bell delay raising long distance telephone rates. We bore much of the expenses ourselves, but we did receive support from outside at critical times. The Penrose Fund of the American Philosophical Society provided a grant that facilitated some travel in Europe.

The Società Esercizi Aeroportuali of Milan provided a grant that supported the graduate assistants working on the Italian site. The Western Societies Program and the Program on Science, Technology, and Society at Cornell University supplemented research expenses in Montreal, Toronto, New York, and Dallas–Fort Worth, and the Centre for Transportation Studies at the University of British Columbia financed most of the field research in Vancouver and in Ottawa. The German Marshall Fund of the United States granted one of us a fellowship that proved to be the turning point in the overall effort; we would not have been able to complete the study in its present form without the time provided by the Fund. We would not have been able to complete the book, however, without a Visiting Scholar appointment for one of us to the University Consortium for Research on North America. This latter grant afforded us our only extended opportunity to work together in the same place during the entire course of the project.

A question that we have been asked frequently is, *How did you do so many interviews in so many places? Who paid for all the travel and time involved?* We are all the more grateful to the programs that supported us because of the many that did not. Although we received contributions from six different foundations, agencies, and programs, only two exceeded $10,000 and one was only $500. We think we may have failed to communicate to some potential donors the political significance of airport development, in particular, and the utility of our methodology for social science more generally. Consequently, our extensive data bank, which exceeds in depth and often in breadth the products of research funded at literally millions of dollars, came as much from our own resources as from the resources of others. This study would have been completed at least two years earlier had we received more generous financial assistance. Nevertheless, we are confident this book will please those who helped us, and will communicate our message, finally, to those who did not.

When we first discussed this manuscript with John Harney, Dave Johnson, and Gene Bailey at Auburn House, their publishing program was not yet in place and our book was little more than a completed data set and an outline. Our gamble on a new press has paid off in a superb working relationship with dedicated and serious publishers; we are proud to be part of the prestigious list they have developed in a very short time, and we hope they will find their commitment to our book equally rewarding.

We are both blessed with wives who share our intellectual commitments and interests. They have endured with us the vicissitudes inevitable in a project that takes so long, and they have been unstintingly supportive. This book is rightly dedicated to them.

E. J. F.
J. M.

CONTENTS

Introduction   xxxvii

PART ONE
Comparative Politics and Comparative Policy   1

CHAPTER 1
The Evolution of a Study   3

Choosing the Technology   5
Choosing Political Systems and Cases   9
  Dallas–Fort Worth   11
  London   12
  Milan   13
  Montreal   14
  New York   16
  Paris   18
  Toronto   19
  Vancouver   21
Observations, Explanations, and Unsettled Problems   21
Choosing a Methodology   24
Framework of the Study   29

PART TWO
Technology and Policy   39

CHAPTER 2
The Technological Imperative   41

Formulating the Hypothesis   43
Common Strategies   46

Identifying the Problem   46
Choosing a Solution   49
Selecting a Site   51
Acquiring Land   54
Assessing the Technological Imperative   56
An Alternative Explanation   57
The Technological Imperative and the Business   60
    Mentality
Conclusion   62

CHAPTER 3
Forecasting and Policy Choice   67

Reliability and Utility   68
Inverted Pyramids   69
Theory   71
Practice   72
Explaining Errors   81
Common Assumptions   82
Fighting the Previous War   85
Hired Guns   86
Applications of Forecasting   89
Forecasting and Decision Making   90
Forecasting and Legitimacy   92
Conclusion   94

PART THREE
Planning and Policy   99

CHAPTER 4
Success, Failure, and Rational Planning   101

Rational Planning and Its Discontents   102
Conflict and Conflict Resolution   102
Governments That Do Not Work   104
The Airport Cases and Rational Planning   105
The Builders   106
The Failures   109
Rational Planning and Fragmented Authority   113
Additional Explanations of Outcomes   115

Judging Success and Failure 117
The Impact of Economic Criteria 122
The Quest for Alternatives 124
Technocracy and Bureaucracy 125

CHAPTER 5
The Technocratic Servants 131

The Locus of Expertise 132
  Central Agencies 133
  Specialized Agencies 134
  Outside Consultants 134
Experts in the Policy Process 136
  Inappropriate Credentials 136
  Disciplinary Biases 138
  Limited Data 139
Elites or Servants? 140
  Satisfying Client Interests 141
  Exceeding Client Expectations 143
The Impact of Expertise 145
  Technical Rhetoric 145
  Disputes Among Experts 146
  The Price of Expertise 147
The Case for Independent Expertise 148

PART FOUR
Citizens and Protest 153

CHAPTER 6
Property and Protest 155

The Dilemma of Compulsory Purchase 156
  Consequences of the Dilemma 157
  Rules of the Game 158
The Airport Cases 159
  France 160
  United States 163
  Canada 165
  Italy 170
Competing Objectives and Strategies 172
Consumers or Citizens? 176

CHAPTER 7
Citizen Action   181

The Democratic Challenge   182
  Equity   183
  Substance vs. Process   184
Citizen Groups   185
  Objectives   188
  Structures   189
  Resources   192
Channels of Participation   196
  Formal Participation   197
  Informal Participation   199
Strategies and Tactics   200
  Of Citizen Groups   200
  Of Governments   204
Outcomes   207
International Protest   210
Challenges   211
  To Government   211
  To Political Science   215
Conclusion   218

PART FIVE
Lessons and Theories   223

CHAPTER 8
Politicians and Bureaucrats   225

Subjects and Objects   227
Lessons for Civil Aviation   228
  An Uncertain Future   229
  Cross-National Experiences   231
  Dealing with the Public   233
Technocracy vs. Democracy   235
  Inevitable Conflicts   236
  Resolving Conflict   238

APPENDIX 1
A Methodological Approach to Comparative Policy   241

APPENDIX 2
Case Synopses   251

Index   279

INTRODUCTION

Vancouver International Airport is situated on Sea Island in the Fraser River estuary, seven miles from downtown. The airport was built in the 1930s, but the island was more a farming and recreation area than an airport until it was used by the military during World War II. The air field was purchased by the federal government in 1954, and additional land was expropriated on the island for the development of an international facility.

The federal Veterans Land Administration (VLA) built homes in various cities to resettle Canadians who had fought in World War II. Two subdivisions of Sea Island were acquired in 1953 for this purpose. The VLA did not know that the Department of Transport (DOT) intended to develop most of Sea Island as an airport. Soon after many of the houses were built by the VLA and purchased by veterans in 1954, they were expropriated by DOT and torn down.

The 1954 expropriation did not eliminate the veteran population on Sea Island. Some veterans bought back their homes from the government at salvage prices and moved them down the road beyond the lands designated for immediate airport development. Most of the land acquired by the federal government in 1954 then went unused until 1967, when new transportation officials resolved to develop Sea Island into Canada's gateway to the Pacific. Plans were drawn to add a runway, doubling the airport's capacity for aircraft movements. The veterans and their families remaining on Sea Island were all in the path of the runway. Procedures again were initiated by DOT to take their homes.

The runway plans for Vancouver International Airport were formulated by DOT's Air Administration. A separate division of DOT decided to construct a new bridge to improve access to the airport from the metropolitan area. Working separately, the bridge designers planned to build near what was to be the foot of the new runway. Moreover, they designed an arching bridge to assure the passage of large boats along the river below. The bridge was under construction when the runway planners, working in the same government department, discovered that aircraft could not clear the height.

New plans were drawn to move the runway west on the island. Sea Island, however, is small, and a runway designed to accommodate all aircraft must be long. The revised plans brought the runway beyond the island's edge. It would be necessary to dredge and build up the western end of the island with landfill. Dredging, and the breach of a dike beyond the island's edge, threatened the ecological balance in one of the world's great salmon breeding areas. So the veterans were expropriated and forced to move, the high-arching bridge to serve an expanded airport was built, and a political battle in which environmental issues were among the most important produced stalemate. Thirteen years after land acquisition had been initiated, no runway construction had taken place.

What kind of planning involves two agencies of the federal government failing to communicate so badly that one tears down homes almost as quickly as the other builds them? What kind of planning involves one department of an agency foreclosing the options of another department, in the same agency, while in the process disrupting communities and displacing families? The answer, all too often, is typical planning. This story is neither isolated nor peculiar to airport development; examples such as the experience at Sea Island abound throughout the industrial world.

This book concentrates on the development of the infrastructure upon which civil aviation depends. The controversies that have jeopardized the future of the industry are the product of countless small decisions that affect both the logic of development and the prospects for competing interests. These decisions seem technical and economic; they are always political. The balance of technical, economic, and political considerations, and how the balance is achieved, is this book's central concern.

As social scientists, we have tended to present our work to people who are not knowledgeable about transportation and civil aviation but who have been intrigued about various aspects of these sectors from their own travel experiences. Because we spent a good deal of time interviewing officials in the aviation industry and in relevant government departments and ministries, our audiences often have assumed that we could provide answers to many questions about airports and civil aviation. Many of these subjects are not treated elsewhere in the book, but the questions and answers do offer some sense of the book's mood, intention, and style.

Did you come here to study the airport? It seems that wherever we went during the 1970s, and for whatever reason, local inhabitants guessed that we might have come to study *their* airport problem because everyone had one. This question was asked in cities we did include in our study (New York, Vancouver) and in cities we never intended to include (such as Boston; Naples, Italy; Columbus, Ohio; Chicago; Rome). In fact, we often did not know about the local problem until local people told us, but the urgency of their questions on the subject constantly reminded us of the passion involved and the universality of the problems.

You must really like airports. Do you fly a lot? Both of us like to travel, but this study required more than usual, and we confess that we grew weary of airports. In Europe Elliot Feldman began avoiding airports and relying on trains because it was too easy as an airline passenger to complain about inadequate facilities and services. To maintain neutrality, it seemed better to make formal visits to the airports. Jerry Milch visited the Montreal, Toronto, and New York sites by car, also avoiding the influence of the travel experience as much as possible.

I really like Charles de Gaulle Airport, from the passenger's point of view. What's wrong with it? We are critical of decisions governing Charles de Gaulle Airport, but we recognize that many travellers enjoy the facility. On a sunny day, when arriving without too many other passengers, and with all the mechanical devices working, the airport is a marvel. However, an arriving passenger mounts six stories from the satellite arrival lounge to the airport exit. When the electricity is down, which does happen, it is a long, hard walk, and when the electricity is working the energy expenditure to move passengers and to raise luggage six stories is exorbitant. Furthermore, the arrival areas were not designed effectively for wide-body aircraft, and it is impossible to form a proper queue for immigration when a fully loaded wide-body plane comes in. The errors resulting from the absence of consultation between rail and air authorities during the airport's development made the train to Paris inconvenient at best, and the failure to develop effective road networks has made the airport a questionable travel objective in rush hours. Finally, in an era when flexibility is the key to effective airport design, the round terminal is the only style that cannot be modified to accommodate changes in traffic. It is elegant, perhaps, but it is also impractical and expensive, and those costs are passed on to consumers through airport charges on the airlines and in the boutiques.

Why is access to many airports so difficult? Airport authorities build airports. They do not build railroads, subway systems, or roads. Even in the apparently most centralized systems, they cannot produce access by themselves. In France Aéroport de Paris drew numerous elegant schemes for access, but they did not consult with the RATP and the SNCF (authorities responsible for the Métro and the railroads) and they counted on the Minister of Equipment to build roads whose principal purpose would be service to Charles de Gaulle Airport. The result was a traffic jam on the airport's opening day. In Italy years of discussions between SEA (the airport authority) and the MM, FNM, FS, and ATM (explained in Tables 4-1 and 4-2) (authorities responsible for various surface access) yielded stalemate, with SEA and the Commune of Milan lacking authority to force construction of rail and roads. In Canada the federal government relies on the provinces to build roads and metros, and the adequacy of access usually depends on provincial good will. Even when the federal government tried to share costs for a bridge to Sea Island by providing extra space for rapid transit, British Columbia refused to cooperate and the bridge's grand design led to underutilization. Although much of the value of airports derives from speed and urban access, complex political systems have low tolerance for simple criteria of economic efficiency.

What is an example of a good airport? Different airports are designed for different purposes. International facilities that must accommodate immigration and customs have different design requirements from facilities handling primarily domestic traffic. Airports carrying 30 million passengers per year have different problems than airports carrying 3 million. We have come to admire the terminal at Orly Ouest, for example, whose simplicity makes it efficient and inexpensive to operate. Heathrow Airport, which undergoes a permanent revolution of construction and development, is not particularly attractive or pleasing for most passengers on busy days, but it has increased its capacity over the years at modest cost and with remarkable efficiency. A "good" airport can be judged only according to specified criteria and in reference to the particular facility's purpose. Overall, there are perhaps no good airports, but there are some that are more accommodating than others for travellers, and more efficient and cost-effective for operators. Because the technology keeps changing and the facilities on the ground must be permanent, there probably cannot be more lasting and satisfactory solutions.

When governments plan to build an airport, don't speculators move in to buy up land? We heard reports of speculation everywhere, but we were able to track down very few examples. Government compensation tends to be unpredictable. The French, for example, paid the rich farmers of the Plains of France well, but frequently have been less generous with poor urbanites. Hence, it is hard to know in advance whether speculation will pay off. Officials in Italy and Canada complained frequently and publicly of speculation, but they offered few examples. Innuendo was more common than evidence.

Doesn't property value decline near airports? Owners everywhere asserted that development would harm the value of their property. In cases where residential property was sold for residential use, certainly value did not increase with proximity to airports. However, price climbed considerably with changes in land use. As generously as the French paid to acquire land for airport development on the Plains of France, adjacent land sold for ten times as much to developers of the Holiday Inn. Commercial and industrial values can exceed the price for residential property and rezoning around airports does not appear to be an obstacle anywhere. Hence, owners who want to move and are willing to be patient may find commercial buyers and realize a profit from airport growth.

Aren't airports economic growth centers? Probably no single view is held more commonly than this one. Unfortunately, the evidence is not very supportive. Airports logically should have the attraction of port facilities; commercial enterprises can reduce their transportation costs by locating near the port. However, enterprises near Malpensa Airport told us their greatest expense was in loading, unloading, and maintaining trucks. The distance they travelled between the airport and the warehouse was not so important. Industries near Charles de Gaulle Airport were attracted by the trucking development at Garonor and the concessionary rents offered by Aéroport de Paris to induce development. Mirabel and Malpensa have not generated significant economic growth. Where growth has appeared, it seems to have been drawn by the construction of roads opening new lines of access to the city. Land distant from the city but along the road tends to be vacant and cheap—and coincidentally, near the airport.

Several economic factors are involved in the inducement of satellite growth. Airports are merely large centers of employment, like other businesses. They have modest spillover. It is difficult to promote building airports as particularly significant for economic development.

Why did urban development encroach everywhere on airports? Urban encroachment lent credibility to the concept of airports as magnets for development. Most international airports were sited before or during World War II, and the urban boom of the industrial world came after 1945. Vancouver International Airport seemed to be in the distant countryside in 1945; the same can be said for Orly, Heathrow, Le Bourget, Linate, La Guardia, Kennedy, Love, Dorval, and Malton—all airports considered in this book. All are within fifteen miles of the center of the metropolitan area. A circle with a fifteen-mile radius from the urban center of any of these cities would reveal growth in all directions. The airports were inevitably in the path of development.

These airports were not protected by effective zoning, but they were not unique in this respect. Similar patterns may be found in Boston, Berlin, Rome, Los Angeles, Tokyo, and indeed everywhere there has been an airport controversy. The pressure on politicians to permit the construction of homes and offices comes from a broad constituency; the pressure to insulate airports from encroachment has a much narrower base. Sometimes the consequences are absurd, as in the construction of highrises surrounding Tempelhof in Berlin and Ciampino in Rome. But the tendency appears to be universal.

Does this study mean you know about anything besides airports? We have become so identified with airports that it has been difficult to shed the image of narrowness. This book is ample demonstration, we think, that the object of our study has been airports, but the subject has been broader. We made a methodological choice for a single technology suitable to inquire about the future of democracy. We learned a great deal about airports, and that knowledge helped us control the parameters of discourse across different cases and countries. We have, however, looked constantly to the relationship between technocracy and democracy. The organization of the book should clarify somewhat this response.

Part One explains how the study was conceived and organized, and it sets out the issues and objectives of the study. The influence of technology on decisions is the theme of Part Two. Similar phenomena in airport development were observed in many different countries during the same period of time. Chapter 2 examines the hypothesis that a technological imperative is responsible for these results, and Chapter 3 exposes the role of a single technique, forecasting, in the determination of development strategies. Part Three is concerned primarily with aspects of decision making. The emergence of rational planning as the key tool of decision making throughout the advanced industrial world is explored in Chapter 4, and the technocratic servants, those officials and private consultants responsible for many of the most important decisions, are the focus of attention in Chapter 5.

The cases studied in this book were all controversial. In Part Four, we assess both the causes and effects of public protest. Chapter 6 examines the origins of most protest, the expropriation of private property, and Chapter 7 concerns the protest of prospective airport neighbors. We consider whether the appearance of *ad hoc* single-interest groups has had an impact on public choice. The final part of this book consists of a concluding essay that summarizes the argument and tentatively offers a final theoretical explanation for the similar conflicts, yet different outcomes, that we have observed in eight cases in the five countries.

In each chapter we have reviewed pertinent literature. We examine the relevant works on comparative politics and political systems (Chapter 1), the technological imperative (Chapter 2), forecasting (Chapter 3), planning techniques (Chapter 4), the role of scientific advice (Chapter 5), land-taking (Chapter 6), and participation (Chapter 7). We offer modest theory in each chapter, but these separate contributions are designed as part of an overall assessment of the utility of political science (and, to some extent, economics) in the cross-national comparative study of public policies.

The diversity of topics examined in *Technocracy vs. Democracy* is the product of a wide range of questions that we posed at the outset of the study. We wanted to explore how governments conceptualize the problems of air travel demand and why the solutions they adopt are so uniform. We wanted to know how citizens respond to these solutions and why some are more effective than others in expressing their views. And we wanted to understand how and why governments respond as they do to the expression of citizen discontent. We have answered the questions with which we began, but we did not foresee a sustained argument emerging out of these answers. We were surprised to discover such an explanation.

In an ideal world where technical choices might be made exclusively on the specific merits of a case, a public interest in economic growth and greater equality would be served constantly by technological advancement. The real world of airport development bears no resemblance to the ideal world. Technical choices never depend exclusively on merit; they are always political. They always serve particular interests, and stalemate results from the competition of interests in political systems where power is fragmented. Technique is a tool of economic interests animated by what we call a "business mentality." The criteria for choice are the product of narrow economic assumptions, not scientific evaluations. No matter how sophisticated the justifications for seizing land and building facilities, we can identify consistently non-technical motives.

Technique also serves, in the real world of airport development, to limit the democratic rights of citizens and enhance the role of specialists. The pattern of all political systems is to reduce the influence of laymen by declaring them unqualified to participate in technical discussions. Their land may be taken for the public interest; their rights to enjoy property may be attenuated. The whole composition of their environment may be changed without permitting them access to the specialists who declare growth to be the essence of public welfare.

Despite the often ruthless character of public power and the dubious criteria by which it can be guided, governments frequently do not get their way. Critics of pluralism have hypothesized that the most important obstacle to the implementation of policies in the public interest is the existence of single-interest groups and the permissiveness of political systems that provide broad access to decision processes. *Ad hoc*, single-interest citizen groups opposed to airport development were active in these cases, but the critics who credit them with the defeat of projects do not appreciate fully this newer form of participation. Citizen activists sometimes delayed projects, but responsiveness to them was never the decisive factor in airport development.

Do governments succeed, then, in serving the public interest? According to conventional criteria, the public interest can be defined by the construction of aviation infrastructure. However, we question the wisdom of these criteria. Successes, upon analysis, often are failures; failures, ironically, often are more successful in achieving a reasonable balance among the competing interests of the public. The criteria by which public choices are made need to be influenced by greater wisdom, and by a more fundamental commitment to the principles of democracy.

Some comparative analysis is undertaken to demonstrate similarities among different countries, as in the many efforts to formulate general development theories in politics and economics. Other comparative analysis, deriving from an area studies tradition, strives to highlight differences among societies and cultures. This study began with an assumption about the probable differences among different countries. The argument outlined above, however, applies with equal force to all five countries we studied. The problems the argument addresses, therefore, appear to carry a measure of universality. Perhaps the lessons that may be drawn can be universally applied.

E. J. F.
J. M.

Part One

COMPARATIVE POLITICS AND COMPARATIVE POLICY

Chapter 1

THE EVOLUTION OF
A STUDY

This book began as a dialogue in 1972 about the relationship between technology and public (or citizen) participation in the democratic states of the advanced industrial world. We identified two conflicting perspectives on this relationship. According to one, the growing importance of technical issues in public policy and the rise of a technocratic elite within government is reducing decision making to the pursuit of technique.[1] Experts trained in a particular technology seek out the one best solution to problems. Public participation is subordinated to the requirements of technology, thereby limiting the number of voices and interests that play a role in decisions. Advances in technology, according to this view, have contributed to the end of ideology and, implicitly, to the end of politics.

A second perspective, which focuses on either the cultural or the structural basis of political choice, challenges the importance of technocracy in limiting public participation. According to advocates of a cultural view of politics, values and preferences continue to determine choices, despite the development of a technocratic elite, and the extent of citizen participation is determined by cultural attitudes.[2] Proponents of a structural view of politics, by contrast, argue that institutions shape and mold choices, regardless of technological demands; participation becomes a function of the opportunities provided by political institutions.[3] In either case, according to this second perspective, technology does not—and indeed cannot—replace political choice, even though it might impose constraints on decision makers.

3

The authors inclined toward opposite sides in this dialogue, yet on many points we found each other's arguments compelling. Hence, we set out to examine how different political systems and cultures, with different structures and values, solve common technological problems. If technology is the key to technical decision making, then all political systems should be driven by the same forces, and toward the same outcomes, in technological issues. If, however, culture or political structure determines choices in technical decisions, we might expect different perceptions as well as different outcomes.

Although the empirical evidence available at the outset was incomplete, and although our own perceptions diverged, we suspected that the second perspective would be vindicated by our inquiry. More than a decade after Daniel Bell had declared an end to ideology, different societies and cultures still appeared to accomplish apparently similar goals in very different ways.[4] Moreover, proposed solutions to common problems were debated vigorously by ordinary citizens as well as public officials in most of the countries we observed, thereby challenging the technocratic assumption that democratic participation in public policy issues was declining. We inferred a link between visible citizen activity and the different solutions to common problems, but refutation of theories about a technological imperative would not establish an alternative causal interpretation. Our objective, to build theory concerning the relationship between technical decision making and democratic systems, with particular reference to public participation, could be met only if we understood first how technical decisions are taken, why conflicts emerge, and how disputes are resolved. We had to address the implicit debate of the second perspective: Technology aside, which is more decisive in producing the outcomes of technological choice, political values or the institutions that define political structure?

These questions about the relationship between the procedures of choice and their outcomes necessarily invoked central questions of judgment that became fundamental to our inquiry: What are the criteria for the determination of success or failure in problem solving, and why do some efforts succeed and others fail? Do the criteria for success and failure vary from place to place? Might such variation affect choices and outcomes? Alternatively, if the criteria are the same, why do there seem to be substantial variations in the quality of outcomes?

The nature of our proposed inquiry dictated the choice of comparative analysis, which in turn afforded additional analytical advantages. To test the independence of technology as a variable, it is necessary to consider its role in more than one system. Comparative analysis makes it possible to recognize a range of choices, to discover whether all choices involving technology are perceived in any given system, or whether different cultures and structures afford such different perspectives that perceptions are of different choices. Comparative analysis thus helps us discover a range of possible solutions to a technologically defined problem—an aid to policy choice—and to identify the extent to which structure and culture mitigate the influence of technology—our intellectual objective.

Choosing the Technology

We sought a technology that could provide a high degree of comparability across different political and cultural systems. We employed three criteria. First, the technology had to be deployed in different places at the same time. The inclination to explain investment and development choices according to international conditions can be limited if each society makes its choices during the same brief span of time, under essentially similar international economic conditions. The implications of a technology can be radically different when surrounding conditions are varied by time, and we wanted, therefore, to hold chronological conditions constant.

Second, our issue was to be defined universally as a public sector problem in order to facilitate the comparative examination of government intervention in the deployment of technology. The choice of a public sector problem necessarily meant the responsibility of some particular agency of government, even if different bureaucracies might assume responsibility for a problem in different systems. Comparability was still possible as long as the bureaucracies defined the problem in the same way.

Finally, the technology most suitable for this study had to be involved in the democratic process by generating public conflict; its deployment plainly had to be affected by non-institutionalized groups. Controversy would not necessarily be evident everywhere, and we therefore might be able to determine whether the technology caused controversy, or whether it was merely the most visible feature of conflict stimulated by other issues.

The ideal technology satisfying these criteria is civil aviation infrastructure in major metropolitan areas. No issue aroused more passion in different countries in 1972 than the construction of airports. The noise produced by aircraft had been magnified both by the commercial introduction of the jet plane and by a rapid increase in air travel. Airports were expanding; new ones were being built. The quantities of land they consumed threatened the suburbs of many major metropolitan areas. There seemed to be construction in almost every major city in the industrial world, and construction was accompanied almost inevitably by protest.

The common problem perceived by public authorities responsible for the provision of airport services was to satisfy passenger demand. The expansion of existing infrastructure was increasingly difficult, for there was no longer sufficient undeveloped land adjacent to airports. Once-isolated airfields were now surrounded by development because local authorities had failed to enact or enforce zoning restrictions. Furthermore, the noise burden of jet aircraft had stirred neighbors to oppose expansion schemes. Clearly, other solutions to the common problem seemed desirable.

The emergence of airport development as a common problem in the same time frame throughout the advanced industrial world was inherent in the technology itself. An airplane operates between two distant points, and the facility from which it takes off must be as sophisticated in certain technical requirements as the facility where it lands. As airplanes became faster and heavier, requiring longer and stronger paved runways, runway development had to occur at the same time everywhere the planes were to fly. Moreover, an increase in traffic at one airport necessarily meant traffic increase somewhere else; demands on infrastructure for aircraft and passenger movements necessarily escalated simultaneously in at least two places. As long as any government authority would choose to interpret air traffic growth as a legitimate popular demand requiring a positive response, the logic of growth itself would affect different places simultaneously. Thus, any pair of international airports with growing traffic between them (such as Paris and London, Montreal and New York, Paris and Milan, Toronto and Vancouver) would involve the imposition of the identical problem—meeting the technologically and economically induced demand—in both places at the same time. Airports, of course, are not built for paired service but for operation in a network of many facilities. A selection of cities within the same growing international network would enable us to observe different governments trying to solve the same problem at the same time.

As the aircraft that commute between international airports impose similar infrastructure demands, they also impose similar technical burdens with political, economic, and social consequences. Despite variations in climate and geography, the noise impact of aircraft is largely the same from place to place. International air travel, premised on speed, requires similar proximity to urban centers for airports, creating similar problems of ground access everywhere and, along with problems of noise, creating similar challenges to the management of the urban environment. And international airports are the largest land-using facilities on the urban periphery. Their impact is concentrated on heavily populated residential communities because of market requirements to operate within metropolitan areas.

Civil aviation is a very big business and an essential component of the economies of the advanced industrial world. The industry generates thousands of jobs and billions of dollars in revenue, and it plays a critical role in international trade. American aerospace exports in 1981 may reach $18 billion, second only to agriculture among all exporting industries in the United States. Civil aviation is also an important generator of revenue for the economies of Western Europe and Japan. Airbus Industrie, an increasingly significant European competitor for U.S. aerospace companies, expects to earn $50 billion during the 1980s.

These revenues are impressive, but the costs of operation and fleet development often exceed available resources. The world's airlines spent nearly $55 billion in 1978 to operate and maintain their fleets. A single Boeing 747 costs approximately $50 million, and its Lockheed and McDonnell Douglas competitors cost $40 million. Over eight hundred such planes were in commercial operation in 1979. Moreover, 1100 aircraft, valued at $35 billion, were on firm order as of early 1981, and options were held on an additional 725 planes with a price tag of $26 billion. Although $1.9 billion in accumulated revenues had been set aside for the new fleet, the one hundred ten members of the International Air Transport Association forecast a deficit of $700 million for 1981 and an additional $1.7 billion for 1982.

Investment in civil aviation infrastructure is of an equally high order. New airports in the 1970s began with $100-million price tags, and some climbed close to the $1-billion mark. The most expensive facilities, moreover, often involved the most land. Dallas–Fort Worth Regional Airport, built at an initial cost of over $700 million, is as large as Manhattan Island. Charles de Gaulle is one-third the size of Paris, the city it serves, and the one hundred forty square miles acquired for Montreal's Mirabel Airport covers more surface than most of the world's cities.

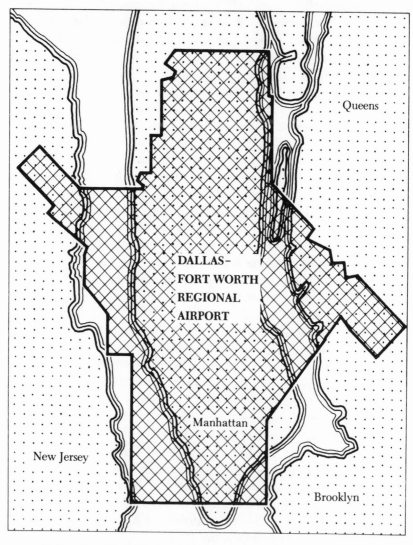

Dallas–Fort Worth Regional Airport in Size (1973 Opening Phase)

The stakes in civil aviation are high; competition is keen and national prestige is on the line. Decisions involving aviation have become extremely sensitive and controversial. In airport development, the lines of political conflict are clear. Development challenges basic citizen rights in land ownership and the peaceful enjoyment of property, while appealing to elite concerns about international standing in technology and industry. Other public works involving high technology, such as the construction and operation of nuclear power plants, would likely yield similar conflict. In the early 1970s, however, airport development was the predominant concern of citizens in major metropolitan areas throughout the advanced industrial world.

Choosing Political Systems and Cases

In selecting specific countries for comparative analysis, we considered two methodological factors important in narrowing the range of choice. First, we wanted only democratic systems where participation may be initiated legitimately outside, as well as within, institutions. We would not be able to identify or study public conflict over airport development in non-democratic systems, and some of our principal concerns lay with the participatory features of public policy formation. Second, we decided to concentrate our analysis on the advanced industrial world. The conflict between technical decision making and democratic participation, to be sure, is relevant to lesser developed countries, and there have been several important airport development cases in the Third World, notably in East Africa, Barbados, and, until the overthrow of the Shah, in Iran. Moreover, we suspect that an important audience for this book may be in the Third World, both because the industrialized countries seek to export their technology and because Third World representatives frequently indicate at international conferences a desire to copy many of the experiences of more prosperous countries. Nonetheless, we decided to limit the variables that could affect cases by controlling the broadest lines of structure, values, and culture.

Practical considerations, unavoidable in a project of this scope, were also valuable in limiting the choice of cases. We decided to confine our study to countries and cases where detailed information could be collected reliably. Two central factors affected this concern: language and money. We wanted to conduct all interviews ourselves or through research assistants we ourselves had trained. For linguistic reasons, then, we decided to forego Munich, Frankfurt, and Tokyo; for financial reasons, we ignored Sydney, Melbourne, and Wellington. All would qualify for detailed analysis within the methodological and intellectual framework of this study.

Concentration on the democratic systems of the industrial world still left a number of choices. We decided to narrow further the possibilities by considering cities already endowed with international airports but where conflict had arisen due to plans for the development of new aviation infrastructure. We selected cases of expansion only when the project was conceived as an explicit alternative to the construction of whole new facilities.

These criteria enabled us to select cities in five countries (Great Britain, France, Italy, Canada, and the United States) for systematic analysis. A single site in each of the European countries met our criteria. In England, the battle for a third London international airport was entering its second decade; across the channel, the French were finishing a third international airport for Paris. In Milan the airport authority had acquired all the land necessary for expansion of its second international facility, but various protests seemed to prevent any implementation of plans.

Several cities in North America appeared appropriate for our inquiry, and we decided to study three sites in Canada and two in the United States. This decision enabled us to introduce an additional set of issues into this inquiry. We wanted to consider whether federal systems promote a range of procedures and outcomes, and we thought a most appropriate test of federal systems would involve the pursuit of common problems in different regions of one country.

Of all possible tests of federal systems, Canada offered the most promising lessons.[5] There are only four airports that Canadian authorities categorize as international in character; one in British Columbia, one in Ontario, and two in Quebec. The Canadian federal government, unlike the West German and American, owns and operates the country's principal airports. Not even the most centralized systems have so much control, for local Chambers of Commerce own and operate all French airports outside Paris, and a variety of organizations and agencies—none controlled by Rome—owns and operates Italian airports. The British Airports

Authority does control seven of the most important airports in the United Kingdom, but the Authority (like its Paris counterpart) is autonomous and not operated out of the central government. In Canada, the federal Ministry of Transport's own Air Administration governs directly. During the period of our study, the Canadian government pursued major construction programs for air transportation facilities in the three largest cities of Canada: Montreal, Toronto, and Vancouver. Consequently, it seemed useful to consider all three cases.

In the United States, consideration of more than one experience offered us the opportunity to examine the variations possible within a single country and outside federal control. Constraints on our resources and capacities required us to limit this inquiry to two regions, the southwest and the northeast.[6] Dallas–Fort Worth was an inevitable choice because of its size and international visibility. In addition, we considered the aborted plans for a fourth international airport for New York. As the world's busiest airport system, linked with all the other potential airports in our study, New York was also an inevitable choice.

We have detailed the case experiences elsewhere.[7] In this volume we will only sketch the case histories; brief notes follow here, and some details are in the appendix. However, our objective is to answer our initial questions by utilizing effective comparisons. We do not intend here to highlight the intricate, although often fascinating, experience of each case.

Dallas–Fort Worth

Both Dallas and Fort Worth developed air facilities in the late 1920s and continued to operate them through the early 1960s. Love Field in Dallas carried the bulk of the traffic but was surrounded by residential development and could not be expanded. By contrast, the Fort Worth facility, Greater Southwest International Airport, was underutilized. Pressure from the federal government to consolidate air facilities was ineffective, but the threat of competition from Houston's new airport forced a compromise in 1965 on a site for a new facility midway between Dallas and Fort Worth.

There was no public opposition to the project, but airport neighbors objected strenuously to the flight patterns introduced in 1974 when the facility was completed. Despite a flexible design and

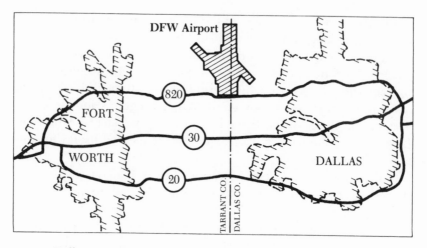

Dallas–Fort Worth Regional Airport with Dallas and Fort Worth

a phased development program, the new airport was overbuilt. However, the Airport Board did succeed in drumming up sufficient business, largely by attracting transfer passengers from other facilities, to justify the development plan.

London

Heathrow Airport, west of London, was planned in 1944. Its Star of David design, with the runways enclosing the terminal and operational areas, made large-scale long-term expansion impossible. Gatwick, over thirty miles south of London, was linked directly to the city by rail, but for political and economic reasons was never envisaged as a principal commercial facility potentially equal to Heathrow. In the late 1950s pressure developed for a third London airport that would absorb the growing traffic demand on Heathrow and Gatwick. Among other concerns, British politicians spoke frequently of the balance of payments and the need to compete with the Continent.

Many sites were proposed in numerous studies and by a royal commission. Each proved controversial. Citizen objections were frequent and forceful; continuous bureaucratic reorganization repeatedly changed the criteria for site selection. No site was developed despite growth in traffic and the operation of several other London area facilities, but millions of pounds were spent on plans and schemes which still have not been entirely abandoned.

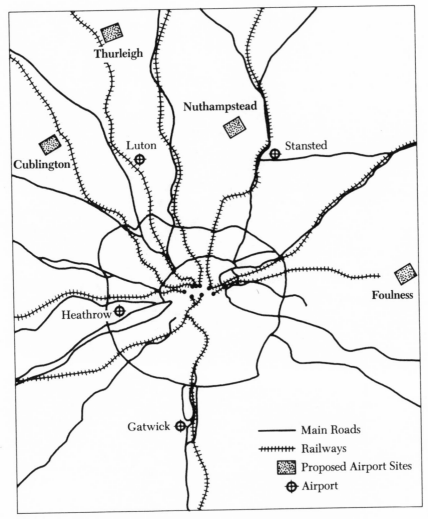

London Area Airports and Final Roskill Commission Sites

Milan

Linate Airport, Milan's principal facility, lies only seven miles southeast of the downtown area. It is surrounded by urban development. The city's intercontinental facility, Malpensa, is over forty miles north of the city, nearly half-way to the Swiss border. Efforts to develop Milan as Italy's main international air terminal encouraged plans to develop and expand Malpensa.

No scheme was ever developed to rationalize traffic between Linate and Malpensa. Although land was expropriated for Mal-

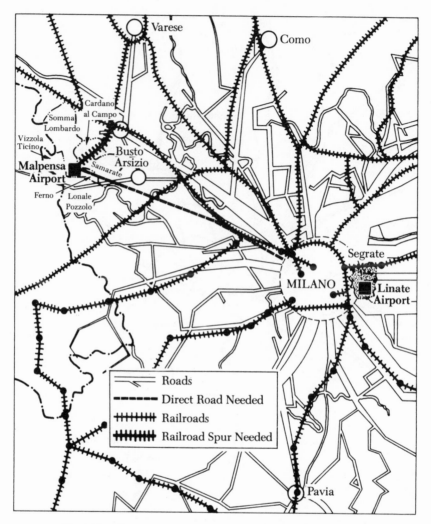

The Milan Region, Linate and Malpensa Airports, and Access

pensa's growth, funds ran out during development delays resulting from citizen resistance and bureaucratic inefficiency. No effective access to Malpensa was built despite decades of plans and discussions. Fourteen years after initial plans for construction at Malpensa, Linate continued as Milan's main airport, with no growth potential and considerable conflict with neighbors.

Montreal

Plans for a new airport to replace Dorval were developed during 1967 and 1968 by the Ministry of Transport, following the rec-

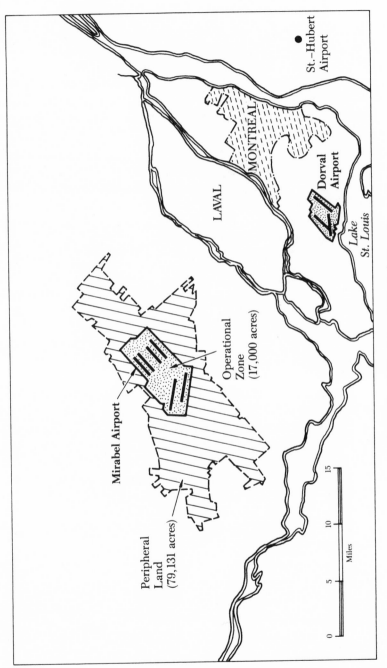

Montreal with Dorval and Mirabel Airports

ommendation of consultants that existing air facilities could not be expanded to meet demand beyond 1985. The selection of Ste. Scholastique, forty miles north of the city, as the site for a new airport was attacked by provincial officials but accepted by local residents. Nevertheless, a major protest erupted several years later when expropriated farmers became conscious of the prices the federal government had paid for land in Ontario to develop another airport there.

Mirabel Airport opened in 1975, but Dorval has not been closed. Air traffic has not approached early projections, and both facilities are operating at a fraction of capacity. The 78,000 acres of "peripheral" land taken as a buffer zone for the new airport have become an additional burden for federal resources, and Ottawa in 1981 is seeking divestiture.

New York

In late 1959, the Port Authority of New York and New Jersey announced its intention to construct a fourth airport in the Great Swamp of Morris County, New Jersey to supplement Kennedy (Idlewild), LaGuardia, and Newark Airports. Opposition from local residents and competition between the two states delayed construction for more than a decade; when the Port Authority agreed in 1969 to seek a new site, no site was available. The quest was abandoned finally in the early 1970s when traffic projections declined.

The battle was not over, however. A second government agency, New York's Metropolitan Transportation Authority, proposed to expand Stewart Airport, a former Air Force base, into the fourth metropolitan air facility. Legal battles over expropriation led by airport neighbors delayed initiation of the project. The land finally was taken, but Governor Nelson Rockefeller's resignation and the continued decline in New York's share of the air market led to the quiet demise of the project in 1974.

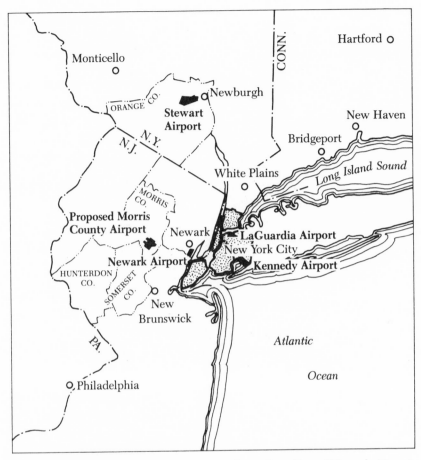

Stewart Airport and Its Region with Kennedy, LaGuardia and Newark Airports
and Proposed Morris County Airport

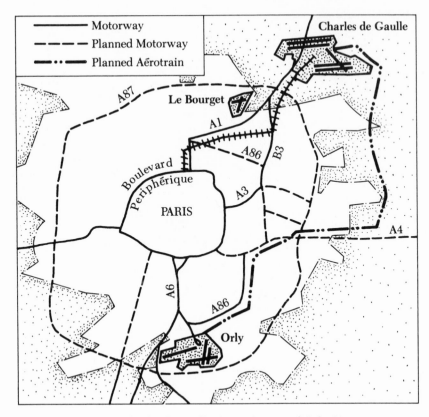

Paris with Charles de Gaulle, Le Bourget, and Orly Airports

Paris

Since World War II Paris has operated at least two international airports, north and south of the city. In the late 1950s proposals to create open space north of Paris led to plans for the closure of Le Bourget and the construction of a new and larger facility further north, on the Plains of France.

The facility built a decade later and opened in 1974 far exceeded the city's air capacity requirements and created numerous problems of access and coordination with Orly Airport south of Paris. The French Government has struggled to suppress criticism of the airport and advertises it as a symbol of French technological and planning achievement.

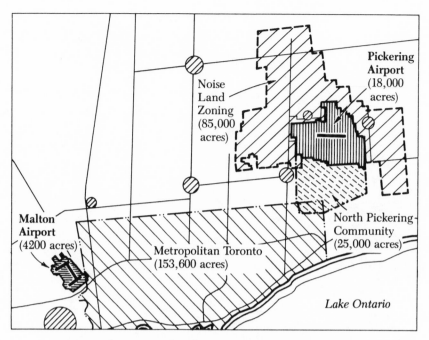

Metropolitan Toronto with Malton and Pickering Airports

Toronto

Malton Airport was built in the 1930s and modernized two decades later. Expansion plans, which included the expropriation of 3000 acres of land, were drawn up in 1968 principally to protect the facility against future urban encroachment. Opposition from provincial politicians and airport neighbors, however, encouraged the federal government to abandon expansion plans in favor of a new airport elsewhere in the metropolitan area.

A site for the new facility was not selected until 1972, and land acquisition was complicated by opposition in Pickering Township and a requirement for formal public hearings on expropriation. An additional delay accompanied minority government in Ottawa, and construction plans were not confirmed until 1975. When the provincial government withdrew its support for development in the fall of 1975, the project was shelved, but the federal government retains ownership of the land.

Vancouver International Airport, Sea Island, and Environs
Copyright © Her Majesty the Queen in right of Canada.
Department of Energy, Mines, and Resources.

Vancouver

Vancouver International Airport occupies most of Sea Island in the Fraser River estuary seven miles from downtown Vancouver. The federal government planned the facility as Canada's gateway to the Pacific, but local and regional interests concerned themselves more with slow growth and environmental protection. Federal development plans threatened the estuary's ecological balance, the city's growth objectives, and the airport's wealthy neighbors.

Vancouver's geography makes an alternative site impractical. Plans for a second parallel runway on Sea Island, however, aroused conflict between the federal government and the Greater Vancouver Regional District, and also among federal agencies with competing responsibilities for transportation, the environment, and regional planning. Deadlock ensued. The land on Sea Island was expropriated in 1970, but in 1981 no planned construction had been accomplished.

Table 1–1. Case Summary

	Start of Issues	Major Citizen Protest	Planned New Facility	Planned Expansion	Status in 1980
Dallas–Fort Worth	1961	No	X		New airport built
London	1963	Yes	X		Nothing
Milan	1967	Yes		X	Land taken
Montreal	1968	After develop-ment	X		New airport built
New York	1959	Yes	X		Land taken
Paris	1963	Suppressed	X		New airport built
Toronto	1968	Yes	X		Land taken
Vancouver	1966	Yes		X	Land taken

Observations, Explanations and Unsettled Problems

When we began the case studies, the controversies over airport development in these five countries were unsettled but obviously not headed toward a common outcome. As we scanned our choices, we saw a third international airport in Paris about to open, yet the third international airport in London (which seemed to be more required in terms of traffic growth) was still on the drawing boards. A second Montreal airport was under construction, yet a second Toronto airport (again where projected traffic growth was greater) remained in fierce dispute. Certainly, we reasoned, when different societies and cultures face a similar problem, they generate different solutions because they have different values. The social science literature, with an emphasis on Western Europe for comparisons in the industrial world, pointed to this assessment.* A modest structural-functional literature suggested that different states, at different levels of development, would have differential capacities for getting things done, but the argument was generated in the context of modernizing states and seemed inappropriate to an already industrialized world.[8] An assessment of the state of the art made us expect that different social and cultural values would explain best the variations in outcome we observed. Moreover, this expectation was comforting to seekers of choices and options, for it suggested that technology did not dictate decisions as long as cultural diversity prevailed.

We developed elaborate hypotheses, based on casual observations, in order to confirm the prevailing view and thereby refute the theorists of technocracy and the end of ideology. The French, we thought, translated their fabled *horreur du face à face*[9] into a site selection which preferred great distance from Paris to conflict with property owners. In contrast, we reasoned, the British put an excessive premium on efficiency;[10] measuring distance travelled as time, and time as money, they required a site close to London despite possible conflict with neighbors and residents. We extrapolated similar cultural explanations for the elements that precipitated conflict and solutions in all the cases we observed.

These hypotheses suggested a defense of cultural and political differences against the advocates of social and political convergence. We were persuaded by our observations of different results in different places that we would prove the cultural defenders to be correct. The "iron law of oligarchy," one of the most revered social science findings, suggests that all organizations tend toward

---

* The United States generally has been excluded from these comparisons in the belief that experiences there are unique in some way, and Canada has been ignored by everyone but Canadians.

the same decision-making arrangements and potentially to the same decisions on like issues.[11] We thought, however, that different bureaucrats would be prepared to make different choices when posed with similar problems in different cultural settings. The very existence of different choices not only would undermine the power of the "iron law," it would also weaken interpretations of technology as an independent variable that dictates outcomes. We would demonstrate the persistence of competing values and even suggest that the competition increases the number of perceived options. Released from the constraints of culture and structure within any one society or state, the analyst could discover a new range of possibilities.

Despite the different outcomes, other observations were inconsistent with hypotheses that emphasized differences. Why were so many new airport projects, for example, proposed at the same time in so many different places? The growth in air travel demand, after all, did not dictate additional construction. The demand could have been given lower priority than other social requirements, thereby deflecting into other modes of transport any apparent growth in the penchant to travel. Scheduling could be reorganized to redistribute traffic growth through the day, the week, and even the season, thereby increasing the capacity of existing facilities without new construction. Pressure could be put on aircraft manufacturers to increase the size of aircraft, thereby reducing the number of planes required to carry a given number of passengers and, consequently, reducing the pressure to build additional runway capacity. Private aircraft could be displaced to smaller, less crowded airports, creating more room at the major facilities. These solutions, and others, were no less available at the beginning of the decade than at the end. Yet, in every visible case, within our sample and beyond, the choice was to build. Was Daniel Bell right? Were the different values in different societies subordinate to a more common impulse? Was strategic decision making a function of general convergence of industrial and capitalist societies, removing the peculiarities of culture or even political structure from the final calculus?

Still another observation that troubled us was the reluctance of the public in most places to accept the solution proposed by policy makers. Why did construction plans encounter so much vigorous and effective opposition in so many different places? According to the prevailing theory in the study of comparative politics, significant variations in political culture from one country to another, determined by levels of political development, dictate degrees of public participation.[12] The capacity to organize and sustain political demands is believed to be far more advanced in the United States than elsewhere. Scholarly work on Italy, notably by Banfield, LaPalombara, and Almond and Verba, suggested that sustained citizen protest focusing on a particular issue was unlikely, if not impossible.[13] Moreover, the social scientists who favored cultural explanations for the differences among countries would have thought it unlikely that protest would arise in several countries at the same time over what appeared to be the same issue; different values, they would argue, give apparently similar problems different character and different definition in different countries.[14] Yet active, organized opposition to airport plans appeared everywhere, in Italy as well as in the United States, in France as well as in Canada. Everywhere the same issues triggered simultaneous protest, in all kinds of democratic political systems and in countries at different levels (or stages) of economic and political development.[15]

We also observed a patterned recourse to expertise. Officials claimed to have knowledge and understanding unavailable to laymen. They said that citizens should entrust decisions to the experts. And citizens, unhappy or uncertain about these decisions, turned also to experts to attack official positions. This dependence on expertise involved a pattern that denied democratic procedures; experts would evaluate a problem and propose a solution that could not be debated in the public arena because technique was more important and more reliable than politics. Any unfortunate consequences for some citizens of projects recommended by experts were to be understood as an imposition on the minority in behalf of the public interest. The public interest was to be served by the advance of technology and the public works therein required. This pattern of expertise was visible in all the countries we studied.

Choosing a Methodology

How could we explain the pattern of airport controversies we observed? Were variations in outcome the result of different perceptions of a common problem, as we had originally speculated, or were they merely the product of the differential capacities of the experts, as the theorists of technocracy proclaim?

Our search for an explanation took us first to the traditional approaches of comparative politics, because the phenomena we observed were cross-national and political. One popular approach is concerned generally with political sociology and focuses specifically on the attitudes of large sectors of the population. Accordingly, political phenomena can be explained persuasively in terms of the underlying attitudes of the population.[16] These attitudes, in turn, can be ascertained through a large-scale survey of the relevant population groups in each country.

We recognized that this approach could provide us with information helpful in comprehending and explaining our observations. We could discover, for example, the identity of the apparently new protestors in places such as Milan, and we could distinguish their attitudes and values from their less politically involved compatriots. Nonetheless, we rejected this approach for both practical and theoretical reasons. A large-scale survey at eight different sites in five countries would have required very substantial resources, and the information we would have obtained from it could be procured in other ways. We did not believe that a survey could provide us with the data necessary to understand the issues that generated protest, the strategies of the activists, or the decision making that triggered these activities.

More generally, the theories that have emerged from cross-national survey research did not correspond to our observations. They did not serve to predict protest activity because their assumptions about participation embrace conventional, formal, and legal modes to the exclusion of street protest and informal organization.[17] Populism emphasizes electoral procedures, and the interest group literature looks to formal organizations working within the traditional ground rules of political systems. Popular protest is understood in terms of class and ideology. Popular protest in these cases, however, appeared to be concentrated among particular groups, not consistently defined by class or ideology, who resorted to nontraditional participatory activity. Additional surveys did not promise answers to the questions we posed.

A second tradition in the study of comparative politics involves the analysis of institutions and political structures, such as legislatures and parties. Several methods of analysis are available, but two of the principal approaches are systems analysis and a variant, structural-functional analysis. They treat government institutions as "black boxes" that process inputs and produce outputs, and they are particularly suited to a comparison of the policy-making capability of different systems.[18] Accordingly, this approach would direct our search for an explanation of the observed political phenomena to the differential capacity of government structures to fulfill specialized functions.

We recognized, once again, that this approach has certain advantages. Systems analysis, in particular, emphasizes the interconnections among issues which are too frequently overlooked in studies of political phenomena. But the assumptions inherent in this analytical approach, principally the notion that popular demands are processed by unchanging government structures into policies, did not correspond to our observations. Decisions involving aviation infrastructure were the subject of protest and apparent popular dissatisfaction with the responses of governments. Popular pressures had not produced the decisions to build; it appeared from our observations that these decisions were often taken in secret. It would be important, then, to penetrate the "black box" which brought about these decisions.

This realization encouraged us to adopt a non-traditional approach to the explanation of the observed phenomena by marrying the perspectives of policy analysis to the problems defined by comparative politics. Policy analysis, with its focus on the processes, choices, and strategies of government, offered a more appropriate framework than either the sociological or the traditional institutional approach.* But the application of policy analysis to problems of comparative politics required substantial innovations in methodology. We found it necessary, in particular, to abandon the sectoral approach of policy analysis and to introduce strict controls on the definition of the comparative problem.

Policy analysis and program evaluation commonly concentrate on policy sectors.[19] Sectors are defined by the programmatic responsibilities of agencies and departments. Problems in a policy which lie outside the sector have been called "spillover" by po-

---

* "Policy analysis" does not offer a single method, and there is great disagreement over units of analysis, particularly with reference to divisions between planning and implementation. There is general consensus, however, that policy analysis refers more to what governments do, whereas political analysis looks more to what governments are and behavioral analysis to what people think or believe.

litical scientists and "externalities" by economists.[20] Yet, most problems are necessarily cross-sectoral. We began, for example, with the literature on airport development. It was written by transportation specialists, and its perspective consistently adopted the prevailing official assumptions about the need for additional facilities and the technical requirements of construction.[21] This literature, in all the countries we studied, considered environmental problems, for example, as a by-product of the main task of airport development. Given the commitment to develop, analysts would say, how might the environmental problems be treated? Cost-benefit and other analytical techniques were employed to choose among sites for construction, not to weigh construction against other potential land use. Yet, airport development necessarily implies an increase in traffic which necessarily will mean more noise and pollution. The environmental implications may not seem important to aviation planners seeking to meet passenger demand, but they are inherent in the decision to build, affect seriously other actors, and therefore constitute a direct—not a secondary—trade-off in decision making.

Even when the policy makers in all these countries began to appreciate environmental issues by requiring some form of environmental impact statement, they isolated the environmental questions from the initial decision and policy review, and they continued to disregard other issues raised by other affected parties. For example, airports are the largest land users on the peripheries of major metropolitan areas and therefore constitute a land-planning problem as much as a question for transportation. Within the transportation sector itself, civil aviation is a distinct branch whose operation is dependent upon another separate branch, that of surface transport providing access to air facilities. Transportation agencies or departments, or port authorities, were assigned in all five countries to plan, build, and operate airports. We found these agencies usually unwilling or unable to coordinate with others responsible for access, land use, or for that matter any other implication of development. No decisions could be enacted without cooperation from local planners, environmental agencies, justice departments for land taking; public works agencies for construction; regional economic planners for site location; local councils for zoning; surface transit and rail authorities; and highway departments. The policy assessment of costs and benefits could not account for these various inputs and their corresponding and often competing interests. The sectoral approach—whether for transportation, health, education, welfare, or environment—implied confrontations strictly between line agencies and local citizens. The most cursory observation of the controversies warned us that the issues were far more complex.

We would examine the policies as well as the politics of airport development, but not from the perspective of sectors. We did not want to wear the lenses of the bureaucrat, wrestling with his mandate and his definition of problems. Rather, we wanted to see the issues more comprehensively. When he might ask, "How do I get the facility built?" we asked, "Why build it?" When he would ask, "Where will it serve the travelling public?" we asked, "Where would it help the economy and cause the least damage for neighbors?" The entire frame of reference we adopted deviated from one strain of traditional policy analysis. A more traditional approach would never have helped us understand why conflicts arose everywhere, and why there were different outcomes in different places.

A second tradition in policy analysis fastened on process but at the expense of effective comparison. Case studies of decision-making procedures, even within the same sector, have been assembled for different countries, but no methodological attention has been paid to the significance of examining the same issue—and asking the same questions—in different systems.[22] In this sense, the use of case studies in policy analysis has followed the path blazed by students of comparative politics. There are too few examples in the comparative politics literature of cases chosen deliberately because of their similarity in different settings.[23] Cases thought to be illustrative of a culture or system were assembled but never compared.[24] Textbooks in comparative politics reported on different countries with different country specialists, but no one compared systematically what was reported about each case.[25]

We found the case method appealing, in light of our particular concerns and interests, but we could adopt that method only if we were prepared to depart from traditional practice. We did not think the study of airport site selection in one country could be compared reliably with the decision process for rail or highway development elsewhere, although generalizations might be derived from a more tightly controlled study that might be expanded eventually into useful comparisons across problems and even conventionally defined sectors. We would have to study intensively the similar conflict over airport siting in different countries, treating each controversy as a case in decision making and in conflict resolution. The strategy was not to compare decision making broadly but rather to build the comparisons specifically around a common problem of advanced industrial societies.[26]

The conditions within which a problem is set necessarily affect the character of the problem itself. No problem can ever be precisely the same in more than one setting. However, we chose a common technology that is necessarily international and has been understood in apparently the same way by responsible officials in different countries. This choice seems to minimize the usual difficulty of establishing validity in comparative analysis.

If scholars want to understand the sources of conflict, they need to study conflict. Attitudes toward conflict do not provide the same focus. If scholars want to understand why different governments choose different solutions to common problems, they must study the problems and the processes of arriving at solutions. The study of traditional political structures does not necessarily reveal how and why governments act, because it assumes that the answers must be found within certain institutions. The evaluation of solutions through specialized techniques, such as cost-benefit analysis, does not reveal the range of potential choice when cultural and structural constraints are overcome, chiefly because the evaluation must be confined to criteria derived from a sectoral definition of the problem and its solution. Why did development occur simultaneously in different countries? Why did conflict occur everywhere? Were there patterns in the choices of governments and in the reactions of citizens? To pursue these questions we had to adopt a new comparative policy methodology with a focus on problem-solving cases. We had to move policy analysis toward cross-sectoral as well as cross-national approaches, and we had to liberate the analysis from both the identification of attitudes and the presumed functions of political structures in favor of activity and conflict inside and outside government.

Framework of the Study

These considerations led us to undertake a series of detailed and systematically comparative case studies of airport development decisions in eight major metropolitan centers in the industrial world. Between 1974 and 1978 we completed some 350 interviews in five countries and examined hundreds of documents. We spoke with critical participants: presidents of major airlines, directors of airports, aviation specialists, government ministers, regional and municipal authorities, civil servants, and citizens whose land was taken for development projects or who had opposed government plans. A more detailed description of the methodology is included in the appendices.

We decided to test some of the central theories governing the study of comparative politics—the discipline most centrally implicated by our questions—and the development of technology in democratic countries by focusing on four specific issues in each case: (1) decision-making processes, (2) the role of experts, (3) citizen protest, and (4) the bureaucratic response to conflict. These four categories framed our inquiry, although they did not determine the organization of our analysis.

1. The Decision-Making Process. The literature of politics is replete with theories of decision making. Pluralist theory, which suggests numerous decision centers and actors, chiefly interest groups, has been popular in the United States.[27] Elite theories have gained growing acceptance in the industrial world, with variants proposed by C. Wright Mills in the United States, John Porter in Canada, and Pierre Birnbaum in France, among others.[28] Models of bureaucratic politics focus attention on bureaucrats as key decision makers.[29] Theories of the firm assess government decision-making processes in organizational terms,[30] while technological determinists ascribe to technology the ultimate responsibility for choices.[31]

Our initial observations raised some questions about all these approaches and persuaded us to abandon any generalizations about the impact of bureaucrats, politicians, interest groups, or conventional structures. There was no obviously consistent pattern for choices and outcomes in the different countries we studied or, for that matter, in the different cases we examined within a single country. Whereas in France a single autonomous agency exercised enough authority to override the potential wishes of a ministry, in Britain competing ministries appeared to succumb to the persistent opposition of local amenity groups. In Canada one provincial government could prove critical in the decision process, whereas provincial authorities elsewhere were unable to influence the choices of a single division of a single ministry in the federal government. We decided, therefore, to ask an empirical descriptive question: how, in fact, are decisions made? By tracing these decisions in each case, we could discover whether bureaucrats had more clout in some systems than in others, and we could observe the conditions under which countries invite or encourage democratic participation.

2. *The Role of Experts.* A common theme in the literature on technology and government concerns the growing power and influence of the new class of technocrats.[32] Some critics have argued that specialists with particular training control decisions in technical areas.[33] In France and Italy these technocrats function within the government itself;[34] in Britain, Canada, and the United States experts outside government provide consulting advice, and this professional work is often crucial in decision making. By comparing the use of expertise across countries, we could assess whether specialists are more likely to affect choices in some systems than in others, and we could inquire whether such involvement of experts distorts democratic participatory procedures. Most important, perhaps, we could inquire whether differences in the flow of information to decision makers, determined by the availability of expert advice and counsel, accounted for differences in the character and quality of policies.

3. *Citizen Protest.* Theories of non-conventional participation are not well developed in the literature of comparative politics. Citizen participation became a popular buzz word in industrial societies in the late 1960s and early 1970s, as both organized social groups and *ad hoc* alliances of citizens discovered innovative ways of voicing their discontent with government policies. These new forms of participation have escaped serious analysis, for reasons which we have indicated in this chapter, and we sought to develop theory through a systematic comparison of protest activity and opposition in five countries. Citizen participation implies a new, active role for laymen previously excluded from the political process. We wanted to establish whether the activists indeed were new to political participation, and whether citizen groups could affect decision processes and outcomes. By comparing activism cross-nationally, with a focus on the same issue, we could inquire, too, whether there are common sources of protest. Is there an intellectual objection to growth, as Galtung and others implied,[35] or are there other factors motivating the demonstrations and other protest activities?

4. The Response to Protest. We observed readily that the construction of airports was proceeding more easily in some places than in others. Did protesters sometimes win? If so, why and how? What determined official responses to protest? Students of participation have concentrated on the organizing and strategic side and not on the process of achieving results.[36] Through comparisons, we could observe the relative responsiveness of different systems and cultures.

The decision-making process could be defined, we found, by two very distinct phenomena. First, the tendency to identify common problems in common ways stemmed from similar analytical approaches, especially to forecasting, in all the countries. Yet, the common definitions of problems led to uncommon ends, often because the process of decision and the influence of institutions varied significantly from case to case. Hence, we have divided the decision-making discussion between perceptions of problems and the procedures for solving them.

Citizen protest constituted an important influence on decision making. However, we discovered a common thread to protest which casual observation had not exposed. We found that despite the public prominence of environmental lobbies, the process or threat of land acquisition through expropriation triggered most citizen action. Hence, we decided to give land acquisition separate attention, in addition to a broader assessment of protest movements and their impact on the decision process.

Experts, we found, were marshalled by both public officials and citizen activists. They influenced the process of decision making and outcomes at various points. Analytically, we could not place this role in a chronological order, as if it intervened critically at some consistent point in all our cases. We chose, therefore, to separate the subject entirely.

This order of presentation corresponds more to the notion of interrelated essays than to the telling of a story. There are, of course, other ways to organize the presentation, including a rough tracing of the development process: forecasting and the decision to build, site selection, expert advice, citizen protest and more expert advice, official adjustments in decisions, and final solutions. Although such an order of presentation might illuminate the airport development process, it corresponds less well to answering the central questions we have posed. Although airport development is treated in detail, it is treated as a case of technology and decision making in democratic industrial states.

Every government we studied chose initially a strategy of major new construction; protest occurred in some form everywhere, despite different provisions for citizen participation, different perceived levels of political development, and different attitudes toward activism. Hence, theories based on cultural values could not be sustained across the cases. The character, source, and interpretation of demands rendered structural-functional approaches of little use. Yet, the outcome of conflicts generated by similar problem definitions varied significantly from place to place, thereby precluding any simple application of technocratic or bureaucratic theories. In sum, the results of our research forced us to derive theory; we could not rely on the popular theories of comparative politics that had stimulated our first hypotheses.

We have derived middle-range theory in each of the areas of our inquiry. Such theory is the product of a comparative policy approach unlike more established methods either in comparative policy analysis or in comparative politics. In Chapter 8 we tentatively offer a more encompassing theoretical explanation for our observations, but a grander or more global theory, with greater articulation in addressing the future relationship between democracy and technocracy, awaits more empirical study and probably greater insight than we have been able to muster so far.

Endnotes

1. The classical roots of this viewpoint can be found in the writings of Francis Bacon, Henri de Saint-Simon, and Thorstein Veblen. Among the more contemporary statements of the political role of technocrats are those by Don K. Price, *The Scientific Estate* (Cambridge, Mass.: Harvard University Press, 1965) and John K. Galbraith, *The New Industrial State* (New York: New American Library, 1968). A useful analysis of their views can be found in Langdon Winner, *Autonomous Technology: Technics-out-of-Control as a Theme in Political Thought* (Cambridge, Mass.: MIT Press, 1977), pp. 135–172.

2. An excellent example of this approach may be found in Stanley Hoffman, et al., *In Search of France: The Economy, Society and Political System in the Twentieth Century* (New York: Harper and Row, 1962); also, see Samuel Beer, Suzanne Berger, Guido Goldman and Adam Ulam, *Patterns of Government: The Major Political Systems of Europe*, Third Edition (New York: Random House, 1972), especially Beer's opening discussion, "Modern Political Development."

3. A critical example is Samuel P. Huntington, *Political Order in Changing Societies* (New Haven: Yale University Press, 1968).

4. Daniel Bell, *The End of Ideology: On the Exhaustion of Political Ideas in the Fifties* (New York: Free Press, 1960).

5. An entire separate volume is devoted to the Canadian experience; see Elliot J. Feldman and Jerome E. Milch, *The Politics of Canadian Airport Development: Lessons for Federalism* (Durham, N.C.: Duke University Press, 1982).

6. We were able to accumulate data on airport controversies in other cities of the United States including Miami, Chicago, Minneapolis–St. Paul, and Los Angeles, but we were unable to conduct interviews at any of these sites. We were able, however, to test some of our ideas by employing the data collected by Dorothy Nelkin in her study of the conflict in Boston. See Dorothy Nelkin, *Jetport: The Boston Airport Controversy* (New Brunswick, New Jersey: Transaction Books, 1974).

7. Feldman and Milch, *The Politics of Canadian Airport Development, op. cit.*; Elliot J. Feldman, *Airport Siting as a Problem of Policy and Participation in Technological Societies: The Case of Milano-Malpensa* (Cambridge, Mass. and Torino, Italy: Center for International Affairs and Fondazione Luigi Einaudi, 1978); Elliot J. Feldman, *White Elephants and the Albatross: French and British Planning in the Supersonic Age* (Cambridge, Mass.: MIT Press, 1982).

8. See particularly Gabriel Almond and G. Bingham Powell, *Comparative Politics: A Developmental Approach* (Boston: Little Brown, 1966), and Gabriel Almond and James S. Coleman (ed.), *Politics of the Developing Areas* (Princeton: Princeton University Press, 1960).

9. This idea refers to the inability of French officials to deal in face-to-face confrontations. The bureaucratic tendency is to avoid conflict by raising the administrative level assuming responsibility. The concept was first developed by Michel Crozier in the French edition of *The Bureaucratic Phenomenon* (Chicago: University of Chicago Press, 1964).

10. The reputation for this concern regarding airport site selection emerged clearly in the Roskill Commission study. See Commission on the Third London Airport, *Report* (London: HMSO, 1971).

11. Robert Michels, *Political Parties: A Sociological Study of the Oligarchical Tendencies of Modern Democracy* (Basel: 1916). Although Michels' argument was developed from the comparative observation of political parties, especially with reference to parties on the political left, the iron law of oligarchy seems to apply to all organizations.

12. Gabriel Almond and Sidney Verba, *The Civic Culture: Political Attitudes and Democracy in Five Nations* (Princeton: Princeton University Press, 1963). A series of volumes published in the Little Brown series in Comparative Politics followed the "civic culture" method and theme for single country analyses.

13. Edward C. Banfield and L. F. Banfield, *Moral Basis of a Backward Society* (New York: Free Press, 1958); Joseph LaPalombara, *Interest Groups in Italian Politics* (Princeton: Princeton University Press, 1964); and Almond and Verba, *The Civic Culture, op. cit.*, pp. 102, 170.

14. See particularly Beer, Berger, *et al.*, *Patterns of Government, op cit.*

15. Concepts regarding "stages" of political development are complex, ambiguous, and not followed in this discussion. Dependence on the concept and

on the idea of development for political systems may be found in A. F. K. Organski, *Stages of Political Development* (New York: Knopf, 1965); Lucien Pye, *Aspects of Political Development* (Boston: Little Brown, 1966); Lucien Pye and Sidney Verba (eds.), *Political Culture and Political Development* (Princeton: Princeton University Press, 1965); W. W. Rostow, *Politics and the Stages of Growth* (New York: Cambridge University Press, 1971); and Myron Weiner (ed.), *Modernization: The Dynamics of Growth* (New York: Basic Books, 1966).

16. Almond and Verba, *The Civic Culture, op. cit.,* and Almond and Powell, *Comparative Politics, op. cit.*

17. A critical view of this bias, with a plea to consider other forms, may be found in Samuel P. Huntington and Joan Nelson, *No Easy Choice: Political Participation in Developing Countries* (Cambridge, Mass.: Harvard University Press, 1977).

18. The principal statement remains David Easton, *A Systems Analysis of Political Life* (New York: Wiley, 1965); also Karl Deutsch, *et al., Nerves of Government* (New York: Free Press, 1963). The structural-functional approach is to be found especially in Almond and Powell, *Comparative Politics, op. cit.*

19. For a criticism of the sectoral approach see Elliot J. Feldman, "Comparative Public Policy: Field or Method?" *Comparative Politics* (January 1978), especially pp. 298–302.

20. Economists consider externalities as distortions in private economic activities that affect third parties. Thus, aircraft noise is perceived to be an externality in the operation of an airport rather than an integral part of the operation of the facility. It should be noted, however, that there has been discussion among economists during the past decade concerning revisions in this perspective. See for example Jon Nelson, *Economic Analysis of Transportation Noise Abatement* (Cambridge, Mass.: Ballinger, 1978), pp. 13–14; also, Robert H. Haveman and Julius Margolis (eds.), *Public Expenditures and Policy Analysis* (Chicago: Rand McNally, 1974). On the concept of spillovers see Arnold J. Heidenheimer, Hugh Heclo, and Carolyn Teich Adams, *Comparative Public Policy: The Politics of Social Choice in Europe and America* (New York: St. Martin's Press, 1975), p. 213.

21. A typical example is Robert Horonjeff, *The Planning and Design of Airports* (New York: McGraw-Hill, 1962).

22. Particularly grievous examples of this failure may be found in T. Alexander Smith, *The Comparative Policy Process* (Santa Barbara: Clio Press, 1975).

23. Important exceptions include Christopher Leman, *The Collapse of Welfare Reform: Political Institutions, Policy, and the Poor in Canada and the United States* (Cambridge, Mass.: MIT Press, 1980), and Theodore Marmor, Amy Bridges, and Wayne L. Hoffmann, "Comparative Politics and Health Policies: Notes on Benefits, Costs, and Limits," in Douglas Ashford (ed.), *Comparing Public Policies: New Concepts and Methods* (Beverly Hills: Sage Publications, 1978), pp. 59–80.

24. Examples include James Christoph (ed.), *Cases in Comparative Politics* (Boston: Little Brown, 1965), and Gwendolen Carter and Alan Westin (ed.), *Politics in Europe: Five Cases in European Government* (New York: Harcourt Brace, 1965). Even for the Third World this traditional failure seems to

persist. For example, Merilee S. Grindle (ed.), *Politics and Policy Implementation in the Third World* (Princeton: University Press, 1980) draws
different cases from seven different countries with no rigorous comparative
control.

25. Beer, Berger, Goldman and Ulam, *Patterns of Government, op. cit.*; Roy
C. Macridis and Bernard E. Brown (ed.), *Comparative Politics: Notes and
Readings*, Fourth Edition (Homewood, Illinois: Dorsey Press, 1972); and
Stanley Rothman, *et al.*, *European Society and Politics* (Boston: West, 1976).

26. Our case strategy is consistent with the ideas put forward by Alexander L.
George, "Case Studies and Theory Development: The Method of Structured,
Focused Comparison," in Paul Gordon Lauren (ed.), *Diplomacy: New Approaches in History, Theory, and Policy* (New York: The Free Press, 1979),
pp. 43–68; and Adam Przeworski and Henry Teune, *The Logic of Comparative Social Inquiry* (New York: Wiley, 1970).

27. The leading proponent of this view is Robert Dahl. See in particular, *Preface
to Democratic Theory* (Chicago; University of Chicago Press, 1956). The
most thorough critique of pluralism is probably Theodore J. Lowi, *The End
of Liberalism: Ideology, Policy and the Crisis of Public Authority* (New York:
W. W. Norton, 1968).

28. C. Wright Mills, *The Power Elite* (New York: Oxford University Press, 1956);
John Porter, *The Vertical Mosaic: An Analysis of Social Class and Power
in Canada* (Toronto: University of Toronto Press, 1965); Pierre Birnbaum,
Les Sommets de l'état: essai sur l'élite du pouvoir en France (Paris: Seuil,
1977).

29. Graham Allison, *The Essence of Decision: Explaining the Cuban Missile
Crisis* (Boston: Little Brown, 1971). Bureaucratic explanations of decision
making have become particularly popular in Canada in recent years, as critics
have linked the growth of government and government projects to aggran-
dizing civil servants. Walter Stewart, *Paper Juggernaut: Big Government
Gone Mad* (Toronto: McClelland and Stewart, 1979), provides a particularly
exaggerated version of this model.

30. Richard M. Cyert and James G. March, *A Behavioral Theory of the Firm*
(Englewood Cliffs, N.J.: Prentice Hall, 1963); Herbert Simon, *Administrative
Behavior: A Study of Decision-Making Processes in Administrative Orga-
nizations* (New York: Free Press, 1965).

31. Futures research, in particular, abounds with deterministic arguments based
on technology. See for example Herman Kahn and Anthony Wiener, *The
Year 2000: A Framework for Speculation* (New York: Macmillan, 1967);
Dennis Gabor, *Inventing the Future* (New York: Knopf, 1964); and Daniel
Bell, "The Year 2000: The Trajectory of an Idea," *Daedalus* 96 (1967), pp.
639–651.

32. In addition to the literature cited earlier see Jean Meynaud, *Technocracy*
(New York: Free Press, 1964).

33. See particularly Daniel Bell, *The Coming of Post-Industrial Society: A Venture in Social Forecasting* (New York: Basic Books, 1973).

34. Jean-Claude Thoenig, *L'Ere des technocrates* (Paris: Editions Organisations,
1973).

35. Johan Galtung, "Limits to Growth and Class Politics," *Journal of Peace
Research* (1973). Galtung's thesis is presented as a response to Donella L.

Meadows, *et al.*, *Limits to Growth: A Report for the Club of Rome's Project on the Predicament of Mankind* (New York: Universe Books, 1972).

36. This criticism is made effectively by Huntington and Nelson, *No Easy Choice, op. cit.*

Part Two

TECHNOLOGY AND POLICY

Chapter 2

THE TECHNOLOGICAL
IMPERATIVE

Governments in Western Europe and North America have become increasingly involved since World War II in the promotion of technology. Both military requirements and economic logic are cited frequently as explanations for this phenomenon. Technological sophistication is related closely to military capability. The countries of the NATO alliance, interpreting the international system as a balance of military power, made clear commitments to develop technology in their contest with the Soviet Union. At the same time, government institutions in capitalist countries observed a positive relationship between technology and economic growth. In their effort to enhance the economic performance of the market, they searched for appropriate tools to promote the development and deployment of technological innovations.[1]

The extent to which the state can direct the development of technology in pursuit of military and economic objectives is not entirely clear. Many observers have questioned the ability of governments to control technology, and some have suggested that government policies are more likely to respond to technological change than to influence the flow of innovation. How could it be otherwise, some argue, when the environment in which governments operate is influenced, to a great extent, by the technologies which they seek to control?

The notion that technology is a determinant of public policy has been widely accepted in contemporary social science. The convergence theory, which postulates a growing similarity among

41

advanced industrial societies regardless of their dominant ideology, was predicated largely on the influence of technology.[2] Similarly, the modernization literature of the 1950s and 1960s emphasizes the political impact of technologies on developing societies.[3] Most social scientists agree that the relationship between technology and politics is complex and that technology influences policy choices in a multitude of ways.

Theories of technological determinism vary considerably from author to author, but one of the more popular views is embodied in the concept of a "technological imperative." The basic idea, according to Langdon Winner, is that "technologies are structures whose conditions of operation demand the restructuring of their environment."[4] Political actions must conform to the requirements of technological systems if innovations are to be exploited. Advanced industrial societies are particularly subject to the imperative, because "beyond a certain level of technological development, the rule of freely articulated, strongly asserted purposes is a luxury that can no longer be permitted."[5] In theory, political leaders may choose among different strategies for employing technology; in practice, their choices are defined by the technology.

Both methodological and moral objections have been raised to the idea of a technological imperative, and most social scientists have been inclined in the past decade to regard it as a considerable overstatement of the role of technology in society. Public policy, it is often asserted, varies systematically from country to country, thereby demonstrating the limits of the technological variable as an explanation for policy choice.[6] Structural and cultural factors modify the impact of technology and are responsible, in the final analysis, for critical decisions. As John Zysman argues with respect to the electronics industry in France, "the efficient use of technology was required by certain strategies, but the choice of strategy was affected by the action of other institutions such as the state, the banks, and competing firms."[7]

The preference of social scientists for structural and cultural explanations for policy choice is understandable, but they offer insufficient evidence to justify this peremptory rejection of the technological imperative. Single-country analyses make it difficult to isolate technological influence from cultural and structural factors; cross-national study becomes essential. However, cross-national assessments of different technologies offer no test of different approaches to a common problem.[8] Our study's systematic cross-national comparisons of policy choices taken in the same time frame for the same technology allow us to explore, at least in one critical case, the relative importance of social, cultural, and technological variables. The limits of the technological imperative, after all, would be evident if different countries adopted different strategies to deal with a common technology.

Formulating the Hypothesis

International airports process air traffic in the form of passengers, cargo, and aircraft movements. They involve various technologies concerned with the movement of goods and people, and they must be understood as complex systems that integrate several functions for the single goal of efficient movement. When the system's capacity is calculated to be exhausted, additional calculations are made for the expansion of capacity. Such calculations require consideration of the entire complex system, and the consequences of any technological change affecting any part of the airport must be analyzed for impact on all other parts of the operation. The entire airport complex constitutes the "technology" to which this study refers.

Advanced industrial states promoted aviation technology and financed the development of infrastructure for many years without serious conflict. Aviation was regarded as a wholly positive technology, and public support seemed boundless. Airport development became controversial only when governments sought to balance their commitment to aviation with growing conflict over the expansion of facilities.

Both military and economic factors were responsible for the strong commitment of governments to civil aviation technology. Major advances in commercial air transportation originated in military research and development. Aircraft of various sizes, shapes, and ranges, guidance systems, and air traffic control capabilities were developed by the military divisions of major aircraft manufacturers. National security provided one justification for expenditures on civil as well as military aviation, at least through the mid-1960s,[9] but economic concerns were equally important. Government authorities reckoned that innovations in aviation technology were critical to maintaining international economic competitiveness.[10] Indeed, European governments embarked on joint development projects such as the Concorde and the Airbus in order to compete with the aviation industry in the United States.

The development of civil aviation infrastructure was shaped by the same factors. Airport development often was stimulated by strategic considerations. The locations of many major airfields in continental Europe are products of decisions made by German military authorities during World War II. Early impetus for airport location and development in Canada and Britain came from the use of bases during the war, and many commercial airports in the United States were built on abandoned military sites or in connection with military airfields. At the same time, the prospect of economic gain prodded public officials to anticipate the demand for air services and provide the infrastructure necessary to satisfy business clients. Local government authorities were persuaded that inadequate air facilities would discourage private investment in the local economy and would siphon off business and industry to neighboring and competitive cities. Internationally, the British Airports Authority exhorted the government to build a third London airport because French construction at Roissy-en-France threatened London's competitive advantage.

The commitment of significant resources to aviation technology and infrastructure development was accepted without question in Western Europe and North America. Citizens willingly taxed themselves to finance the development of air facilities, even though a relatively small minority could profit directly from them. Aviation retained its glamour for the public through most of the 1960s, and few individuals questioned the inequities in the distribution of costs and gains. Resistance to the growth policies of governments was inhibited, in any event, by the issue of national security; public debate was perceived as unpatriotic during the height of the Cold War.

Opposition to airport development emerged in the latter half of the 1950s and mushroomed in the following decade as costs and the demand for scarce land increased dramatically. Noise and pollution became more serious problems with the introduction of commercial jet aircraft, and airport neighbors were no longer willing to tolerate these penalties to support the travelling preferences of other, usually wealthier, segments of the population.[11] National security arguments were no longer sufficient to prevent open conflict; indeed, military aviation became controversial in its own right as the costs of defense contracting in projects such as the C-5A and later the B-1 bomber (in the United States) soared.

Conflict over airport development is part of a growing concern with the consequences of unbridled technological innovation. Survey data indicate that the public has become more wary of technology and less inclined to regard all changes as progress.[12] Public officials, both political and bureaucratic, have recognized the growing malaise and have talked of the need for caution and foresight in the introduction of innovations or the spread of technology. The formal recognition of a problem, however, does not necessarily imply the development of an effective response, and policy makers have not compiled an enviable record in assessing the impact of technology or in restraining policies of growth.

How have the governments of advanced industrial states responded to the increasing opposition to airport development? What efforts have they made to deal with public concerns over the costs of development and the unwanted by-products of technology? Theories of the technological imperative predict that governments will pursue policies of expansion and growth despite opposition. As long as public officials are committed to aviation technology, they can neither reject the development of infrastructure nor impose serious constraints on planners. The economic and social costs of development may be recognized, but the range of policy responses which governments can offer is limited. The technological imperative predicts that the growing demand for air services, which depends in part on technological innovation, will be met through the expansion of infrastructure, regardless of the economic and social costs of the policy.

Over the past two decades, public officials in the United States, Canada, the United Kingdom, France, and Italy, as well as in many other countries not examined in this study, have fashioned policies for civil aviation infrastructure in the face of serious and growing opposition. If there were no technological imperative, we would expect the governments in different countries to define problems differently and to respond to conflict by formulating strategies consistent with their own underlying political values or institutional norms. Alternatively, if there is a technological imperative, significant variations in the definitions and strategies adopted by these governments are unlikely to emerge; policy makers will opt for similar solutions, regardless of differences in structures and cultures.

Those who challenge peremptorily the notion of a technological imperative might find this exercise in hypothesis testing unnecessary. There is, however, an analytical problem that emerges from these cases. The strategies from place to place are similar despite great differences in culture. The theory of the technological imperative might be metaphysical, but those who are unwilling to accept it must offer an alternative explanation for the results. If there is no imperative in technology itself, what drives decision makers in different countries toward such similar choices?

Common Strategies

The formulation of strategies for airport development involves a number of discrete, sequential decisions. Each decision involves basic assumptions and value judgments. A range of solutions is available at each stage of the process, and policy makers can choose, at least in principle, among the alternatives. Over the past two decades, however, policy makers in Western Europe and North America, as we have indicated, adopted remarkably similar strategies. At each decision stage they made similar assumptions based upon similar values, and in the end they opted for similar technological solutions.

Identifying the Problem

The spectacular growth in the demand for air travel during the past generation occurred worldwide. In the decade following 1960 the number of passengers utilizing the terminals of the world's busiest airports increased approximately threefold (Table 2–1). This demand was fueled by a steady decline in fares relative to disposable personal income and by the increasing affluence of advanced industrial societies. The reduction in the real costs of air travel was facilitated, in turn, by advances in aviation technology. The patterns of growth have been more erratic in some countries, and metropolitan areas have not experienced equally the demand for air transportation. Still, the volume of passengers, cargo, and aircraft utilizing major airports throughout the industrial world expanded consistently in the post-war era.

By the middle of the 1960s, crowded passenger terminals and

Table 2–1 Growth of Air Travel

	Passengers (millions)					Movements (thousands)				
	1960	1965	1970	1975	1980[e]	1960	1965	1970	1975	1980[e]
London	6.2	12.7	22.0	28.8	39.6[f]	190.0[a]	255.0[a]	347.0[a]	381.1[a]	439.0[a]
Paris	3.6	6.6	12.6	18.1	25.8	126.6	178.3	277.1	320.3	353.0
Milan	0.7	1.7	3.4	4.9	6.3	33.0	55.0	92.0	114.2	118.0
New York (includes JFK, LaG. & Newark)	16.0	25.8	37.4	40.4[b]	53.5	603.8	764.1	868.1	767.9[b]	820.0
Dallas–Fort Worth	2.8[c]	5.6[c]	10.5[c]	15.2[c]	21.6[c]	258.7	266.2	410.2	603.6	463.0
Montreal	2.2[d]	2.7	4.6	6.8	8.0[g]	185.3[d]	233.7	263.8	192.7	224.0[g]
Toronto	2.6[d]	3.3	6.4	10.5	14.5	124.2[d]	151.2	234.2	238.2	255.0
Vancouver	0.9[d]	1.2	2.6	4.7	7.3	145.2[d]	102.4	152.6	203.3	268.0

SOURCE: International Civil Aviation Organization.
[a] London figures include Heathrow, Gatwick, Stansted, and Luton Airports for all years except 1975 and 1980, which include only Heathrow and Gatwick.
[b] 1974 figures.
[c] Scheduled passengers × 2. 1975 figures include DFW Regional Airport and Love Field.
[d] 1963 figures. No reliable figures were retained before 1963.
[e] 1980 figures are provisional.
[f] Includes 1979 figures for Stansted.
[g] The figures for Mirabel were 1.5 million passengers and 49 thousand movements.

queues of aircraft had become a common sight during peak travel hours. Aviation planners, who define congestion as an excess of demand over supply at any moment, concluded that air facilities were rapidly approaching capacity. Moreover, newer aircraft were larger and heavier than existing fleets, posing additional technological constraints on existing airport operations. In many instances, runways would have to be lengthened and reinforced, and the distance separating parallel runways sometimes was insufficient for the simultaneous operation of new planes.

The adequacy of aviation infrastructure has been a problem throughout the brief history of manned flight, as steadily increasing demands for services and rapid innovations have exerted pressure on air facilities.[13] Indeed, the American Society of Planning Officials and the American Municipal Association called the first "airport dilemma" to the attention of federal policy makers as early as the 1930s.[14] Existing airports have been modernized and upgraded frequently to cope with changing requirements. Aviation planners were persuaded in the 1960s, however, that this strategy was no longer adequate. Most airports were developed for an earlier flight technology (that is, smaller, slower, and lighter aircraft) and could not absorb development without the acquisition of additional land. This time, major new projects were required to keep pace with the demands.

Two additional considerations heightened the sense of urgency with which planners addressed the problem. First, forecasters predicted a constant rise in demand for the foreseeable future. During the 1960s and early 1970s, there was little variation from country to country in forecasting techniques, interpretations of trends, or conclusions (see Chapter 3). Forecasters everywhere were persuaded that rapid growth rates would continue unabated and that the market for air travel was essentially bottomless. Consequently, continuing adjustments in facilities offered only an incremental response to a dilemma which would grow more serious over time.

Second, systems planners warned of the intricate interrelationships in the modern airport that made the upgrading of facilities in only one aspect of airport operations disfunctional. Runways and taxiways, passenger terminals and aircraft hangars, parking facilities and access roads are interrelated components of a modern airport; a deficiency in any single facet can upset the entire system. An additional runway might attract passengers exceeding terminal capacity; a new terminal might reduce cost-effectiveness without additional runway capacity. Neither could serve well without other new facilities such as taxiways, curb space, and parking. No solutions could be simple.

Public officials with decision-making responsibilities in all five countries were inclined to accept these arguments. They shared with aviation planners the assumption that the adequacy of aviation infrastructure is defined in terms of consumer demand and that government is obligated to anticipate and satisfy demand.

Other assumptions certainly were possible. If adequacy were defined in terms of air safety rather than congestion, for example, government action would be triggered only when significant dangers for air passengers or airport neighbors would appear. Problems of air safety, of course, do increase with congestion, and concern for safety was expressed by air controllers and pilots as traffic at metropolitan airports increased. Moreover, planners subsequently employed this argument to justify the expansion of infrastructure. But if air safety issues had served to identify the problem, a wide range of solutions, including quotas or priorities at busy airports or the banning of general aviation during peak hours, might have been contemplated. Such alternatives were not considered seriously anywhere before the impulse to build and expand was checked.* Public officials everywhere believed that the obligation of governments was to anticipate and satisfy consumer demand, not to respond to questions of air safety.

Choosing a Solution

The identification of the problem in these terms restricted the range of solutions available to policy makers, but the expansion of infrastructure still was not the only available alternative to the direct imposition of priorities on the use of facilities. Even if policy makers were unwilling to discriminate actively among consumers, they might have permitted the market to allocate the available resources. The obvious market solution to a sharp increase in

---

* Quotas were introduced by the Federal Aviation Administration in 1968 to deal with peak-hour congestion in New York, Washington, and Chicago. They were employed only briefly in the New York area. A queuing system has operated at London's Heathrow Airport for more than a decade. In both cases, however, responsible authorities perceived these measures as temporary and undesirable, not as permanent alternatives to expansion.

consumer demand when supply remains relatively constant is to increase the price of services. The pricing mechanism, as economists have pointed out frequently, can allocate scarce resources efficiently without the direct imposition of government controls.

A variation on this strategy is to manipulate the price structure at crowded air facilities in order to encourage a redistribution of consumer demand. Traffic at air facilities is characterized by peaks and valleys. Even if airports approach saturation at peak hours, they are inevitably underutilized at other times. By providing economic incentives to consumers, capacity could be increased without an expansion of facilities.[15]

These solutions were not considered serious alternatives to expansion anywhere in the advanced industrial world.* For one thing, policy makers had absorbed the planners' definition of airport saturation, making it difficult for them to appreciate that reduced demand during off-peak hours constitutes excess capacity. But solutions which called for altering consumer preferences also seemed to violate an ideological article of faith. Policy makers everywhere believed that government was obliged to encourage the free movement of people and to refrain from interfering in the expression of consumer preferences.

The decision to increase the availability of air services did not eliminate the necessity for choice. Governments could acquire additional land for the construction of runways, terminals, access roads and parking facilities at existing airports; or they could build entirely new airports at other sites in the metropolitan area to replace or supplement older facilities. Expansion at existing sites generally is less expensive than the construction of new facilities and, therefore, is preferable for most policy makers. By the late 1960s, however, the differences in cost had been reduced sharply as airport expansion *in situ* had become an expensive and difficult task. Urban growth had altered the character of the airport environs and increased significantly the cost of land acquisition. The fierce competition for land on the metropolitan fringe had converted inexpensive pasture into expensive residential develop-

---

* After the Labour Government in Great Britain dropped plans for a new air facility, the British Airports Authority modified a pricing scheme at Heathrow which had been introduced originally for the purpose of increasing revenues in order also to redistribute demand. In the mid-1970s the Association of European Airports studied the impact on other airports of the British operations and the potential for implementation elsewhere in Europe.

ments and commercial enterprises, often in a very short time.[16] Economic factors alone could not provide a sufficient basis for choosing between these alternatives.

Of the eight cases examined in this study, six were decided eventually in favor of airport development at a new site in the metropolitan area; a seventh, Malpensa Airport in Milan, differed little in scope and nature from the others, even though it was technically an expansion project at an existing facility.[17] Only in Vancouver, where geography precluded the development of a new airport, was the alternative of expansion adopted.[18] The preference for construction at new sites included cases where expansion was recognized by planners as a viable alternative (Montreal) or even as a superior choice (Toronto). Policy makers, it appears, rejected the expansion of facilities in favor of new construction whenever and wherever possible.

Several factors contributed to this preference. It is possible that policy makers paid some attention to the social costs associated with the expansion of infrastructure. They were conscious of the increasing unpopularity of air facilities and of local opposition to expansion projects. The interests of airport neighbors, however, did not play a significant role in the decision process, even though choices were justified frequently in these terms. The most important factors everywhere were bureaucratic and political, as we shall see in Chapters 3 and 4. The development of entirely new facilities was preferred, ultimately, because it contributed to national or local prestige, protected the economic dominance of the metropolitan area, or satisfied the most powerful and vocal political elites.

Selecting a Site

A third stage in airport development involves the selection of a site for new facilities. Ideally, this decision should reflect consideration of three types of factors. First, certain physical characteristics of potential sites are conducive to airport development. Planners seek large tracts of relatively level and undeveloped land, situated preferably in an environment free of mountains or immovable structures. The quality of the soil and the drainage of rain waters are factors that may affect construction and operation; similarly, planners consider the frequency of fog and snow as well as general climatic conditions in evaluating potential sites. Traffic

patterns at existing civil and military air facilities within a metropolitan area may restrict operations at some potential sites. The
construction of airports is technologically feasible in virtually any
location, but the costs of construction may be prohibitive and the
operation of facilities severely curtailed if these considerations are
ignored.[19]

Economic factors are also critical in site selection. Planners often
are concerned with accommodating consumer demand for air
travel by placing facilities in appropriate "catchment areas" where
access to major markets is simplified. A different type of economic
calculation is based on the notion that airports are "growth points"
and that the construction and operation of air facilities stimulate
regional economic development. These two factors may generate
contradictory evaluations of the same site; regional development
criteria suggest construction at sites remote from primary markets.

A third category of factors relevant to site selection is the social
costs of airport development. The environmental consequences
of airport construction will vary according to site; some potential
locations are in, or adjacent to, ecologically fragile zones. Airport
development on agricultural land may reduce the supply of a
potentially scarce commodity. Opportunity costs are important
and planners, ideally, would consider alternative uses of land in
the process of evaluation. Finally, population density in the immediate neighborhood of a potential site can be a factor of some
importance; although catchment area criteria encourage proximity
to populations, the displacement of residents and the burdens of
noise and pollution imposed on neighbors are broadly calculable,
and contradictory, human costs.

Each of these factors should be considered in the process of site
selection, but there is no agreement in the technical literature
on the significance to be assigned to any single factor. The evaluation of a wide range of factors is difficult and contentious. Even
the elaborate methodologies such as cost-benefit analysis, created
to facilitate this type of decision making, cannot resolve all the
difficulties.[20] Variations in decision-making patterns from country
to country would seem likely under these circumstances, as technical arguments are filtered through institutions and cultural
norms.

Some differences in processes and decisions do appear in these
cases, but a careful analysis of decision making reveals similar
responses. One consistent pattern was secrecy; site selection

everywhere was shrouded in mystery. Airport planners and policy makers justified secrecy as a necessary measure to prevent land speculation, but they were equally reluctant to discuss criteria after decisions were reached and the land acquired. Vagueness and ambiguity characterized *post facto* discussions of the relative importance of different criteria, even in countries such as the United States where secrecy is not considered an acceptable norm for decision makers.

One plausible explanation of this universal pattern is that irregularities in the process of site selection were sufficiently embarrassing to discourage the disclosure of information. Indeed, critical decisions rarely were characterized by rational analysis of relevant variables. In several instances, sites were selected for reasons that had little to do with the technical criteria of airport planners. The original site for London's third airport was chosen primarily because the government already owned the land and operated a runway. A political agreement between the cities of Dallas and Fort Worth was the critical factor in locating the new regional airport. The cities were prepared to cooperate with each other and with the federal government only if the facility would be located precisely midway between their central business districts.[21]

Although a prime directive in site selection is the consideration of all possible locations, it was the exception rather than the rule. French aviation planners never considered seriously alternatives to Roissy-en-France as the site for a new Paris airport. That location had been selected several years before construction was authorized, as planners were determined to retain control over the last major tract of land on the urban fringe.[22] The report issued by the Port Authority of New York and New Jersey in connection with the selection of the Great Swamp in Morris County, New Jersey indicated that alternative sites had been considered and rejected. But no study, in fact, had been conducted; only when plans were stalled did the Port Authority actually undertake the effort.[23] British authorities visited only Stansted when choosing it for London's third airport, and alternatives were considered only when concerted opposition necessitated the abandonment of existing plans. Dallas–Fort Worth planners had no serious alternative to consider.

Even when efforts were made to evaluate criteria for site selection, relevant factors were weighed unequally. Planners everywhere emphasized proximity to catchment areas while virtually ignoring the regional economic impact of facilities. The Ministry of Transport chose sites for new airports in Montreal and Toronto following a study of alternative locations, but the results infuriated provincial officials in Quebec and Ontario whose economic development concerns had been entirely ignored. The same phenomenon occurred in New York where Port Authority planners opted for a site opposed by the governors of both New York and New Jersey. Political opposition eventually reversed priorities for Toronto and forced the abandonment of expansion plans in New York; only in Montreal was an effort made to seek a compromise between these two conflicting criteria.[24]

Physical criteria, such as hilly terrain, fog, and air space conflicts, served frequently as sufficient justification for rejecting certain sites, but these criteria, in fact, were never important enough to rule out locations preferred by planners and policy makers. Charles de Gaulle Airport is plagued by fog and by air traffic control conflicts with Le Bourget and a military base at Creil. Malpensa Airport is fog-bound and hemmed in by the Alps. Both sites were preferred by planners despite these drawbacks because construction was cheap and easy; the area around Roissy-en-France (where de Gaulle Airport was built) was large, flat, and undeveloped; the basic facility was already in place at Malpensa.

In no instance, apart from Britain's Roskill Commission, did the site selection process deliberately consider the social costs of airport development. Planners, to be sure, were determined to avoid the errors of the past by obtaining a sufficiently large tract of land to ensure a buffer against urban encroachment. They sought vacant or underdeveloped land to minimize conflict over acquisition. But they were not particularly concerned with the use of agricultural land or the environmental consequences of airport development, and they chose to ignore completely opportunity costs. In site selection, experience in all cases reveals that poor technical choices are not the product of a social conscience.

Acquiring Land

The acquisition of private property for public purposes may involve voluntary sales by landowners, but expropriation remains a viable alternative in the absence of agreement. Policy makers in all five countries shared similar perspectives on expropriation. They agreed that airports are public utilities and that governments are entitled to seize property from individuals for development. They alleged a technical process for choosing land to be taken, and they believed that private owners of designated land are entitled to "just compensation" according to legal formulae based on current market value. The actual procedures employed in expropriation were not identical (as we shall see in Chapter 6), and some governments chose to exceed the legal requirements of compensation in order to facilitate the acquisition of land. Policy makers, however, believed uniformly that compensation according to market value constitutes just and equitable treatment, even when property owners suffer visibly from expropriation.

The actual definition of site boundaries was always justified in terms of specific, technical need. Never, however, was a master plan for land use ready before the commencement of land acquisition. In every case, planners took as much land as they possibly could. Airport design under such a decision rule often was haphazard. After the Canadian Ministry of Transport had acquired 88,000 acres in Quebec, for example, planners observed that they had no suitable site for the runways; two additional packages of 3000 acres each were added. In France, a land parcel one-third the size of Paris proved insufficient when a site plan was prepared, necessitating a second expropriation.

Policy makers throughout the industrial world assumed that their responsibility for the consequences of development and operation terminated at the airport boundaries. The impact of airport facilities, however, exceeds their physical space, even when quantities of extra land are taken for a buffer zone. Airport design errors exposed residents of Roissy-en-France to so much noise that the airport authority eventually bought most of their homes; but even after the French government accepted some responsibility for such problems, it refused to extend the procedures employed for the few residents near Charles de Gaulle Airport to the far more numerous and long-suffering neighbors of Orly. The Dallas–Fort Worth Regional Airport Board acquired 18,000 acres of land and introduced operational procedures at the new airport in order to protect residents of Irving, Texas from excessive noise; but when the airlines servicing the airport sought to reduce their operating costs by ignoring these rules, the Board raised no objections.

Assessing the Technological Imperative

Theories of the technological imperative predict that policy makers everywhere will define technical problems the same way and adopt similar strategies to deal with them. The results of this inquiry into airport development strategies in five industrial states are consistent with that prediction. Some differences emerged in the lengthy process of decision making, but the initial formulation of government strategies was identical everywhere. Problems were diagnosed and solutions adopted on the basis of similar criteria and value judgments. None of the governments paid much attention to the social costs of airport development in fashioning policies or in responding to opposition. With respect to this technology, at least, the vaunted concern of governments in the industrial world for the costs as well as benefits of technological developments has had no apparent impact on policy.

These results are striking in light of the obvious differences in political structures and cultures among these states. Responsibility for airport development is concentrated within a single agency of the federal government in Canada; responsibility is only slightly more diffuse in the United Kingdom, and the Paris airports are similarly controlled. The role of the central state, however, is less significant in Italy and, even more apparently, in the United States.[25] Local planners, one might have assumed, would have been more sensitive than national authorities to the social impact of development. Similarly, the fear of face-to-face relations in France, long regarded as a decisive cultural feature, might have encouraged planners to place relatively more emphasis than their counterparts elsewhere on the avoidance of conflict with property owners and potential neighbors during the site selection process. Yet, neither structural characteristics nor cultural patterns appear to have influenced the formulation of strategies in any significant way.

What conclusions can be drawn from these observations? Is it true that a technological imperative generated similar strategies for airport development in these five industrial states? Certainly, a broad commitment to technological development was evident, and experts within the aviation community pressed their case in terms of a technological imperative. Arguments about technological determinism, however, are not entirely persuasive, and there are alternative explanations for common strategies which do not require metaphysical interpretations of human behavior.

In all phases of decision making, governments demonstrated that they were not bound by the dictates of aviation technology. Technical constraints on decision making often were ignored; the advice of experts was not always heeded. The secondary role of technical criteria in decision making was most evident in the site selection process, but public officials were also influenced more by political than technical factors in choosing between expansion of existing facilities and new construction elsewhere. Preferences for technological solutions involving public works were universal, but technological arguments justified, rather than shaped, policy.

Perhaps a more important objection to the theory of a technological imperative is that the common interpretation of the requirements of air transportation, and the similar strategies for airport development in Western Europe and North America during the 1960s and early 1970s, did not lead to similar results. Major new air facilities were planned for six of the eight cities in this study, but by 1981 only three were realized. In New York and Toronto, detailed development plans were abandoned, although the Metropolitan Transportation Authority and the Ministry of Transport still retain land purchased originally for development. Construction of a third London airport, the proposed expansion of Vancouver International Airport, and the modernization and expansion of Malpensa remain delayed. Arguments about technological imperatives cannot be restricted to the initial formulation of strategies. The failure to implement development policies, especially when technology allegedly made development imperative, demonstrates the role of human actors in the deployment of technology.

An Alternative Explanation

Common strategies were the product of different actors with different interests. Members of the aviation community, public officials in air transportation agencies, and government authorities with broad responsibilities for public policy approached the problem of airport development with different objectives. All agreed, however, that technological solutions were warranted despite possible social costs. Airport development financed through the public treasury, they agreed, was in everyone's interest, and even the otherwise fractious aviation community of manufacturers, traffic controllers, pilots, commercial and public operators could unite in support of this objective.[26]

At the pinnacle of the aviation community is a small professional elite, with strong international links, which is responsible throughout the advanced industrial world for air transportation services. This elite meets often to exchange information through organizations such as the International Civil Aviation Organization, the International Civil Air Transport Association, and the International Airports Association (plus corresponding regional groupings centered in the industrialized countries), and it shares a professional ideology committed to the growth of air transport and the maximum development of aviation technology. This international community encourages common perceptions of solutions as well as problems.

Public officials in air transportation agencies have no direct economic interest in development, but they are equally committed to the growth of air services. A common pattern in industrial societies is to staff these agencies with former pilots who share an ideological commitment to aviation.* Occupational incentives are equally important in encouraging them to equate the interests of the aviation community with those of the public.[27] These incentives generate aggressive development strategies, based on the premise that the expansion of infrastructure will attract more traffic, generate more revenue, and thereby relieve the financial burdens of a beleaguered industry. Bureaucratic empires are constructed on such premises.

Governments tended to support the development of civil aviation in the 1960s and 1970s largely because they perceived high-quality air service as essential for general economic development. Policy makers were not swayed entirely by arguments about the need to satisfy consumer demand and to protect the health of the industry. Indeed, some elected public officials and civil servants—especially those responsible for government activities other than aviation—opposed actively the implementation of development policies. Support for airport development, however, remained strong at critical levels of government. Officials believed that superior air services, handsome airports, and national flag carriers are necessary to attract private capital and to protect the local or national economy.

---

* An excellent and typical example outside the agencies is the "Interdepartmental Committee" assembled to study the third London airport in 1961. Only two of fifteen members did not come directly from an aviation agency or company.

The different interests of public and private actors could be satisfied through a common strategy of growth and development. Widespread faith in prosperity made development of civil aviation infrastructure appear financially attractive, and an ideology borrowed from the business world made it possible to ignore social costs. Aviation was considered a business that should operate like any business, responding to market conditions, not social concerns. Economic and commercial criteria alone are relevant in decisions concerning infrastructure; if consumer demand is strong, and if a reasonable return on investment (however measured) can be expected, development is warranted.

This perspective on aviation infrastructure can be found in all advanced industrial countries. The establishment of airport authorities in the United Kingdom and Italy was premised on explicit commercial considerations. The British Airports Authority was organized in 1965 expressly to put airports on a profitable business footing,[28] and the Società Esercizi Aeroportuali was launched in 1948 (originally under private auspices) to promote the economic and financial interests of industrialists in the Milan region.[29] The charter of Aéroport de Paris, the autonomous public authority that owns and operates all civilian airports within fifty kilometers of Notre Dame Cathedral, requires the exploitation of airport facilities for commercial profit.[30] In Canada, the Air Administration in the Ministry of Transport identified cost recovery at major airports as a reasonable objective of government and created a "revolving fund" as a first step in implementing the new policy.[31]

Airport planners, developers, and managers in the United States, where the clientèle of public agencies is designated frequently by statute, were especially attracted to a business orientation. The Federal Aviation Administration was instructed in 1958 "to make long-range plans and formulate policy with respect to . . . the orderly development and location of land areas . . . as will best meet the needs of, and serve the interests of, civil aeronautics."[32] In some instances, growth strategies are written into the law. The mission of the Port Authority of New York and New Jersey, for example, is to "make recommendations to the legislatures of the two states . . . for the better conduct of the commerce passing in and through the port of New York, the increase and improvement of transportation and terminal facilities therein, and the more economical and expeditious handling of such commerce."[33] The legal arrangement for the Dallas–Fort

Worth Regional Airport is in the form of a business contract between the two cities. The contract specifies in great detail the
financial obligations of each party, but it does not identify the
"public purpose" for which the agreement was made.

Airport authorities, of course, are not businesses. They can—
and often do—appeal to their responsibilities as public servants
in order to draw public subsidy. In the United States, they pay
no taxes and, because interest on their bonds is tax-exempt, they
are able to borrow at government rates. The British Airports
Authority is particularly proud of operating in the black, but it
has never paid for the infrastructure it inherited in 1966. Aéroport
de Paris borrows on the state's credit and, like other government
authorities, at reduced rates of interest. Airport authorities are
exempt from regulation because they are officially public utilities.
With the power of the state they possess to take land, they are
required to pay only condemnation prices.

The capacity to water at the public trough seems to exacerbate
a tendency to make choices and commitments no sound private
business would make. Public officials may have adapted a business
mentality from the private sector, but they did not behave as
responsible businessmen. Sound business practice accepts the
market and satisfies demand in many different ways; the business
practices of civil aviation often ignored the market and repudiated
alternative strategies. Throughout the 1950s and 1960s, airport
authorities developed facilities at their own discretion with little
interference from governments, citizen groups, or even the market. They enjoyed the ideology of business without always having
to read the proverbial bottom line.

The Technological Imperative and
the Business Mentality

The decisions governing the development of air transportation
infrastructure are characterized by a business, not a technical,
mentality. Economic and commercial considerations, rather than
technological arguments, dominated the decision process. Technical analyses were influential as long as they made good economic
sense, but public authorities had no difficulty in rejecting those
that did not.

This mentality enabled governments to scrap development plans
when costs escalated and commercial considerations changed.

Popular protests and political difficulties contributed to these decisions, as we shall soon see, but the abandonment of elaborate construction projects was the product, in each case, of economic logic. Planners for the Port Authority of New York and New Jersey recognized, in the early 1970s, that aviation forecasts for the New York area were grossly unrealistic and that existing facilities were more than adequate to cope with passenger demand for the foreseeable future. The Labour Government in the United Kingdom dropped plans for a third London airport (later resurrected by the Conservatives) when the Cabinet discovered that the final site selected for the facility, Maplin Sands on the estuary of the Thames River, was too far from London to attract business and much too expensive to build and service. In Toronto, too, economic factors led the federal government to abandon plans for a new air facility. The decision of the Ontario Cabinet to withdraw participation in the project increased the financial burden on Ottawa to a level that federal authorities did not choose to accept.

The importance of economic and commercial considerations in these decisions is not surprising. Aviation planners and government authorities responsible for air transportation view the airport as facilitating the transfer of passengers and cargo between one mode of transport (aviation) and another (surface transit). The decision to build additional infrastructure was predicated on expectations of increasing demand. When market conditions changed and forecasts became more pessimistic, business criteria dictated avoidance of investment on which return would be extremely slow.

The decisions of public officials, of course, were never dictated solely by business considerations. They believed that civil aviation was a public good, and they had considerable success in persuading the public that cost should not be an issue. Their faith in the historic inevitability of growth allowed them to advocate unlimited financial sacrifice in the short term, a position no respectable businessman would take. Nevertheless, criteria borrowed from business ultimately were critical in many of the judgments concerning aviation infrastructure, for projects planned with economic justifications must be able to withstand changes in economic conditions.

Technological arguments cannot account for the results described here. If policy makers were governed by a technological imperative, they could not elevate short-term economic consid-

erations over long-term technological criteria. During most of the
1960s and early 1970s, policy makers believed that the development of aviation technology and the expansion of infrastructure
were conducive to economic growth. In this sense, technology
did influence choice. But policy makers never believed that their
decisions were truly technical in the sense that there are specific
requirements which offer few or no options.[34] In every phase of
decision-making there were choices, and when commercial considerations eventually dictated a more flexible approach to technology, policy-makers were prepared to comply.

Conclusion

The decision in many different countries to deploy the same technology at the same time in similar economic and political circumstances suggests that variations in political structures and cultures
did not influence initial decisions in any significant way. Policy
makers everywhere shared a common perception of aviation requirements and developed common strategies accordingly. But
governing criteria rarely were technical. A business mentality and
common politico-economic views adopted the data of technology
to support policies in aid of frequently narrow interests.

If there were a technological imperative, common outcomes
would have followed the common plans. However, two essential
factors deny this relationship. First, outcomes varied significantly
from case to case. Second, the criteria governing policy changes
were economic and reflected a judgment that civil aviation must
be treated as a business—albeit of a special kind. Hence, a common view of economics dictated the common strategies, derived
from a faith in technology's ability to solve economic problems.
Economic capacities, as managed institutionally, then adjusted the
technological faith, encouraging great variation in the techniques
of moving people within different airport facilities.

Different political systems gave different opportunities to different actors, and they precipitated differences in policies and
outcomes. Hence, the formulation of common strategies tends to
deny the significance of cultural differences across countries, and
the differences in outcomes tend to deny technological determinism. In the following chapters we shall see how technology has
been applied to support the illusion of a dominant role, and we

shall discover how political structures, more than any other factor, assured different solutions to common problems.

Endnotes

1. For a simple summary see J. Herbert Holloman *et al.*, "Government and the Innovation Process," *Technology Review* (May 1979), pp. 30–41.
2. See for example S. Huntington and Z. Brzezinski, *Political Power: USA–USSR* (New York: Viking Press, 1964).
3. Early examples of this literature are Daniel Lerner, *The Passing of Traditional Society* (New York: Free Press, 1958) and Karl Deutsch, "Social Mobilization and Political Development," *American Political Science Review* 3 (September 1961), pp. 493–514.
4. Langdon Winner, *Autonomous Technology: Technics-Out-of-Control as a Theme in Political Thought* (Cambridge, Mass.: MIT Press, 1977), p. 100.
5. *Ibid.*, p. 238.
6. Arguments about the systematic variation of policy from country to country can be found throughout the literature of comparative public policy. See for example A. Heidenheimer, H. Heclo, and C. Adams, *Comparative Public Policy* (New York: St. Martin's Press, 1975). Much of the literature also points to the unique character of public policy in the United States. One attempt at a cultural explanation for this phenomenon can be found in Anthony King, "Ideas, Institutions and the Policies of Governments: A Comparative Analysis," *British Journal of Political Science* (July-October 1973).
7. John Zysman, *Political Strategies for Industrial Order* (Berkeley: University of California Press, 1977), p. 161.
8. A typical anthology concerning different technologies in different countries, with no effective comparisons, is Ron Johnston and Philip Gummett (ed.), *Directing Technology: Policies for Promotion and Control* (New York: St. Martin's Press, 1979).
9. Interview with Holden Withington, Vice-President of Boeing Aircraft Corporation, Renton, Washington, October 31, 1977.
10. For an analysis of the role of aeronautics in the formulation of French policy for science and technology see Robert Gilpin, *France in the Age of the Scientific State* (Princeton: Princeton University Press, 1968).
11. Jerome Milch, "Feasible and Prudent Alternatives: Airport Development in the Age of Public Protest," 24 *Public Policy* 1 (Winter 1976).
12. Todd Laporte and Daniel Metlay, "Technology Observed: Attitudes of a Wary Public," 188 *Science* (April 11, 1975). Also, by the same authors, "Public Attitudes Toward Present and Future Technologies: Satisfactions and Apprehensions," 5 *Social Studies of Science* (1975). A different data set is assessed in "Attitudes of the United States Public Toward Science and Technology," research report prepared for the National Science Foundation by Opinion Research Corporation, Princeton, New Jersey (July 1974).
13. The impact of technological innovation on the design of airports is discussed in Jerome Milch, "Coping with Technological Change: Political Responses

to the Evolution of the Airport," in Joel A. Tarr (ed.), *Retrospective Technology Assessment–1976* (San Francisco: San Francisco Press, 1977).

14. American Society of Planning Officials and the American Municipal Association, *The Airport Dilemma* (Chicago: Public Service Administration, 1938).

15. Ross D. Eckert, *Airports and Congestion: A Problem of Misplaced Subsidies* (Washington: American Enterprise Institute for Public Policy Research, 1972), and Michael E. Levine, "Landing Fees and the Airport Congestion Problem," 12 *The Journal of Law and Economics* (April 1969).

16. When the expansion and modernization of Malton Airport in Toronto was completed in the early 1960s, the surrounding land was undeveloped. A few years later, consultants for the Ministry of Transport recommended further expansion of the airport before the entire area became urbanized. They were too late. Elliot J. Feldman and Jerome Milch, *The Politics of Canadian Airport Development: Lessons for Federalism* (Durham, N.C.: Duke University Press, 1982), Chapter 4. The experiences at Orly in Paris and at Heathrow in London after World War II were almost identical.

17. The major airport in the area was Linate; the expansion of Malpensa was the equivalent, for all intents and purposes, to developing an entirely new airport. Elliot J. Feldman, *Airport Siting as a Problem of Policy and Participation in Technological Societies: The Case of Milano-Malpensa* (Cambridge, Mass. and Torino, Italy: Center for International Affairs and Fondazione Luigi Einaudi, 1978).

18. Feldman and Milch, *The Politics of Canadian Airport Development, op. cit.*, Chapter 5.

19. A good discussion of these criteria can be found in Robert Horonjeff, *The Planning and Design of Airports* (New York: McGraw-Hill, 1962).

20. The application of cost-benefit analysis to airport site selection has been haphazard and, consequently, prone to errors. Even the best of these studies, however, have not escaped criticism. The Commission on the Third London Airport (Roskill Commission) produced the most serious and careful studies, but it also precipitated the most effective criticisms. Perhaps the best summary is John G. U. Adams, "London's Third Airport: From TLA to Airstrip One," *Geographic Journal* (1971).

21. George Edward Burlage, "Federalism's Expanding Dimensions: A Case Study of Decision Making of the Dallas–Fort Worth Regional Airport," unpublished M.A. dissertation, North Texas State University, January 1969.

22. A detailed account may be found in Elliot J. Feldman, "The Parisian White Elephant: The Case of Charles de Gaulle Airport,"2 *The Tocqueville Review* 3(Autumn 1981).

23. The original report prepared by the Port Authority, "A New Major Airport for the New Jersey–New York Metropolitan Area," was released hastily in December 1959 when word of the planning process leaked to the media. David B. Gladfelter, "Jets for the Great Swamp?" in Richard T. Frost (ed.), *Cases in State and Local Government* (Englewood Cliffs, N.J.: Prentice-Hall, 1969). Two years later a multi-volume study, "A Report on Airport Requirements and Sites in the Metropolitan New York–New Jersey Region," was released. This time, the Port Authority's consultants paid greater attention to an analysis of site alternatives.

24. The adoption of different solutions by the same ministry for two airport-related controversies which were identical in all essential respects is analyzed in Feldman and Milch, *The Politics of Canadian Airport Development, op. cit.*

25. For a discussion of these structural differences see Elliot J. Feldman and Jerome Milch, "Options on the Metropolitan Fringe: Strategies for Airport Development," in Douglas Ashford (ed.), *National Resources and Urban Policy* (New York: Methuen, 1980).

26. When commercial airlines were required to pay for redundant and expensive facilities, however, the coalition broke down. Knut Hammarskjold, Director-General of the International Air Transport Association, argues that his organization seeks to prevent governments "from turning airports into monuments, with frills, which are not functional." IATA, however, does not oppose the development of new airports; it merely prefers that the governments, rather than the airlines, pay for construction. Judy Lindsay, "New Airports 'unfunctional, frilly'," *Vancouver Sun* (March 16, 1976).

27. For a discussion of these incentives as they operate in the American context see Jerome Milch, "Inverted Pyramids: The Use and Misuse of Aviation Forecasting," 6 *Social Studies of Science* 1 (February 1976).

28. Chapter 16, Section 3, Article 1 of the Airports Authority Act of 1965 states that: "The Authority shall so conduct its business as to secure that its revenue is not less than sufficient for making provision for the meeting of charges properly chargeable to revenue, taking one year with another."

29. The Commune of Milan entered the company as a majority shareholder in 1951, but the only change it introduced was to secure adequate representation on the governing councils of the company. SEA, whose original name (Società per l'Aeroporto di Busto) was not changed until 1955, remained, to all intents and purposes, a private company with public shareholders. Elda Stifani, "Società Esercizi Aeroportuali: A Case Study in the Italian Airport System," unpublished paper, the Bologna Center of Johns Hopkins University, November 1974.

30. The commercial orientation of Aéroport de Paris is established in Ordonnance 45–2488 of 24 October 1945, Article 3–L–251–3, which created the authority, and it is reinforced by Décret 47–11 of 4 January 1947. According to Article 22, Title 3 of the decree, "the recovery of debts and payments is to be accomplished according to the practices employed by commercial operations."

31. The policy of cost recovery is written into the general guidelines of the Air Administration, but it is not applied across the board. Canadian officials believe that airports in Montreal, Toronto, and Vancouver can pay their own way, and the revolving fund therefore is limited to those facilities. Interview with William Huck, Assistant Deputy Minister, Air Administration, Ministry of Transport, Ottawa, May 11, 1976.

32. Federal Aviation Act, Section 312. Similar wording can be found in the Civil Aeronautics Act of 1938.

33. Article XII of the Port Compact of 1921.

34. These distinctions are made, with emphasis on physicists in Germany, by Otto Keck, *Policy-Making in a Nuclear Program: The Case of the West German Fast Breeder Reactor* (Lexington, Mass.: Lexington Books, 1981).

Chapter 3

FORECASTING AND POLICY CHOICE

Planning for major public investments, such as metropolitan air facilities, begins in principle with forecasting. Forecasting is a technical tool and—like all tools—must be employed properly by both technicians and policy makers. Forecasters must provide accurate and unbiased technical data, and policy makers must rely on this information to make decisions.

The application of aviation forecasting to the planning of major metropolitan airports in the advanced industrial world has not conformed with these requirements. Systematic biases are evident throughout the process, as forecasters have overestimated consistently the demand for air services while underestimating the capacity of existing facilities to accommodate demand. The assumptions that underlie the forecast process are often unrealistic. Forecasters treat government as a neutral actor, for example, even when they acknowledge that it is not, and they assume that demand is a product of impartial market forces even when they recognize that it can be manufactured. The resulting forecasts are almost always consistent with the preferences of the agency or organization commissioning the study.

Policy makers have used forecasting for their own purposes. Plans for the expansion of aviation infrastructure rarely were triggered by forecasts of impending congestion. Detailed projections were either unavailable when crucial choices were made or, if available, they were ignored by policy makers. The decision to proceed with development has not been predicated anywhere, in any significant way, on estimates of supply and demand, but forecasting has been employed universally to justify these decisions.

Indeed, forecasting has proved to be an effective political device rather than an instrument of technical rationality.

Reliability and Utility

Policy decisions always depend on assumptions about the future, but accurate and explicit forecasts are vital when decisions involve a significant allocation of resources or long lead time for execution. Market signals alone, such as the rise or fall of prices as a result of an imbalance in supply and demand, are less useful than forecasts in determining investment choices because they provide little advance warning for decision makers.[1] Detailed forecasts of market behavior and consumer preferences have become an indispensable component of planning, and governments everywhere have responded by institutionalizing forecasting for most public sector activity.

The most competent forecasters, equipped with the most sophisticated techniques, cannot provide policy makers with guarantees of the future. William Page and Howard Rush, for example, examined a series of forecasts for non-ferrous metal production developed over a period of seventy years and concluded that the most accurate forecasts were the most vague—those providing no quantifiable data and little explicit information.[2] J. Scott Armstrong suggests, on the basis of a review of forecasts in a variety of fields, that there are "no studies that showed an important advantage for expertise" in predicting the future.[3] Indeed, recognized and respected experts in forecasting have compiled a poor record in all fields over the years.

There is no specific training to be a professional forecaster. In civil aviation, few of the forecasters have studied economics. Many have been schooled in aviation and have adapted their skills; most are statisticians. The skills involved obviously are quantitative, but the craft often is more an art for which most forecasters are ill-prepared. Although it is not obvious that any training would dramatically improve forecasting, many current professionals have essential disadvantages.

The key to successful forecasting lies in the accuracy of core assumptions, not in the application of sophisticated techniques.[4] Experts have no advantages here; their assumptions are not necessarily more accurate than those of non-experts. Economic forecasters in the United States, for example, consistently have projected growth at a higher rate than the American economy has been able to sustain; nor did the accuracy of their forecasts improve as their methods became more sophisticated or as the target date drew near. The errors stemmed from faulty assumptions: Forecasters argued that productivity is the major determinant of economic performance, and they minimized the significance of changes in the work week or unemployment patterns.[5] Trade union officials would not have made the same assumptions.

Forecasting, then, remains more of an art than a science: Practitioners are not equipped with a crystal ball, and their assumptions about the future may be woefully inaccurate. But forecasting can still contribute to rational policy choice by reducing "the area of the unpredictable to a manageable series of clear alternatives."[6] Forecasters commonly evaluate the implications of existing trends, projecting current patterns of behavior into the future. These descriptive forecasts provide one scenario for policy makers. By varying some of the underlying assumptions, other visions are possible. Indeed, forecasters can provide a range of scenarios based upon assumptions that are defined clearly and explicitly for policy makers.

Alternatively, forecasters can supplement these descriptive statements with normative visions of the future. Normative forecasting constitutes the effort to "assess future goals, needs, desires, missions, etc. and work backwards to the present."[7] These forecasts allow the policy maker to determine the most desirable future from among the alternatives and to outline the steps necessary to create that future.

The contribution of forecasting to policy choice need not rest on any special insight into the future. Forecasters can contribute to rational decision making by describing alternative futures, and public officials can make choices, based on this information, which reflect a thoughtful analysis and a clear understanding of the range of possibilities. Unfortunately, the application of these techniques in decisions involving aviation infrastructure does not reflect an appreciation of either the limits or the potential contribution of forecasting. It does reflect a different political function.

Inverted Pyramids

There are three basic kinds of forecasting utilized in civil aviation. The most common, and the one to receive principal attention here, focuses on traffic. Forecasters predict numbers of passengers and aircraft movements, tonnage of cargo, and volume of mail that will move through a given airport or be served by airlines or manufacturers during a specified future period. A second type of forecasting concerns likely economic development associated with the construction of new facilities. Here, forecasters assess the total value of public works for job creation, population relocation, and general economic activity. Finally, forecasting for civil aviation—especially in the 1970s—has concentrated on the anticipated environmental impact of traffic and construction, mostly with respect to noise. No matter what the parameters, and no matter what the particular objectives, the phenomenon of forecasting itself follows consistent patterns for the domination of politics over technique.

Civil aviation is very dependent on long-range forecasting. Commercial airline companies require knowledge of the market in order to determine fleet requirments. Wide-body jets make little sense if demand is slack and aircraft cannot be filled. Similarly the purchase of long-range aircraft would be inefficient if the demand for air services were concentrated in the short- and medium-haul markets. Accurate forecasts are imperative because orders for new aircraft must be placed several years in advance of entry into service.

Accurate long-range forecasting is most important in airport planning. Air facilities are costly to build, they are voracious consumers of scarce land, and much time passes between planning and starting operation. The first phase of construction for the Dallas–Fort Worth Regional Airport, for example, required $700 million in public funds and 17,500 acres of land on the periphery of the metropolitan area. The Canadian government spent an initial $600 million and acquired a final total of 98,000 acres of land in order to build the new airport for Montreal. Dallas–Fort Worth Regional Airport opened for business nearly nine years after agreement was reached to build. Charles de Gaulle Airport took seventeen years from the first plan to the commencement of operations. Errors in judgment can have long-term consequences for the public, and policy makers seek to minimize their risks by commissioning forecasts of market demand.

The role of aviation forecasting in airport development is recognized by industry representatives and government planners. Market forecasting is viewed in most quarters as the initial step in airport planning[8] and the basis for facility expansion.[9] The Federal Aviation Administration in the United States claims that its forecasts are "intended to assist in promoting the development of comprehensive, long-range metropolitan airport master plans by airport and local government planning officials."[10] Successful planning, all participants agree, requires detailed forecasts of economic trends, technological developments, and individual preferences.

Theory

Forecasting for airport development is a complex multi-stage procedure. The techniques of aviation forecasting may differ modestly from place to place, but there are three basic steps involved in arriving at policy recommendations for airport facilities. The first step is a forecast of the number of passengers who will use the airport system in the target years. This figure is important for determining terminal size, baggage handling facilities, and parking space. Planning for runway development, however, requires a second stage. Passenger figures must be translated into aircraft operations and added to estimates of military, cargo, and general aviation flights. Finally, forecasters must estimate the future capacity of the airport system, for technological developments may affect the ability of existing facilities to cope with demand.

Each stage is replete with assumptions about economic trends, business decisions, technological changes, and consumer preferences. Estimates of passenger demand, for example, are predicated on such factors as population growth, occupational distribution, economic development, disposable family income, and price structures. The determination of aircraft operations requires a forecast of the air carrier fleet in the target year and an estimate of the average load factor for each aircraft. Airport capacity is even more difficult to gauge, because it requires some idea of the state of technology in some future year.

Forecasters are aware of the role of these basic assumptions in the preparation of their projections. There are, however, other equally important and subtler premises. The demand for air travel may depend on market conditions, but government actions can encourage or dampen demand. The deregulation of the air industry in the United States in the late 1970s, for example, generated competition and increased the traffic at some air facilities.

Taxation, zoning regulations, quotas, and increased charges for airport services have the opposite effect on demand. Forecasters must make some assumptions, whether implicitly or explicitly, about the likely role of government in the process.

The reliability of the projections made at each stage in the process depends both on the precision of previous calculations and on the accuracy of forecast assumptions. Incorrect assumptions are particularly significant when they occur at an early stage in the procedure, for they are then reproduced at each stage in the calculation. Moreover, long-range forecasts are more hazardous than short-term predictions of demand patterns.

These characteristics of aviation forecasting invoke the image of an inverted pyramid. The most elaborate and detailed recommendations for airport requirements, developed through the systematic application of scientific forecasting techniques, are still dependent on the accuracy of basic assumptions about the future course of events. The structure of forecasting, like that of an inverted pyramid, becomes increasingly unstable as it grows larger and more complex.

Practice

It is hardly surprising that the history of aviation forecasting is filled with monumental miscalculations. Long-range forecasting— that is, estimates for periods in excess of five to ten years—is erratic. New York's Regional Plan Association, for example, projected in 1947 that domestic air passenger traffic in the metropolitan area would reach 31.6 million by 1960; the actual figure was only 13.1 million.[11] Short-term forecasting has improved greatly in recent years,[12] but these projections are of little help in planning major infrastructure. They also can be hazardous. An airport consultant estimated in 1968 that there would be 322,800 aircraft operations at the Detroit airport just two years later; the actual figure, 260,791, was in error by more than 20 percent.[13]

There are also significant disparities in the projections of demand developed by different forecasters for the same airport or airport network. Forecasts of passenger traffic in the Toronto metropolitan area for the year 2000, prepared between 1969 and 1972, range from a high of 200 million passengers to a low of 30 million.[14] Six different forecasts of total civil air carrier revenue passenger-miles for the entire United States in 1980 prepared during the mid-1960s yielded a range of 283 billion to 507 billion.[15] Short-term projections are less likely than long-range forecasts to generate disagreement, but variations still are not unusual. Five different forecasts of passenger traffic for Milan in 1980 produced a range of more than 100 percent, even though all the projections were made in the late 1960s.[16]

Miscalculations and disagreements arise in the forecast process because of uncertainty over the precise figures to be employed in calculating future demand. But if the size and frequency of errors as well as the wide variations in projections are understandable, other characteristics of aviation forecasting are more disquieting. For one thing, forecasting errors are not random, as one might expect in light of these many uncertainties. Until the late 1960s, aviation forecasts prepared by governments, businesses, and academic institutions consistently underestimated the demand for air travel; the forecasts prepared since that time have just as consistently overestimated growth. Only two out of twenty-four forecasts of U.S. domestic airline revenue passenger-miles prepared between 1950 and 1969 overestimated demand; by contrast, eighteen out of twenty-six forecasts for 1975 overestimated demand, and not a single projection made after 1966 fell short of the mark.[17]

Forecasters have tended to update their projections whenever growth patterns suggested that they had underestimated the demand for travel. Yet, they have been reluctant to reverse their estimates when the demand for services did not reach expected levels. Rapid growth in air travel, even over a relatively short period of time, commonly was regarded as an indicator of future market demand. A decline in growth rates, conversely, was viewed as a short-term wave in an otherwise steady sea of growth. Projections of future demand are based invariably on the period of the most rapid growth in air travel (typically, the mid-1960s), even when stagnation or slow growth in subsequent years has suggested that the demand for air services may be more cyclical than linear.

These patterns appear in all five countries of this study. Forecasters for the Port Authority of New York and New Jersey predicted in 1957 that 24.7 million passengers would pass through New York's three airports in 1965. The actual growth rate fell below expectations for most of the intervening years, but a spurt in air travel beginning in 1962 brought the 1965 figure slightly above the projected demand (Figure 3–1). As a result, forecasters

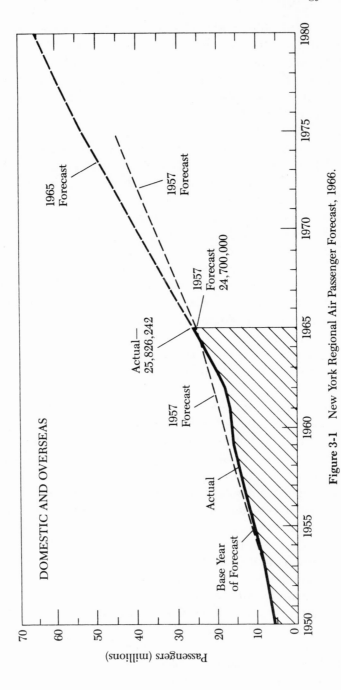

Figure 3-1   New York Regional Air Passenger Forecast, 1966.

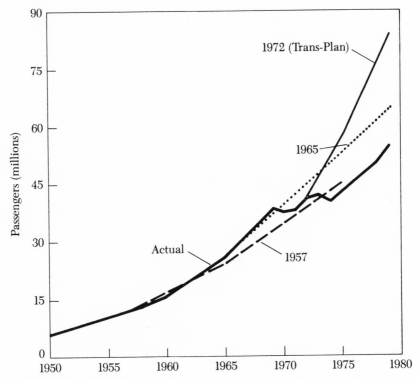

Figure 3-2 Actual versus Predicted Passengers: New York Airport System.

updated their projections in 1966, calling for 53.5 million passengers in 1975 instead of the 45.3 million predicted in 1957. The new forecasts proved much less accurate because the growth rate declined sharply in the late 1960s and early 1970s. Undaunted, Port Authority forecasters developed a new batch of forecasts that ignored the downturn in travel. They projected 81 million passengers in 1980 instead of the 65 million forecast in 1966. In 1980, 53.5 million passengers passed through the New York airports (Figure 3–2).*

In London, aviation forecasts were produced by the British Airports Authority (BAA), the Civil Aviation Authority (CAA), the

---

* No serious forecasts were prepared in Dallas–Fort Worth before decisions were made. However, in 1965 the site selection team provided short-term forecasts that underestimated growth rates. These forecasts appear as an exception to the patterns described here, but they were not the product of any serious effort to estimate the supply or demand in the area and cannot be compared with the more sophisticated efforts of forecasters elsewhere.

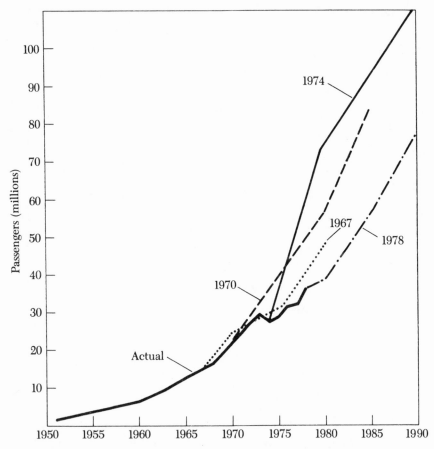

Figure 3-3   Actual versus Predicted Passengers: London Airport System.

Department of Trade, and the Roskill Commission. The different forecasters produced similar results. 31.9 million passengers utilized London area airports in 1977, and all but one of the forecasts generated over the previous decade overestimated demand (Figure 3–3). The Government's 1967 White Paper calling for a new four-runway airport for London presented "high" and "low" estimates rather than a single "most likely" figure. During the next three years, demand approximated the "high" figure; consequently, the Roskill Commission in 1970 assumed that rapid growth rates were well established and projected a sharp increase in the demand for air services. Ironically, the "low" estimate in the White Paper would have provided a more accurate picture of London area traffic in 1977.

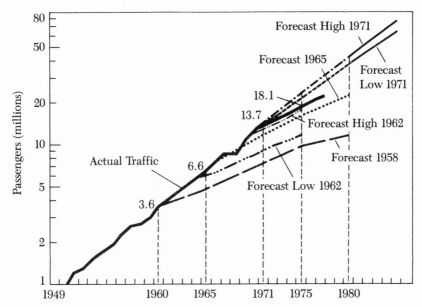

Figure 3-4   Actual versus Predicted Passengers: Paris Airport System.
(N.B.: The *y*-axis of this graph is logarithmic, rather than linear.)

The experiences of French forecasters were similar in most respects, even though the earliest forecasts seriously underestimated passenger traffic in the Paris region (Figure 3–4). The forecast developed in 1965 projected the demand at approximately 23 million in 1980. A spurt in traffic in the late 1960s encouraged planners to develop new forecasts; this time, they estimated that 39–44 million passengers would pass through Paris airports in 1980. In 1978 passenger traffic in Paris had reached the 23 million of the earlier projection.

Of the five forecasts for passenger movements in Milan, Alitalia's was the most optimistic, estimating that 12 million passengers would use Linate and Malpensa Airports in 1978. The forecasts produced by the Ministero dei Transporti e Aviazione Civile, by contrast, were much more conservative, calling for 7.2 million passengers in 1978. All the forecasts overestimated demand; only 5.8 million passengers passed through Milan in the target year (Figure 3–5).

Forecasts prepared for the Montreal area by both private sector and government experts were no better. Estimates of demand prepared by the firm of Kates, Peat, Marwick and Company in 1966 projected a figure of 8.3 million in 1975 and 16.4 million in

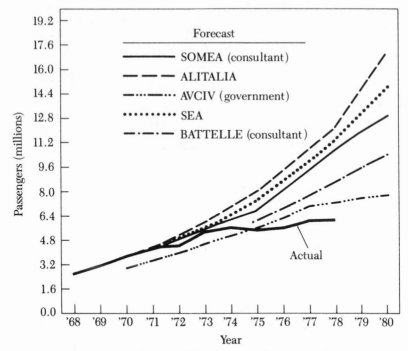

Figure 3-5   Actual versus Predicted Passengers: Milan Airport System.

1985. Several years later Transport Canada's own forecasters increased the estimates to 8.9 million for 1975 and 20.6 million for 1985 (Figure 3–6). But the growth in traffic levelled off in the mid-1970s, and the 1980 figure was only 8.0 million—well below expectations.

Short-term forecasts prepared in 1972 by Transport Canada for Toronto and Vancouver provided reasonably accurate estimates of demand through the 1970s (Figures 3–7 and 3–8). Long-range projections, on the other hand, are more questionable. In 1969 forecasters projected the demand in the Toronto area for the year 2000 at 96 million passengers; two years later they revised their estimate up to 198 million—a figure more than five times greater than the number of passengers using New York area airports when this forecast was made.*

Forecasts of rapid and sustained growth have been accompanied everywhere by predictions of impending saturation of air facilities

* The figure of 198 million passengers was proposed by the Bureau of Management Consulting in a May 1971 report to Transport Canada.

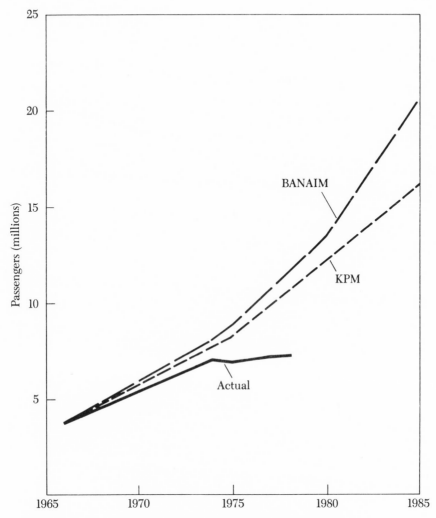

Figure 3-6   Actual versus Predicted Passengers: Montreal Airport System.

and recommendations for the immediate expansion of infrastructure. Forecasters understood that the increase in aircraft movements would not keep pace with the rise in passenger traffic, but
they were confident that the capacity of existing airports to service
both aircraft and passengers would soon be exhausted. The most
egregious errors were made in New York, where Port Authority
forecasters predicted in 1959 that area airports would be unable
to cope with the 24.7 million passengers expected in 1965. Although traffic actually exceeded predictions by 4.5 percent, the

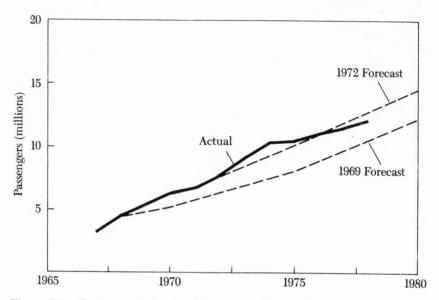

Figure 3-7   Short-term Forecasts of Passengers: Toronto International Airport
(Malton).

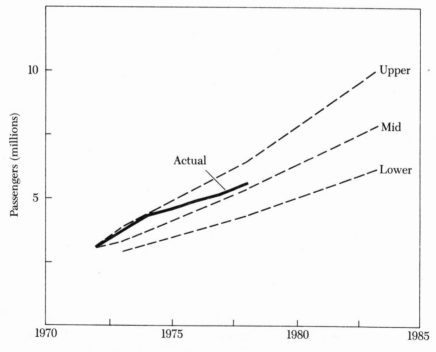

Figure 3-8   Short-term Forecasts of Passengers: Vancouver International
Airport.

airport system had no major difficulty in coping with demand. By 1978 traffic in New York exceeded 50 million passengers with no visible airport saturation. Forecasters had predicted a 62.5 percent increase in the number of peak-hour aircraft movements during the decade of the 1970s; instead, the total number of aircraft movements actually declined by 10 percent.

Milanese forecasters were almost as bad as the New Yorkers. The Società Esercizi Aeroportuali (SEA) predicted a 15 percent average annual growth rate in passenger traffic and a 10 percent increase in aircraft movements during the 1970s. Linate, they argued, could not accommodate the traffic. But the actual number of movements in Milan in 1977 (115,600) was 38 percent below the forecast for that year. Between 1970 and 1977 passenger traffic increased by 55 percent, substantially below the 166 percent predicted by forecasters, while the number of aircraft movements increased by only 20 percent compared with the estimate of 95 percent.

Aéroport de Paris had projected a growth rate in aircraft movements of approximately one third the increase in passenger traffic. The 14 percent annual growth rate in demand, planners expected, would be accommodated by a 5 percent growth in movements. The predicted 3:1 ratio proved to be an accurate measure for the late 1970s, but the increase in passenger travel was only 9 percent per year between 1974 and 1978. Consequently, aircraft movements increased at less than 3 percent annually.

British forecasters were more accurate in estimating aircraft movements for London area airports. The 1967 White Paper predicted a 34–78 percent increase in movements during the 1970s, and the actual increase was 60 percent. But the White Paper also predicted that Heathrow would be saturated by 1970, at the latest, when demand reached 250,000 movements per year. Heathrow registered nearly 300,000 movements in 1978.

Explaining Errors

What accounts for this pattern of errors in the aviation forecasts produced throughout the industrial world during the 1960s and 1970s? Why did forecasters generate projections of rapid and sustained growth in air travel despite evidence of erratic or cyclical

demand, and why did they predict airport saturation, even when
existing facilities were capable of handling increased traffic? Systematic errors are the product of common assumptions about the
nature of air traffic demand, economic trends, and technological
developments. These assumptions, in turn, derived both from a
conservative bias in the forecast process and the structure of incentives under which forecasters operate.

Common Assumptions

Forecasters everywhere perceived the market for air travel as
infinite. Consumer demand, they recognized, is related to economic factors such as disposable family income and the structure
of air fares, but there is no limit to the desire of individuals to
fly. A great untapped market exists both among the majority of
the population of every country who have never flown as well as
among existing air travellers who would fly more frequently if
economic conditions were right. In the long run, growth patterns
in air travel may resemble an S-shaped curve, but forecasters
believed that they did not have to worry for the foreseeable future
about inflection points.[18] Some forecasters have raised questions
about this assumption in recent years, but the notion that market
demand might be limited by non-economic factors remains the
view of a small minority.[19]

In estimating the demand for air travel, forecasters assume that
market conditions prevail. The growth of civil aviation can be
extrapolated from existing technical and social trends, unlike military aviation whose "future depends largely on unpredictable
political changes."[20] The neutrality of government is assumed,
even though forecasters acknowledge that public policy can affect
the operational environment of civil aviation.[21] Demand, of course,
can be manufactured by aviation interests through promotional
fares and tours, but many forecasters do not consider the manip-
ulation of demand in this manner to be interference in market
operations.

The market, then, is almost sacrosanct, and demand must be
accommodated whenever and wherever it arises. Forecasters often
work with peak-hour estimates, both for passengers and aircraft
movements, on the assumption that this "natural" demand cannot
be shifted to off-peak hours, whether by regulation or by economic

incentive.* Passengers choose to travel at 9:00 A.M. or at 5:00 P.M. because the time slot is convenient rather than because flights are scheduled abundantly at those hours. Any attempt to shift traffic to slack periods, they have believed, is doomed to failure.

Assumptions about the economic prospects of the advanced industrial world have been uniformly optimistic. Jacques Block of Aéroport de Paris predicted in 1969 that the average annual increase in income would continue at a rate of 4 percent in major markets for the foreseeable future;[22] FAA forecasters still assumed a 4.25 percent long-term annual average GNP growth in constant dollars as late as 1973.[23] The difficulties experienced by western economies following the sharp rise in oil prices modified expectations, but the Department of Trade in the United Kingdom still predicted in 1974 an average annual growth in Gross Domestic Product of 3.0–3.5 percent during the 1980s.[24]

Forecasters have been equally optimistic about the structure of air fares. Block's 1969 forecast was predicated on a 2 percent annual decline in the costs of air travel,[25] while the FAA predicted a decline of 1 percent per annum.[26] Both assumed that diminishing costs would be passed along to consumers. An increase of 250 percent in the price of aviation fuel between 1972 and 1974 introduced an element of uncertainty into the forecasting process, but the soaring costs of fuel did not alter significantly the assumptions about fare structures. Forecasters believed that the higher cost of fuel would be offset by higher load factors, thereby assuring a continued decline in the real costs of air travel.[27]

Economic growth combined with declining fares would increase both disposable income and the propensity to travel. The continued increase in population, particularly in urban areas, would contribute to the growing demand for air services. More important, continued changes in employment patterns would expand the number of white collar, managerial, and professional occupations. These categories are likely to take advantage of favorable economic conditions, both for personal and business-related travel, and forecasters were confident that economic indicators were "firmly established in long-term upward trends and provide the base for a surging growth in civil aviation."[28]

---

* The formal reports prepared by the Port Authority of New York and New Jersey in connection with its recommendations for a new jetport presented data on aircraft movements strictly in terms of peak-hour traffic. No effort was made to calculate annual movements.

Forecasters were much more ambivalent about the prospects for advances in aviation technology than about the economic future of the western world. Forecasts of technological innovation are even more uncertain and subjective than economic projections,[29] and forecasters generally were more reluctant to make bold predictions of technological advances. Still, they were more conscious of the development of aircraft with increased seating capacity than they were about innovations in air control systems that might increase airport capacity. Improvements in navigation systems and in the method of handling traffic in the terminal area airspace can increase the instrument landing capacity of an airport, but forecasters assumed, almost uniformly, that capacity would not be expanded.[30] Newer aircraft, moreover, would not alleviate problems of congestion despite their larger capacity, because the increased efficiency of the aircraft would reduce passenger costs and expand the market for air travel.

Ambivalent attitudes with respect to technological innovation were reflected, above all, in forecasts of aircraft noise. The second generation of jet aircraft (for example, Boeing 747, DC-10, TriStar L-1011) introduced during the 1970s was quieter than its predecessor, and forecasters assumed that noise levels would be reduced as older equipment was phased out. Aircraft on the drawing board or under development at the time (for example, Concorde, SST, STOL-craft)[31] would exacerbate noise problems, but most forecasters chose to ignore or downplay the impact of these new aircraft in projecting future noise levels.

These assumptions, shared by forecasters throughout the industrial world, produced optimistic views of air traffic demand and pessimistic views of air infrastructure capacity. Irregular growth patterns had little immediate impact on underlying assumptions, as forecasters refused to allow "short-term fluctuations" to alter "long-term and underlying trends."[32] When overestimates proved embarrassing, forecasters stopped publishing growth projections.*

Many of the errors in these common assumptions are evident from the perspective of 1981. Fuel prices continued to soar after the 1973–74 embargo, thereby increasing the costs of air carrier operations well beyond expectations. The demand for air services

---

* Aéroport de Paris, for example, has produced no new forecasts for public consumption since the 1971 air traffic controllers strike contributed to a traffic downturn soon sustained by the first oil crisis.

slackened in the mid-1970s, as economic problems surfaced in every industrial country. Commercial airlines responded by reducing fares to stimulate demand (aided in the United States by the deregulation of the airlines and in other countries by state ownership), by increasing the load factors on aircraft, and by reducing the number of scheduled flights. Purchase of new aircraft was delayed, thereby extending the lifetime of older and noisier equipment. When new aircraft were ordered, air carriers often opted for stretched versions of the first generation of jets rather than the newer, quieter equipment that were too large to operate economically. Passenger traffic continued to rise at most airports, but at rates substantially below those experienced in the 1960s; aircraft movements remained virtually stable. Noise levels remained high. Congestion in terminal areas did increase at peak travel times, but runway capacity—the source of the pressure to build in the 1960s—proved to be adequate two decades later.

Fighting the Previous War

The common assumptions that provided the basis for these common errors were the product, to some extent, of a conservative bias in the forecast process. The bias is reflected in a basic tenet of forecasting—that, "The universe of the future will be much like the universe of the past."[33] Practitioners rely principally on the extrapolation of well-established trends that are modified in light of "expected" changes in critical variables. In the short run, the conservative bias led forecasters to underestimate the growth of air travel; once long-term growth patterns in aviation seemed established, the opposite problem arose. The rapid growth rates of the 1950s and mid-1960s became the basis for extrapolations.

Historical developments have reinforced this conservative bias. Throughout the 1940s and 1950s, forecasters, tending to underestimate the growth in air travel, were embarrassed by traffic congestion. By the late 1960s, stories of circling aircraft with "no place to land" became common.[34] A conservative bias not to predict any significant change in established trends became a sustained concern not to be caught with inadequate facilities in the next decade. Incorrect forecasts also reinforced conservative thinking. Between 1958 and 1961 the pattern of traffic growth in the United States was interrupted by a slight decline in the number of aircraft operations, from 26 million in 1958 to 25.5 million in

1961. A few forecasters assumed that these developments signalled the start of a new era in aviation, and they adjusted their predictions accordingly. In 1961, for example, the Federal Aviation Administration revised its earlier estimate of aircraft operations downward from 45 million in 1964 to 30 million in 1966. The earlier estimate, however, was more nearly correct.[35] In retrospect, forecasters were convinced that the 1958–1961 period had been an anomaly, a short-term fluctuation in a well-established growth pattern. Therefore, any later signs of downturn in aviation were even more likely to be greeted with skepticism.

Still another factor reinforcing the conservatism of forecasters is the influence of fashion. The very fact that reputable forecasters had predicted during the 1960s that aviation would continue to grow at a rapid rate for an indefinite period of time made it all the more difficult for other forecasters to dispute the accepted view. Numerous government economists, as well as many non-government organizations, shared their optimism for the economy.[36] Thus, each individual forecaster was encouraged by the community of forecasters and economists to accept the basic assumptions.

The conservative biases of forecasters represent a methodological weakness in the art of conjecture. By projecting the future as a continuation of the past, forecasters encourage policy makers to avoid the repetition of errors but do not encourage ample preparation for significant departures from established patterns. Various categories of variables are thought to be essential to accurate projections, yet demand elasticities for these are rarely known and even more rarely calculated. Forecasters, it appears, are constantly preparing to meet a prior need—to fight the previous war.

Hired Guns

Forecasters employed by agencies responsible for airport development have been more prone to systematic error than their colleagues employed by other organizations, both public and private. Advocates of growth policies consistently generate more optimistic forecasts of demand and more pessimistic forecasts of supply than do opponents of development. These results cannot be explained entirely in methodological terms.

Systematic—not random—variations always appear where there

are competitive forecasts. A review of several major forecasting studies in the United States in the decade after 1957 revealed that the FAA projected higher long-term growth rates for domestic passenger traffic than Boeing, Douglas, Lockheed, General Electric, or North American Aviation.[37] Only Alitalia was more optimistic than SEA about the demand for air travel services in Milan.* SEA forecast greater demand than government agencies such as the Ministero dei Transporti e Aviazione Civile or private consultants such as the Battelle Memorial Institute and the Centro Sviluppo Transporti Aerei (Figure 3–5). Projections of passenger traffic in the Toronto area were generated by a consultant to the Ontario Department of Treasury and Economics in 1970; his estimates for the year 2000 were nearly two thirds lower than those of Transport Canada.[38]

Airport planners, moreover, were inclined to adjust forecasts of traffic growth when government or agency policies no longer favored expansion. In 1974 the Department of Trade in the United Kingdom, for example, produced more conservative forecasts of traffic growth than either the British Airports Authority or the Civil Aviation Authority had generated in previous years (Figure 3–3). Economic conditions had become less favorable by 1974, and the new forecast was more realistic than its predecessor. It is also true, however, that the forecasts were generated when the Labour Government was in the process of dismantling the Conservative Party's development project for a new airport at Maplin Sands. The Port Authority of New York and New Jersey reduced its forecasts of traffic growth after 1970 when it concluded that a new airport could not be built anywhere in the metropolitan area. The 80 million passengers forecast for 1980 still exceeded the capacity of the New York airport system, according to Port Authority estimates made in the mid-1960s. The agency insisted in 1971, however, that New York could survive without an additional airport, in part because a rival agency, the Metropolitan Transportation Authority, was planning to develop its own airport to compete with Port Authority facilities.[39]

Local governments opposed to airport development occasionally employed forecasters. The City of Toronto commissioned a private

---

* The national airline was negotiating at the time with government officials for permission to buy new and larger aircraft. Alitalia, like SEA, had a distinct interest in optimistic forecasts of air traffic demand.

consultant to examine the impact of the proposed new air facility in nearby Pickering Township; the consultant raised objections to Transport Canada's forecasts, introduced new assumptions into the process, and produced estimates of demand considerably below those of any other forecaster.[40] In Vancouver, local authorities challenged Transport Canada's forecasts indirectly. The Airport Planning Committee, created as a joint venture by three levels of government and several private groups in order to review Transport's plans for the expansion of Vancouver International Airport, established a Forecasting and Economic Subcommittee to consider, in part, aviation forecasts. The subcommittee chairman, representing the Greater Vancouver Regional District, produced a minority report contesting Transport's forecasts. No alternative projections were offered, but the report raised objections to assumptions similar to those raised in Toronto.[41]

Citizen groups opposing the development of airports often have challenged the forecasts of airport planners, but they rarely have had the resources or expertise to generate independent projections. One exception to this rule was the Jersey Jetport Site Association, a private group opposed to the development of a new airport in the New York metropolitan area which hired a consultant firm (United Research, Inc.) to study the need for additional aviation infrastructure. The consultant projected traffic growth at a more moderate rate than the Port Authority had forecast by predicting the development of vertical and/or short take-off and landing aircraft and the introduction of larger jets with greater capacity.[42]

London area citizens challenged the forecasts of noise more than the forecasts of traffic, and they too were prepared to seek out independent experts. Local groups generally accepted overall growth projections, but they doubted noise could be as modest as the government said. The acoustical engineers whom they hired supported their claims. Citizen groups elsewhere could only raise objections to forecast assumptions and propose alternative solutions to the congestion predicted by planners. Vancouver citizens for example, proposed moving General Aviation (private aircraft) out of the International Airport, a solution apparently adopted by Transport Canada in 1980. Opponents of Pickering Airport in Toronto argued that Malton Airport was capable of handling the volume of traffic predicted for 1990 by Transport Canada.[43]

The tendency of forecasters to produce estimates of passenger demand, aircraft movements, airport capacity, economic development, and noise consistent with the preferences of their clients reinforces the idea that the origin of expert forecast errors is not entirely methodological. In formulating projections of demand and capacity, forecasters respond to external cues, such as the mandate of agencies for whom they work or the terms of reference provided by clients. Government agencies responsible for airport development have every incentive to generate optimistic demand forecasts and pessimistic estimates of capacity; the planning process is predicated on the assumption that it is preferable to develop excess capacity rather than discourage the use of air travel through an inadequate airport system. By contrast, government agencies with different mandates or citizen groups opposed to development are inclined to err in the opposite direction. The structure of incentives promotes different responses to the same problem among these different participants.

It is possible that forecasts have been prepared that contradict client preferences, but we have not found them. From the examples in the public domain, one must conclude that forecasters are "hired guns," employed by a variety of agencies and organizations in pursuit of conflicting goals. They respond to the objectives of their clients in generating projections of supply and demand. The process need not be dishonest, as both forecasters and their employers may operate with sincere and common—but narrow—perceptions of the public interest. Unfortunately, the resulting forecasts can be expected to err in highly predictable ways.

Applications of Forecasting

The development of aviation infrastructure involves the commitment of significant resources over an extended period of time. If forecasting were an important decision-making tool, systematic forecasting errors would hinder the decisions to commit resources. However, policy makers have not suffered from the poor quality of forecasts because they have not relied upon them in making critical choices concerning airport development. Decisions have been based largely on political and economic criteria, not the technical information that includes traffic forecasts. Although forecasting proved to be important in all five countries, its primary function was to justify policies rather than to contribute to rational decision making.

Forecasting and Decision Making

Detailed projections of consumer demand were available in four of the eight cities examined in this study at the time critical decisions concerning the expansion of facilities were made. The Port Authority of New York and New Jersey recommended the development of a fourth jetport in 1959 on the basis of forecasts prepared two years earlier, and the Ministry of Transport in Canada submitted proposals for a new airport in Montreal and an expanded facility in Toronto based on forecasts commissioned from outside consultants. The first formal recommendation for the construction of a third London airport was generated (in 1960) by the Hole Committee, which did consider forecasts of demand.

The availability of forecasts did not guarantee decision making based on technical assessments. The governors of New York and New Jersey, whose approval was necessary for the construction of a fourth jetport, were not persuaded that the Port Authority's forecasts of imminent saturation of air traffic in the metropolitan area made new development inevitable. Their support for the jetport was based solely on the regional economic benefits to be derived from development, not a requirement to meet anticipated traffic demand, and was contingent upon agreement on a satisfactory site for the facility. When an impasse developed they withdrew their support, even though the forecasts had not changed significantly in the intervening years.

Policy makers in Canada were no more willing to base critical decisions on forecasts than their counterparts in the United States. Projections of demand prepared for the Ministry of Transport did not justify the immediate development of new airports in either Montreal or Toronto.[44] Transport officials urged the Cabinet to approve the construction of a new airport for Montreal despite the forecasts, on the grounds that Dorval would become saturated with traffic at some future point and that immediate development would save money. Economic, not technical, criteria were the basis of the proposal the Cabinet accepted in August 1968. The Ministry did not favor a new airport for Toronto, because it preferred additional infrastructure. The Cabinet initially accepted this recommendation but reversed its position four months later, approving the construction of a new facility in Toronto. Political factors (for example, organized opposition of Malton neighbors and the demand of Ontario politicians for equal treatment with Quebec) dictated policy choice.

The sole instance of rational application of forecasting in the decision-making process among the eight sites occurred in Great Britain. The delay between the initial recommendation of development (in 1960) and the commitment of the British government to the third London airport (in 1967) was unusually long, and by the time the Cabinet acted a wide range of forecasts had become available. Policy makers opted for a new airport in order to meet the demand for air services which, the forecasters assured them, was growing rapidly and incessantly. In this one instance, unreliable forecasts undermined an otherwise technically based decision process.

Plans for airport development were formulated in Dallas–Fort Worth, Vancouver, Paris, and Milan without detailed forecasts of demand. Local authorities in Dallas and Fort Worth agreed to construct a joint regional airport in 1965 to replace existing facilities in the two cities. The decision was unrelated to either the prospective demand for air services or the capacity of existing infrastructure. City officials were concerned that the new airport under construction in Houston would attract transfer passengers who might otherwise fly through Dallas–Fort Worth. A new and modern air facility, they believed, was necessary to retain the economic viability of the metropolitan area in competition with Houston. Projections of demand were irrelevant; hence, no forecasts were commissioned. The Federal Aviation Administration, which had favored a joint regional airport since 1940, developed forecasts for the Dallas–Fort Worth area based on a share of the national market,[45] but even these forecasts were irrelevant to local authorities.

The Ministry of Transport in Canada commissioned forecasts for Montreal and Toronto in the latter half of the 1960s, but not for Vancouver. As early as 1967 the Minister had indicated his intention to expand the Vancouver airport, and concrete plans for the construction of a parallel runway were developed by 1969. These plans, however, were required to justify a land acquisition program the Ministry had launched in 1967. Transport officials were persuaded that the demand for air services in Vancouver would continue to grow, but development plans were not predicated directly on that belief. Consequently, detailed forecasts were not deemed necessary before decisions could be reached.

The idea of Paris-Nord originated in 1957 with the District of Paris and was conceived as a replacement for Le Bourget. District officials desired to convert Le Bourget into a park and proposed a land exchange with Aéroport de Paris. ADP accepted the exchange and, within two years, the French government agreed to construct a grand new airport on the Plains of France. No forecasts of demand were prepared when the original deal was struck. Some estimates were produced the following year, but the government ignored the results; the 10 million passengers forecast for 1980 was well below the estimated capacity of Orly. Forecasts were irrelevant; the commitment to two great airports to service Paris was predicated on grandeur, not technique.

Plans for the expansion of Malpensa originated in 1967 with the financial problems of SEA. The airport authority sought to acquire state lands in order to increase its capital value, and it proposed modest expansion of cargo facilities on these lands in order to justify acquisition. Detailed forecasts were not available at the time. SEA officials, like their counterparts in France and Canada, were certain that the demand for air services would increase over time, and they did not require forecasts to confirm their faith in the future of air travel.

Forecasting and Legitimacy

Aviation forecasts did not contribute significantly to technical choice, but they did play a vital role in justifying decisions. Both planners and policy makers defended their proposals for the expansion of aviation facilities in technical terms, even though political and economic factors dominated the decision process. Consequently, detailed forecasts were prepared everywhere, but for public consumption.

Forecasts usually were prepared after decisions were made. Airport planners in Dallas–Fort Worth, Vancouver, Paris, and Milan had opted for expansion without technical advice; forecasters were aware of the policy recommendations before they began to develop the data that justified those preferences. Even when forecasts were developed in advance of decision making, planners were not always prepared to release the information to the public. New forecasts were commissioned in many instances to buttress the case for expansion, and these projections invariably were more optimistic than the initial estimates.

Planners and policy makers understood the value of detailed forecasts. They were also conscious of the need for data that could justify expansion decisions. Transport Canada officials realized in 1968 that forecasts for Toronto did not warrant the construction of a new airport. Consequently, the first order of business for the newly established Toronto Area Airports Project (TAAP) was to reconsider existing projections in light of changing circumstances. ADP's 1958 forecasts projected a growth in demand that could be serviced readily by Orly and Le Bourget. When the decision to build a new facility was announced in 1963, however, new and more optimistic forecasts were available. Forecasters may not have altered assumptions or calculations deliberately to guarantee favorable results, but they were aware of the preferences of policy makers and the public commitments that had been made. And in every instance, forecasts were consistent with policy preferences.

Forecasting was not as critical in the justification of choices in Montreal and Dallas–Forth Worth as it was in other sites. Transport officials in Canada based their argument for new construction in Montreal on long-term economic expectations; it is cheaper to build immediately, they argued, even if new facilities are not currently required, rather than postpone construction.* Local authorities in Dallas and Fort Worth recognized openly the political and economic concerns that dictated choice. Even in these instances, however, forecasting could not be ignored; planners and policymakers required technical evidence to justify the rationality of their decisions. Hence, Transport Canada produced new forecasts for Montreal, and local authorities in Dallas and Fort Worth, after failing to commission a single study of demand during the lengthy decision-making process, instructed the site selection team to demonstrate need.

Noise forecasts were also important in justifying expansion proposals. Public officials produced these forecasts when they contributed to the technical argument for growth, but were reluctant to discuss the issue when the forecasts were less favorable. In Paris, authorities stated publicly that noise could not be forecast even as they deposited noise curves secretly with local authorities

---

* Ironically, the recommendation for government policy in the face of inflation contradicts the remedy that public officials propose for ordinary citizens.

and accepted international consulting contracts to predict noise
in other cities. They told the neighbors of Roissy-en-France that
the new generation of jets would be quieter even as they knew
the noise footprints would affect adversely all the Vallée de
Montmorency.

Perhaps the most remarkable example of employing forecasts
for political convenience occurred in Milan. There, authorities
utilized two sets of noise curves, one projecting substantial impact
from airport expansion and one minimizing noise. The high-impact
curves were presented to the government in Rome to justify significant investment, serving as proof that the costs would have
demonstrable effect. The modest curves were employed locally
to reassure neighbors that airport expansion would not be too
disruptive. The first set of curves was drawn by SEA under pressure from Rome; the second set was commissioned by local authorities from Aéroport de Paris, which prepared the study in
secret consultation with SEA.

Projections of economic growth have followed the same pattern,
serving the interests of construction proponents. An egregious
example that had lasting political consequences was in Quebec.
The Canadian federal government predicted that Mirabel would
yield 85,000 new jobs, an economic incentive no Québécois leader
could easily reject. The provincial premier, Robert Bourassa, assumed that the federal government was exaggerating and banked
on only 25,000 jobs, but they were crucial to his political promises
of economic improvement in the province. His political fortunes
were not helped when the airport finally opened, less than a year
before his electoral defeat, with no more than 8000 new jobs.

Conclusion

The commitment to prepare forecasts was accompanied everywhere by an effort to improve technique. The British Airports
Authority established a whole section in the mid-1970s devoted
to sophisticated forecasting methods, and they actively began soliciting contracts from other European authorities. Yet, as the
graphs in this chapter show, greater sophistication did not lead
to greater accuracy. In fact, forecasts have become more inaccurate
over time.

Forecasting relies, above all, on an interpretation of the cause of past behavior. The selection of a point from which to extrapolate depends upon an assessment of the events that led to the particular point. Advocates of the free and unfettered market of industrial capitalism seem to believe in unlimited growth, and political defenders of state intervention in the industrial countries, socialists and communists alike, shared this faith. Downturns are anomalous; upward swings are normal. A decline in traffic is caused by particular and temporary circumstances, hence the French attribution to the controllers' strike of decline prior to the first oil crisis. It did not matter to French officials that the rate of growth was in decline everywhere and that the peculiar French conditions therefore could not provide adequate causal explanation. Conversely, when domestic traffic boomed in the United States in the 1960s, European authorities interpreted the cause as natural western economic development. They encouraged the development of domestic airlines and regional airports, even when their alternative transportation systems were superior to those in the United States and might have been expected to absorb any significant growth in domestic travel demand.

The mentality that calls for construction and expansion has governed the application of technique as well as technology. Forecasters serve employers and clients; growth is considered natural as well as desirable. In this world view the future is almost always rosy and expensive. When the scent fades from the bloom, however, the search for explanation often devolves into a criticism of opponents. And the scent can fade either when construction does not lead to manifest benefit or when the failure to build contributes to a perception of lost opportunity. Technique is rarely blamed. Whatever the technical difficulties, failures are attributed to politics.

Endnotes

1. The private sector has encountered the same problems with market signals as government has experienced in recent years. See for example Mark Abrams, "Market Forecasting," in Tom Whiston (ed.), *The Uses and Abuses of Forecasting* (London: Macmillan, 1979), pp. 54–63.
2. William Page and Howard Rush, "The Accuracy of Long-Term Forecasts for Non-Ferrous Metals," in Tom Whiston (ed.), *The Uses and Abuses of Forecasting, op. cit.*, pp. 201–228.
3. J. Scott Armstrong, "The Seer-Sucker Theory," *Technology Review* (June-July 1980).

4. William Ascher, *Forecasting: An Appraisal for Policy-Makers and Planners* (Baltimore: Johns Hopkins Press, 1978), p. 199.
5. *Ibid.*, pp. 59–92.
6. Andrew Shonfield, *Modern Capitalism: The Changing Balance of Public and Private Power* (New York: Oxford, 1965), p. 67.
7. Dennis Gabor, *Inventing the Future* (London: Secker and Warburg, 1963), quoted in Donald L. Pyke, "Technological Forecasting: A Framework for Consideration," 2 *Futures* (December 1970), p. 328.
8. Robert W. Pulling and Herbert J. Guth, "Forecasting Traffic for Airport Development," in George P. Howard (ed.), *Airport Economic Planning* (Cambridge, Mass.: MIT, 1974), p. 65.
9. Arthur S. De Vany and Eleanor Garges, "A Forecast of Air Travel and Airport and Airway Use in 1980," 6 *Transportation Research* (1972).
10. Federal Aviation Administration, Airports Service, *Aviation Demand and Airport Facility Requirement Forecasts for Large Air Transportation Hubs Through 1980* (Washington: Department of Transportation, 1967), p. 1.
11. Jeffrey M. Zupan, "Do We Need Another Airport?" 1 *New York Affairs* (1973), p. 8.
12. Janet Kiernan reviewed a number of forecasts produced in the United States between 1957 and 1967. She concludes that "these forecasts . . . were consistently accurate on the short-term basis but highly inaccurate for the long-term." Janet D. Kiernan, "A Survey and Assessment of Air Travel Forecasting," IDA-Urban Mass Transportation Project, Research Paper P-540, April 1970, p. 3.
13. "Air Transport: An Environmental Failure Story," *Conservation Foundation Letter* (August 1974), p. 6.
14. These forecasts are discussed in the *Written Summary*, prepared by the Air Administration of Transport Canada for the Airport Inquiry Commission in 1974.
15. Kiernan, "A Survey and Assessment of Air Travel Forecasting." Passenger-miles, a common statistic employed by the aviation industry, refers to the total mileage flown by commercial, passenger carrying vehicles. It is not a measure of the number of trips or the number of passengers.
16. Elliot J. Feldman, *Airport Siting as a Problem of Policy and Participation in Technological Societies: The Case of Milano-Malpensa* (Cambridge, Mass., and Torino, Italy: Harvard Center for International Affairs and Fondazione Luigi Einaudi, 1978).
17. Ascher, *Forecasting, op. cit.*, pp. 142–164.
18. Jacques Block, the Director of Planning and Development at Aéroport de Paris, notes, for example, that "aviation will probably be able to go on developing its market substantially for a very long time to come." J. Block, "Airport Planning For a Place in the Future Environment," 1 *Futures* 4 (June 1969), p. 319.
19. One example of the reassessment of this fundamental assumption is the report of the Secretary of State for Trade of the United Kingdom in 1978. The report notes that "the size of this market for leisure travel is limited not only by economic factors but also by other constraints such as available time and family structure." Secretary of State for Trade, *Airports Policy* (London: HMSO, 1978), p. 15. The Chief of the Aviation Economics Division

of the Port Authority of New York and New Jersey also suggested, four years earlier, that "the growth process from now on is much more likely to be progressive rather than explosive." George P. Howard and Johannes G. Augustinus, "Market Research and Forecasting for the Airport Market," in Howard, *Airport Economic Planning op. cit.*, p. 111. It should be noted, however, that the reassessment of fundamental assumptions took place, in both instances, after policy had changed. This point will be discussed later in this chapter.

20. N. W. Boorer, "The Future of Civil Aviation," 1 *Futures* 3 (1969), p. 207.
21. R. Dixon Speas, a prominent aviation consulting firm, clearly acknowledged the possibility of government action that might disrupt the forecasts the firm had prepared for an interest group representing general aviation. R. Dixon Speas Associates, *The Magnitude and Economic Impact of General Aviation* (Manhasset, New York, 1968), p. 2.
22. Block, "Airport Planning," *op. cit.*, p. 320.
23. Pulling and Guth, "Forecasting Traffic," *op. cit.*, p. 67.
24. Department of Trade, *Maplin: Review of Airport Project* (London: HMSO, 1974), p. 60.
25. Block, "Airport Planning," *op. cit.*, p. 320.
26. Pulling and Guth, "Forecasting Traffic," *op. cit.*, p. 67.
27. Department of Trade, *Maplin, op. cit.*, p. 61.
28. Pulling and Guth, "Forecasting Traffic," *op. cit.*, p. 71.
29. Joseph Windisch notes, for example, that a study of technological developments in civil aviation necessarily is "quite subjective." Joseph Windisch, "Determination of the Average-Size Passenger Aircraft to be Used at Port Authority Airports," in Howard, *Airport Economic Planning, op. cit.*, p. 229.
30. An example of this pessimistic approach is contained in an environmental impact statement, prepared by airport authorities in Detroit, which argues that "operational implementation of a Computer-Aided Approach Sequencing system is not considered possible at Detroit airport before 1980. The effect was therefore not considered in the analysis of runway capacity." Quoted in "Air Transport," *Conservation Foundation Letter*, p. 6.
31. The noise problem associated with vertical and short take-off and landing aircraft are broached briefly in Boorer, "The Future of Civil Aviation," *op. cit.*, pp. 212–213. The noise problems of the Concorde and the SST are legendary.
32. Pulling and Guth, "Forecasting Traffic," *op. cit.*, p. 66.
33. William Fielding Ogburn, *The Social Effects of Aviation* (Boston: Houghton Mifflin, 1946), p. 41.
34. "The Airport Crisis: No Place to Land," *Business Week*, September 30, 1972.
35. "Report of Ad Hoc Congressional Hearing on Air Congestion," *Congressional Record—House* (25 September 1968), pp. 28092–93.
36. Pulling and Guth, "Forecasting Traffic," *op. cit.*, p. 67.
37. Kiernan, "A Survey and Assessment of Air Travel Forecasting," *op. cit.*, p. 21–26.
38. Gerald Hodge, "Regional Impact of a New International Airport for Toronto," report for Ontario Department of Treasury and Economics, Regional De-

velopment Branch and Canada Department of Transport, Air Services (Toronto: March 1970), pp. 81–86. Technically, the report was cosponsored by Transport Canada, but the Ontario government selected the consultant and paid the fees.

39. In the late 1960s the Port Authority had estimated more than 90 million passengers for 1980. For more details see Jerome Milch, "Inverted Pyramids: The Use and Misuse of Aviation Forecasting," 6 *Social Studies of Science* (1976), pp. 22–23.

40. Diamond and Myers, Jack B. Ellis and Associates, and Institute of Environmental Research, *Pickering Impact Study*, prepared for the City of Toronto Planning Board, 17 June 1974.

41. Gordon W. Stead, "Annex to the Report of the Forecasting and Economic Sub-Committee of the Airport Planning Committee for the Vancouver International Airport," Vancouver, 26 August 1974. The Annex was neither published with attribution nor adopted by the full subcommittee.

42. United Research, Inc., "A Study of Requirements for a New Major Airport for the New York–New Jersey Metropolitan Area." The report is summarized in Jersey Jetport Site Association, "White Paper," 1960. Assumptions about the introduction of vertical and/or short take-off and landing aircraft were premature, but the consultant predicted correctly the impact of larger jets. Short-term forecasts underestimated the growth in New York area traffic, but long-range estimates have been quite accurate.

43. Hector Massey and Charles Godfrey, *People or Planes* (Toronto: Copp Clark, 1972), pp. 14–18.

44. The consultants admitted that growth could be accommodated at Malton at least through 1985, but they still argued that "for economic as well as socio-environmental reasons" a new airport should be built. See P. Beinhaker and J. M. Choukroun, "Management of Airport Planning in Canada," paper prepared for the fourth meeting of the Urban Sector Group, Organisation for Economic Cooperation and Development, May 2–4, 1973.

45. The concept of a share of the market is a relatively primitive approach to forecasting in specific cities. It is based on the percentage of air travellers enplaned historically at a given site. The national forecasts are developed through sophisticated techniques, but local forecasts do not take into account specific local conditions. The resulting errors occasionally are spectacular. When New York's Regional Plan Association overestimated passenger traffic by a factor of 3 in its 1947 forecast, it assumed that "the New York region's share of the United States traffic would hold constant, when in fact it declined." Zupan, "Do We Need Another Airport," *op. cit.*, p. 8.

Part Three

PLANNING AND POLICY

Chapter 4

SUCCESS, FAILURE, AND RATIONAL PLANNING

Planners and politicians in the eight sites involved in this study defined the problem of growing air travel demand in the same way and developed common strategies for solutions. The outcomes, however, varied a great deal. New airports were built in Dallas–Fort Worth, Montreal, and Paris. Land was taken, but no construction or development achieved, in Milan, New York, Toronto, and Vancouver. And, despite repeated studies and site selections, land was not even acquired in London.

Cultural differences cannot explain these outcomes, because problems were defined the same way everywhere. Moreover, in the selection of similar strategies, the process of choice also appears common in these cases. In every instance the techniques of rational planning were introduced. Variations in the commitment to these techniques follow no pattern, for the Italians and the Texans relied on them least while the British and the Canadians in Quebec relied on them most. Hence, the explanation for differences in outcomes cannot be detected simply in different applications of rational planning techniques.

The central difference may be found in political institutions. These common problems and strategies were submitted for solution to different political systems. The procedures through which policies were shaped defined different actors in different systems and different possibilities of participation for official agencies as well as for ordinary citizens. Although rational planning was conceptualized everywhere as a method for reducing or eliminating the idiosyncracies of systems (as a method for insuring that "correct" choices would be made according to common criteria of efficiency), its impact varied with the systems into which it was introduced. The introduction of rational planning into different political systems dictated the essential differences in outcomes.

Rational Planning and Its Discontents

Rational planning refers to the systematic and comprehensive assessment and choice of objectives and the formulation of step-by-step procedures for their accomplishment. According to Herbert Simon, father of the concept of rational choice in the study of organizational behavior, "Rationality has to do with the construction of means-ends chains."[1] Originally conceptualized as a process whereby desirable objectives could be pursued through the most efficient and effective methods, rational planning was modified by Simon and James March to apply to the pursuit of satisfactory but less than ideal results. The notion of "satisficing," however, does not alter seriously the premises of rationality in problem solving.[2] The task of the firm still is to enunciate the goal, select the appropriate (that is, efficient) strategy, and marshall resources in a coherent and coordinated fashion.

The application of sophisticated techniques, derived from economic theories, to an articulated decision chain has been taught in business schools for many years. In the decades after World War II it became increasingly a tool of government. Students of public administration and public policy have lauded the virtues of rational planning, and governments everywhere have institutionalized the techniques for problem solving.

Conflict and Conflict Resolution

Rational planning, both in the private sector and in government, requires basic agreement on goals. The early rationalist literature proposed ideal methods for defining and achieving goals, but as Nachmias and Rosenbloom have observed, "Most of it deals with how decisions *should* be made, not how they are made in practice."[3] Indeed, the challenge of bringing large and complex organizations into the common enterprise of pursuing agreed-upon goals is an abiding problem in the study of organizational behavior.

The greater the size and complexity of the firm, the greater the task of concentrating effort on common objectives. Single decision makers with single goals may face obstacles, and the task is greater still for multiple decision makers because of the need to coordinate activities. The job is most challenging of all, however, for multiple decision makers with multiple goals. This situation occurs in the private sector but is most characteristic of government.

Analysts who have applied variants of economic theory to the operations of government have predicted conflict over important interdepartmental decisions. Warner Schilling, for example, in discussing defense policy writes that "not sharing the same responsibilities . . . government organizations will necessarily bring divergent interests and approaches to common problems."[4] Graham Allison, applying the economic theory of the firm to the formulation of foreign policy, argues that large organizations are routinized and follow standard operating procedures; inevitably, the divisions of the "semi-feudal" organizations in his "Model II" description of government have difficulty achieving cooperation.[5]

Students of bureaucratic behavior have concerned themselves with the resolution of conflict among competing objectives and actors engaged in decision making.[6] Interdepartmental conflicts, according to some analysts, are resolved through formal problem solving, compromise, persuasion, bargaining, and politics.[7] Cyert and March perceive a "quasi-resolution of conflict" in which subordinate goals are given priority sequentially.[8] Alternatively, subordinate goals may be distributed for accomplishment by discrete agencies, thereby masking the overall activity and reducing the visibility of conflict-causing issues. Allison notes that incrementalism characterizes the process of conflict resolution,[9] and Lindblom elevates this symptom of response to conflict into "the science of muddling through."[10] Numerous studies of interagency conflict, with many suggestions for conflict resolution often of this kind, have emerged in the decades since World War II.[11] The prevailing assumption, however, is that conflict can and will be resolved, whether through specific goal achievement, compromise, or incrementalism.

Governments everywhere have responded to problems of conflict by deploying the techniques of rational planning. Perhaps the most popular solution has been to formalize coordination among departments that have coincidental interests. Ezra Suleiman has identified an informal coordination in the French *grands corps*

and a more formal effort in the formation of *cabinets* within departments and ministries.[12] The general growth of staff throughout
the United States and Canadian governments has been attributed
to the effort to coordinate and control the activities of line
agencies.[13]

Governments in recent years have formalized coordination most
often through the establishment of interdepartmental committees
that convene planners and technical experts from interested agencies. Guy Peters has noted that "even in those societies that are
not centrally planned and coordinated, each individual agency is
developing its own planning capacity."[14] Interdepartmental committees consisting of these experts are expected to resolve internal
conflicts through rational planning, bargaining, and politics, and
then solve problems through the further application of rational
planning techniques.

Governments That Do Not Work

Efforts to coordinate government activities have increased, but
government performance does not seem to have improved. Richard Fenno has observed the difficulty faced by the Cabinet in the
United States government in its effort to coordinate activities of
the Executive Branch,[15] and Richard Neustadt has described the
dispersion of presidential power in comparison with its earlier
control and coordinating function.[16] Despite the deliberate coordinating efforts, many governments apparently have found it increasingly difficult to accomplish any complex tasks.[17]

Various explanations have been offered by students of organizational behavior for dissatisfaction with government performance.
According to Graham Allison's "bureaucratic politics" (Model III),
individual bureaucrats subvert agency objectives because of personal agendas.[18] Walter Stewart has applied this notion to an
analysis of the Pickering Airport plans, whose failure he attributes
to bureaucratic imperialism.[19] Another popular explanation is that
the techniques of rational planning are not applied enough. If
decision makers were more sophisticated, the argument goes, the
quality of decisions and the performance of government would
improve.[20]

The central idea of these explanations is that government performance must be judged according to criteria defined by the
need for rational planning—by the achievement of pre-determined

objectives in economically efficient ways. The surest cure for the ills of government, according to this logic, is greater dosages of rational planning.

The Airport Cases and Rational Planning

Government agencies in seven of the eight cases in this study engaged in rational planning to define objectives and map strategies for achieving goals. Only in Dallas–Fort Worth was rational planning not considered vital, essentially because decision making was nakedly political and devoid of technical pretense. Nowhere else were forecasts simply ignored, for example, and nowhere else did local government directly oversee and control the development process.

Although important internal debates took place regarding development plans, each agency eventually resolved these conflicts. Some took more time than others, and some changed their collective minds more often, but all arrived at the same long-term goals and the same strategies. Major delays, and important changes in strategy, followed initial choices and were generated everywhere from outside the line agency. The internal process of initial decisions, however important it may have been, did not yield important differences in strategic choice.

Each agency hoped to accomplish its objective through a step-by-step procedure following a rational plan. They all adopted the same strategy for achieving their goal, the construction of additional civil aviation infrastructure. They professed the same ideology in matching goals and strategies. They all began with narrow mandates to serve the travelling public, and they all enjoyed significant public power, including the authority to condemn and seize land, to borrow from the public treasury, and to build within the borders of the land they owned.*

The main difference between those authorities who built these facilities and those who did not may be found in the control they enjoyed over project execution. Those agencies with significant

---

* The case of Dallas–Fort Worth does not conform strictly to this summary. Power remained with municipal officials (not with the Joint Airport Board) for land-taking and building permissions. However, because the two municipalities created the board with a specific purpose, the different locus of power was mostly a technicality.

power, insulation from influence, or freedom from competition (whether intellectual or political) were able to accomplish their objectives. Rational planning, when confined to single agencies with full control over the process and when organized around defined, narrow objectives, can lead to goal satisfaction. But agencies in an environment of fragmented authority which had to negotiate cooperation from interested parties faced delays, opposition, and ultimately stalemate (Table 4–1).

The Builders

The expectations of organization analysts and advocates of rational planning were fulfilled in cases where airports were built. The common characteristics of the decision process in Montreal, Paris, and Dallas–Fort Worth derived from concerted political will to build major airports. Each built a monument. In all three cases, sites were chosen without an articulated plan for land use. Far more land than was required for airport use was seized. In each case, once the decision to build was confirmed, completion rarely was endangered.

The municipalities of Dallas and Fort Worth controlled the development process free of federal interference. They chose the site for the new airport, determined the procedures and designs for building it, and paid prices for land dictated by political convenience. The only constraint on their autonomy was the necessity to seek approval from the legislature and citizenry of Texas for a constitutional amendment that would authorize creation of a bi-county public authority to build and operate the airport. Completion of the project, however, did not depend on that approval. When permission was denied by the voters of Dallas County in a special referendum, municipal officials established a Joint Airport Board to control the project. Neither state and federal agencies nor ordinary citizens ever penetrated the decision-making procedures of the Board.

Conditions generally were similar in Paris and Montreal. Aéroport de Paris (ADP) depended upon the Finance Ministry to supervise land taking, but when the Administration des Domaines objected to the prices offered by ADP, the Minister of Finance personally authorized payments at four times estimated market value in order to avoid delays and political conflict.[21] Approval of the District of Paris was required for site determination, but the site in fact was

Table 4–1 Comparative Decision Processes

Questions:
1. Who defines the problem?
2. Who organizes the strategy for solving it?
3. Who is allowed to participate at the beginning?
4. Are other agencies invited to participate or simply required to perform functions?
5. When/are ordinary citizens permitted to be heard/participate?
6. What are the outcomes?

	1	2	3	4	5	6
British Columbia	MOT Air	MOT Air	BC/DOE/GVRD/DPW	Participate	Exprop. hearings/APC	Stalemate
France	ADP	ADP	Paris District/Ministry of T&CA	Function	Never	Build
Italy	SEA	SEA	Min. of T&CA/FS/MM	Function	Protest	Stalemate
New York (Morris County)	PONYA	PONYA	Governors and Legislatures of N.Y. and N.J.	Participate	Professional lobbying	Project abandoned
New York (Stewart)	Governor	MTA	N.Y. Legislature	Function	Protest/Courts	Project abandoned
Dallas–Fort Worth	Local officials	Local officials	Texas Legislature	Function	Referenda	Build
Ontario	MOT Air	MOT Air	Ontario/Justice/DPW	Participate	Exprop. hearings/AIC	Stalemate
United Kingdom	Min. of Av. (post-1967: Trade/DOE)	BAA/Trade	BAA/CAA/Trade	Participate	Public hearings	Project abandoned
Quebec	MOT Air	MOT Air	DREE	Function	Protest	Build

Key to Table 4–1

ADP	Aéroport de Paris	Min. of Av.	Ministry of Aviation
BC	British Columbia	Min. of T&CA	Ministry of Transport and Civil Aviation
BAA	British Airports Authority	MOT Air	Ministry of Transport, Air Administration
APC	Airport Planning Committee	MTA	Metropolitan Transportation Authority
CAA	Civil Aviation Authority	MM	Metropolitana Milanese
DOE	Department of the Environment	PONYA	Port Authority of New York and New Jersey
DPW	Department of Public Works	DPW	Department of Public Works
DREE	Department of Regional Economic Expansion	Trade	Board of Trade (later Department of Trade)
AIC	Airport Inquiry Commission	FS	Ferrovie dello Stato (national railroad)
GVRD	Greater Vancouver Regional District	SEA	Società Esercizi Aeroportuali

chosen by the District because of its own desire to see Le Bourget closed and converted into a park. Hence, ADP enjoyed the District's support from the very conception of the project. The Ministry of Transport and Civil Aviation, the responsible *tutelle* for ADP (the overseeing government authority for the autonomous public agency), has but three staff members to judge the plans and proposals of the more than three hundred planners and designers employed by the airport authority. French officials cannot recall a single occasion in the lifetime of ADP (since 1946) when a major proposal has been rejected by the Ministry. Opposition might have been expected from the Communist Party in the "red belt" around Paris (because of the disruption for communities), but Party officials shared the commitment to industrial and technological development. Although citizen protest groups did form, the state's commitment to monumentalism combined with the Communist commitment to development guaranteed that no effective participation from outside the agency would be tolerated.

The Canadian Ministry of Transport (MOT) needed Quebec support for the provision of infrastructure, access, and the application of building and zoning codes. However, federal officials did not trust Quebec and preferred not to invite provincial officials to participate in early planning.[22] Instead, MOT exercised the full powers of the state to expropriate land sufficient to build federal roads and to impose federal controls. Apart from modest consideration of the federal Department of Regional Economic Expansion's hopes for a site compatible with Québécois growth, no one outside MOT was permitted to interfere. The federal cabinet wanted a major new airport for Montreal, largely for political reasons, and would not tolerate opposition. MOT received an unequivocal mandate and proceeded to prove that federal powers in Canada can be sufficient for the construction of major public works despite provincial or citizen objections.

These three airports are neither the world's finest nor the most efficient. Neither Mirabel nor Charles de Gaulle Airport enjoys adequate access because, in the end, access lay outside the airport authorities' control. All three airports have been criticized for overconstruction and design failures, and all three have precipitated controversies. But these three cases do show that narrow objectives can be achieved through a zealous pursuit by powerful agencies that are prepared to reject all participation, whether formal or informal, institutional or individual.

The Failures

Analysts of organizational behavior are aware that some cases involve more conflict than others. They are conscious, for example, of objectives other than the profit motive (once thought to dominate all businesses), and they recognize the probability of conflict in the presence of competing objectives.[23] They also acknowledge important differences between governments and businesses, whether in the analysis of municipal budgeting[24] or the defense budget.[25] But they expect conflict to be resolved, through negotiation and bargaining by the actors involved or unilaterally through incrementalism.

In the context of airport development, the goal of satisfying passenger demand is redefined as construction. Compromise or incremental solutions may mean scaled-down plans, adjusted designs (for example, realigning runways), or deferred construction. An option not anticipated in the literature of rational planning, however, is paralysis—the failure to build anything at all. Yet, the most common alternative to the construction of whole new airports is the indefinite delay or total defeat of projects.

Airports have not been built where important aspects of the decision process lay outside the express control of single agencies or where those agencies perceived a need to accommodate participatory demands. The same Canadian Ministry of Transport that denied Quebec an opportunity to participate in decision making believed it necessary for political reasons to cooperate with the Province of Ontario. The federal government was not prepared to seize another 140 square miles, this time near Toronto. Furthermore, a change in the Expropriation Act that followed the Quebec land taking but preceded acquisition in Ontario mandated public hearings. The federal perception of the need to cooperate with the Ontario provincial government and the new legal requirement to give the public an opportunity to be heard, delayed decision making until economic conditions had changed, and the project—at least temporarily—was abandoned.[26]

The Ministry of Transport was involved in a similar situation in British Columbia.[27] Again the new Expropriation Act forced a delay in decision making. So did two new federal ministries entrusted with portfolios that overlapped and competed with the jurisdiction of MOT. Vancouver-based officials in the new Department of the Environment (DOE) shared local environmental concerns and persuaded Ottawa officials to oppose MOT; authorities of the Greater Vancouver Regional District enlisted the aid of Ottawa officials in the new Ministry of State for Urban Affairs (MSUA). Moreover, MOT had to secure close cooperation from the Department of Justice for a complicated and peculiar land taking. Whereas Justice ultimately did Transport's bidding, planners associated with DOE and MSUA employed the techniques of rational planning to articulate with increasing strength, precision, and local political support a systematic opposition, on the merits, to MOT's plans. With the power to build fragmented by competing interests, the project for a parallel runway at Vancouver International Airport was stalemated.

The Canadian cabinet system, with its traditional commitment to the brokerage of provincial interests, contributed to the problems that MOT encountered in Ontario and British Columbia. The countervailing forces of cabinet were neutralized in the Quebec case by a Québécois prime minister, surrounded by Québécois officials, all of whom believed they represented the Province of Quebec and did not require the serious participation of local or provincial officials. The same confidence and the same clout were not present among ministers in cabinet from Ontario and British Columbia; an equivocal prime minister could permit his cabinet members to war over the briefs prepared by their respective ministries. Thus, the Canadian cabinet can centralize power and enforce decisions, but it is more likely to engender confrontation within the federal government itself.

The Milan and London cases involve different actors than those in Canada, but they follow the same pattern. The decision chain was probably longer, more politicized, and more tenuous for the Società Esercizi Aeroportuali (SEA) than for any other authority (see Table 4–2). The central government had to approve project financing; compensation for expropriated land was limited by the central government to prices seriously below market value; access to the airport was determined by contending transportation authorities, not SEA; the Ministries of Defense and of Trade and Industry had greater influence over the process of site selection and design than SEA's own supposed champion in Rome, the spokesman for civil aviation. Despite SEA's many mistakes, it also confronted a process beyond its control.[28]

British authorities never controlled the process long enough to complete a project. Plans shaped by Conservatives in 1961 were reexamined by Labour in 1965; the proposals of statisticians and

Table 4–2   Approval Requirements for Airport Development: Milan and S.E.A.

Project Approval:

Consiglio di Amministrazione: S.E.A.
IGAC (later DGAC)
Consiglio Superiore dei LL.PP. ──────→ Ministero dei Trasporti e Aviazione Civile
ITAV
Ministero della Difesa Aeronautica
Camera dei Deputati (for financing)

Land Acquisition:

Ministero della Difesa Aeronautica,
    Direzione Generale del Demanio
Ministero dei Trasporti e Aviazione Civile
Ministero delle Finanze
Ufficio Tecnico Erariale (evaluation)
Ministero della Giustizia (Malpensa)

Construction:

Consiglio di Amministrazione: S.E.A.
DGAC
Comuni (Ferno, Vizzola Ticino, Lonate
    Pozzolo)

Zoning

Regione Lombardia
Parco del Ticino
Comuni (Somma Lombardo, Cardano al
    Campo, ecc.)

Finances:

Comune di Milano
Provincia di Milano ──────→ ITAV
DGAC
Airlines
Alitalia

Runway Development:

Ministero della Difesa Aeronautica
ITAV
DGAC

Provision of Access:

Ferrovie dello Stato	IRI
FNM	MM
ATM	Regione Lombardia
Comuni	Provincia di Varese

Key to Table 4–2

Consiglio di Amministrazione: S.E.A.	Governing Board of SEA
DGAC	Director General's Office for Civil Aviation (Rome)
Consiglio Superiore dei LL.PP.	Senior Council for Public Works (Rome)
ITAV	Air Traffic Control Agency (Rome)
Ministero della Difesa Aeronautica	Ministry for Air Defense (Rome)
Camera dei Deputati	Chamber of Deputies (Rome)
Direzione Generale del Demanio	Director General's Office for Land (Rome)
Ministero dei Trasporti e Aviazione Civile	Ministry of Transport and Civil Aviation (Rome)
Ministero delle Finanze	Ministry of Finance (Rome)
Ufficio Tecnico Erariale	Technical Office for Land Evaluations (Province of Varese)
Ministero della Giustizia	Ministry of Justice (Rome)
Communi	Local communes
Regione Lombardia	Regional Government of Lombardy
Parco del Ticino	The State Park of Ticino
Ferrovie dello Stato	National Railroads
FNM	Railroad for North Milan
ATM	Milan Tram System
IRI	National Agency for Reconstruction
MM	Milan Subway System

planners in the Ministry of Aviation in 1965 were surrendered to economists in the Board of Trade in 1967; recommendations of a royal commission appointed by Labour in 1969 were delivered to a Conservative Government in 1971; a mammoth Conservative development project including the airport, launched in 1972, was cancelled by a new Labour Government in 1974. The oscillation of parties in power and the constant reorganization of the British bureaucracy—including endless transfers of the airport portfolio—meant that careful, rational plans framed around the assumptions and objectives of one set of actors perpetually fell victim to contrary plans and assumptions. That the plans could not be reconciled from one government to another might suggest ideological conflict, but it might also be a final testament to the incoherent rigidities of "rational" choice.[29]

The New York case is complicated because it involves two separate agencies operating under different guidelines and with different constraints. The Port Authority of New York and New Jersey, whose efforts at construction spanned a twelve-year period from 1959 to 1971, required the initial support of the two state governors and legislatures, all of whom were sensitive to competing demands in their constituencies. Moreover, highly professional and well-financed lobbying reached deep into the system. Despite its vaunted power,[30] the Port Authority did not control the process when the interests of wealthy and influential citizens were affected by its choices.

By contrast, the Metropolitan Transportation Authority, which assumed responsibility for airport development after the Port Authority bowed out, was not limited by these considerations. As a New York State agency, the MTA was not required to consider the interests of New Jersey. With the unrelenting support of Governor Nelson Rockefeller for Stewart's development, there was no problem of competing jurisdictions in state government. Even powerful citizens in Orange County were unable to gain more than a temporary delay in project implementation. Indeed, all the ingredients for the successful completion of the project were present in this instance. There was only one drawback: The project never was economically viable. Although all obstacles to construction were overcome, the project was abandoned once Governor Rockefeller resigned and state government officials with a different economic perspective could control the decision.

Rational Planning and Fragmented Authority

Airports cost money and are the source of noise and atmospheric pollution. They require housing, roads, and sometimes rail access. They use land, restricting neighborhood construction and development and regional economic growth. They also serve as nodes in transportation systems. Many different agencies and departments of government have responsibilities directly affected by decisions to expand facilities or to build new ones. Traditionally, the task of development has been assigned to a single line agency with a narrow mandate to satisfy air travel demand. And traditionally other agencies have been allowed only to assist in the realization of the development goal. However, the cross-sectoral character of development problems has required some interaction because, despite the role of the initiating agency concerned primarily with transportation, airport issues are never confined to a single policy or organizational sector.

In the past, when interdepartmental committees convened to resolve differences over projects, mandarins with generalist training did negotiate, bargain, and compromise as planning theorists predicted. Interaction could be described, as Cyert and March proposed, in political terms, for decisions did emerge from political coalitions built among the firm's competing actors.[31]

The situation changed in the 1960s and 1970s. The commitment to rational planning techniques that occurred in all five countries of this study led almost all line agencies to employ a new cast of people. Throughout the western industrial world new offices, variously called "planning" or "policy," or both, were established at the intermediate levels of agencies and departments. Specialists with training in rational planning techniques were hired. Their job was to formulate comprehensive, rational plans for the achievement of the basic goals of the agency. And these specialists were assigned the task of overcoming obstacles to goal fulfillment.

Rational planners are in the business of achieving predetermined goals efficiently. They are technicians. Their mandate is to improve the evidence and arguments supporting goals that have been set at higher levels, not to compromise those goals. Rational planning is not employed in government to set goals, as the history of forecasting in civil aviation illustrates. Politicians set goals; rational planning is employed *post-hoc*, both to rationalize the goals and to guarantee their achievement.

Airport authorities mandated narrowly to build airports give little or no priority to the financial, environmental, and regional economic implications of construction. They recognize issues of access but consider them of secondary importance, because they rarely control land outside airport boundaries. Apart from the goal of meeting civilian travel demands, only defense is accorded priority consideration in airport development.

In the three cases where new construction was achieved, the powers required to build were bestowed upon Aéroport de Paris, the Ministry of Transport for Quebec, and the Joint Airport Board in Dallas–Fort Worth. Money was no object, and land was thought to be virtually unlimited. Little serious thought was given (despite considerable rhetoric in Paris and Montreal) to environmental concerns, and authorities assumed that the political priority they enjoyed would guarantee cooperation from the providers of access. Except in Texas, they planned in pursuit of narrow objectives, and they built their airports.

In New York, the Metropolitan Transportation Authority was endowed with the same formal powers and provided with the same political support as Aéroport de Paris, the Ministry of Transport, and the Joint Airport Board. An independent judiciary permitted citizen groups to delay briefly the implementation of plans (see Chapter 7), but the Metropolitan Transportation Authority was not restricted by competing agencies with different priorities. The objectives were narrow and authority broad, but economic considerations and political change eventually torpedoed development plans.

In the other cases, competing authorities formulated their own coherent, rational plans in conflict with the plans of the initiating agency. Where authority is fragmented, competing agencies have the power to object as well as to serve. The planners and policy analysts who represented these agencies on interdepartmental committees had no mandate to negotiate or compromise on the respective goals of their agencies. Rather, they informed themselves as to the goals of others so that they could improve their defenses and arguments in behalf of their own. Their improved plans continuously eroded the grounds for compromise. The combination of fragmented authority and rational planning then led to paralysis.[32]

Sophistication, of course, varied from case to case. Cost-benefit analysis was mastered in Britain but was unknown in Italy; it was irrelevant to the purely political process in Texas. Yet, even in

Italy agencies defined objectives and mapped step-by-step strategies for their achievement, and even in Italy the records of interdepartmental meetings reveal increasingly irreconcilable conflict over time.

The examples of confrontation are boundless. In Vancouver the Department of the Environment demonstrated that airport development would harm the ecology of the Fraser River estuary, while the Ministry of Transport demonstrated that failure to build would harm the regional, and potentially the national, economy. The confrontation required a political choice between the travel and fishing industries, because neither side could refute the technical evidence. Politicians, hoping the conflict would resolve itself through the technical superiority of one side, were paralyzed; the technocrats in the two agencies could not compromise, and the politicians were not prepared to choose between them.

Confrontations of this kind took place in Britain between acoustical engineers and airport developers, in New York between economic planners in state governments and transportation planners in the Port Authority, and in Italy between industrial developers and the airport authority.[33] In every instance, interdepartmental committees became uncompromising battle grounds featuring technocrats with sophisticated rationale for their "one best way" to defend the public interest as the mandates of their respective agencies defined it. In all these cases of paralysis there had been previous airport development. But two factors now intervened. First, there was the transition from mandarin to specialist. Second, adjustments in political conditions and structures (such as the mandated public hearings in Toronto and Vancouver, the government reorganizations in Britain, the growing commitment to interdepartmental committees and the introduction of regional governments in Italy*) permitted new contests with, and sometimes within, the lead agency. Paralysis, therefore, has replaced incrementalism.

Additional Explanations of Outcomes

The combination of rational planning and fragmented authority does not account entirely for the differences between the builders

---

* The introduction of the regional governments in Italy involved the transfer of authority over "urban policy." In Milan this change brought the Lombardy government centrally into plans for access, zoning, and general land use.

and the non-builders. Development projects may be abandoned even in the absence of competing authorities if the political will weakens. The determination to construct facilities may be sapped by the departure of political leaders (as the Stewart case illustrates) or conceivably by the activities of citizen groups. The role of these groups will be examined in more detail in Chapter 7.

Two other factors weighed heavily on outcomes: resources and luck. A large land parcel within convenient distance of the central city was available, often through historical accident, in all the cases where new airports were built.* In London, New York, Toronto, and Vancouver the location of a suitable site was especially difficult because of intense urban development and land use. In Italy, land was available but there were powerful competitors seeking to use it for other purposes. The Italian authorities also had no money with which to build—a problem, though less acute, that affected thinking in the United Kingdom. It was easier to proceed when cost was no object.

It is not clear whether construction would have moved ahead had large, convenient, undeveloped, and uncontested parcels been available for London, New York, Toronto, and Vancouver. Certainly in Toronto and Vancouver, public hearings over expropriation exposed the many questionable aspects of MOT plans, whereas the absence of such hearings in Montreal undoubtedly insulated the Ministry. However, assumptions within the critical decision-making echelons of MOT varied significantly over entitlement for participation between Quebec on the one hand, and Ontario and British Columbia on the other. Even before the public hearings, provincial officials in Ontario and British Columbia were invited to participate in the decision process, in complete contrast to proceedings in Quebec. And the New York legislature authorized the expropriation of 8,657 acres near Stewart Air Force Base for development of a jetport, only to learn that the distance was too great, the demand too slack, and the objections from others (including the Port Authority) too numerous to justify construction. If cost had not been important, Stansted might not have been the first choice of British planners and hearings might not have been

---

* The *plaines de France*, for example, had no natural water source and lay on the northern invasion route; beetroot farming prevented any construction. The land northwest of Montreal lay in the only path where development from the city had not yet taken place, largely because of growth concentrated around the St. Lawrence River.

precipitated. But it is also true that the criteria for site selection fluctuated with the movement of the airport portfolio, an event that occurred with even greater frequency than the turnover of governments.

Resources and luck plainly were important. It would not seem, however, that in the cases where new construction did not take place they were decisive. Resources and luck interacted with other factors of greater importance, especially the contest of participants that was determined by the rules and structures governing participation in each respective political system.

Judging Success and Failure

There are two distinct levels at which different outcomes, however temporary they may be, must be assessed.* Decision makers everywhere wanted to build. According to their criteria, authorities in Dallas–Fort Worth, Paris, and Montreal were successful, whereas their counterparts elsewhere failed to achieve their objectives.

The adoption of these criteria reflected a commitment to the fulfillment of strategies. The strategy chosen everywhere for solving the problem of anticipated air travel demand was the construction of civil aviation infrastructure. The intermediate goal of construction effectively supplanted the long-term goal of meeting demand; alternative solutions, therefore, could not be considered until and unless there would be no construction. Success was measured by building infrastructure, not by success in meeting travel demand.

The second analytical level appropriate to a judgment of policy success involves the consequences of government accomplishment and the fulfillment, in the most efficient and just manner, of the original goal. According to these criteria, success and failure must be reversed. The long-term goal, to meet the demands of the travelling public for the rest of the twentieth century, has not been compromised in the cities where construction has not taken place, and present estimated ratios of capacity to forecasted traffic suggest that far more modest plans will assure satisfaction.

It appears from this perspective that the strategy of construction

---

* Proposals are still disputed in Toronto, Vancouver, London, and Milan.

usually was unnecessary and even inappropriate. It was pursued, moreover, at considerable cost. The British spent by 1980 over £6 million ($15 million) on planning, studies, and hearings. The Canadian Ministry of Transport displaced 3000 people to acquire 18,000 acres in Pickering Township and another 650 people to obtain additional land on Sea Island in Vancouver. New York displaced 1200 people at a cost well over $30 million to acquire 8076 acres adjacent to Stewart Airport in Newburgh. Over $15 million were spent on land acquisition and studies in Milan. Yet, in all these cities, existing facilities accommodated demand through the 1970s and likely will do so until the end of the century with only modest changes and additions in infrastructure. Only in Toronto has the problem of traffic congestion become acute. A major reason appears to be the construction of Mirabel; transfer passengers prefer to change planes at Malton rather than travel between Mirabel and Dorval. Hence, both Montreal facilities are under-utilized, while the Toronto airport faces a growing problem.

These "failures" were expensive, but "successes" might have been worse. Apart from construction and development costs, authorities would have borne the expense of operating a multiple airport system. These costs arise from the necessity of assigning different tasks to different airports—for example, the division of intercontinental from international and domestic traffic (Malpensa vs. Linate), mostly commercial from mostly charter (Heathrow vs. Gatwick), or international from domestic and transborder (Mirabel vs. Dorval). This system inherently is inefficient because airlines must duplicate personnel and facilities and reorganize aircraft operations. If each facility is self-contained (that is, capable of handling all transfer traffic), these problems can be minimized. The New York system (LaGuardia and John F. Kennedy International Airports) generally has succeeded in distributing traffic efficiently. Elsewhere, however, the results have been less satisfactory. The division of traffic between Charles de Gaulle and Orly Airports, for example, is incoherent, and both airports are utilized well below their most conservatively estimated operating capacities.* The International Air Transport Association, observing a pattern,

---

* Orly was judged capable of 17 million passengers in the mid-1960s. British authorities estimated this figure to be less than half the real potential. Charles de Gaulle was planned to handle more than 50 million passengers by the mid-1980s. Combined, the two airports handled fewer than 26 million passengers in 1980.

consistently has objected to the development of more than one airport in a metropolitan area.[34]

Existing air facilities have proved adequate in London, New York, Milan, Toronto, and Vancouver, and additional facilities would only have exacerbated the problems of operating a multiple airport system. Had the Port Authority in New York and the Società Esercizi Aeroportuali in Milan succeeded in developing their new airports, they would have created a problem where none had existed before. The third London airport would have been a white elephant, even if the government had selected a less remote site than Maplin. A parallel runway in Vancouver might have reduced the noise level in Richmond, but only by transferring it to Vancouver's Southwest Marine Drive. Even in Toronto, where demand appears to have kept pace with forecasts, a second airport would only have discouraged the transfer passengers who have chosen to bypass Montreal. By "failing" to achieve their objectives, decision makers in these cities were spared the financial costs of construction, airlines were able to avoid the expense of duplicating facilities, and passengers were saved from the agony of additional transfers between airports.

These government failures can be contrasted with the "successes" of construction. The builders of Dallas–Fort Worth, Charles de Gaulle, and Mirabel have become the most visible and important international consultants on new airport development. With the active encouragement of their respective governments, they advise other governments and supervise the construction of airports all over the world. They are especially prominent in promoting facilities in the Third World, where they argue that airport construction is essential for economic development.[35] The general consultants for Dallas–Fort Worth are preparing the Stewart master plan, and the Mirabel consultants won the contract for a new airport in Barbados even though their only previous experience in airport construction had been in Montreal. The consultant services of ADP are in the greatest demand of all. Not only do their own governments believe in the success of these developers, but governments the world over seek to emulate their success.

Although the construction of the new airport did assure Dallas–Fort Worth sufficient capacity to satisfy demand well into the future, the facility has proved of greater value to travellers from other sections of the country than to local residents. Even the Executive Director of the Regional Airport admits that transfer passengers "do not directly contribute much to the local economy."[36] Approximately $65 million of the $700 million price tag for the facility was financed by the taxpayers of Dallas and Fort Worth, but they have received few benefits from their investment. The airport has neither stimulated economic growth in the area nor provided a boost to commerce in the two cities. According to Richard de Neufville, the Dallas–Fort Worth Regional Airport is "a financial and operational misfortune."[37]

The costs of the new airport in Montreal ($500 million) was absorbed by the national government. Nevertheless, traffic at Mirabel has been so much below expectation that there has been serious discussion in government circles of closing the facility entirely.[38] Mirabel, like Dallas–Fort Worth, has not generated economic development in the surrounding communities. Montreal's economic decline, moreover, may have been accelerated by the added incentive for air travellers to bypass the city in favor of Toronto. And the airport won a "black star" from the International Airline Pilots Association because of its distance from hospitals and service facilities. The federal government promised Quebec 85,000 jobs associated with the airport; by 1976 Mirabel employed only 8,000.

Charles de Gaulle Airport is no greater monument to rational planning. ADP turned a deaf ear to the state railway, the Société Nationale des Chemins Fer (S.N.C.F.), because it preferred a possible new technology, the *aérotrain,* to conventional railroads for the provision of access. When the new technology failed, airport construction had begun and coherent options for rail access had been foreclosed. The rail line subsequently built is sadly underutilized and a financial liability. ADP assumed the Minister of Equipment would provide new roads to relieve congestion on the Autoroute du Nord, the lifeline of the new airport, but they were not built. And the need for a flexible design that could be modified with fluctuations in traffic was not served by the construction of a circular terminal, the only design permanently unalterable.

In all three of these "successes" there were early warning signals that planners were on the wrong track. MOT officials seemed oblivious to the irony of building the world's largest airport in the second largest city of an underpopulated industrial country. The S.N.C.F. and the Régie Autonome de Transports Parisiens (R.A.T.P.-Métro) urged ADP to plan traditional access systems

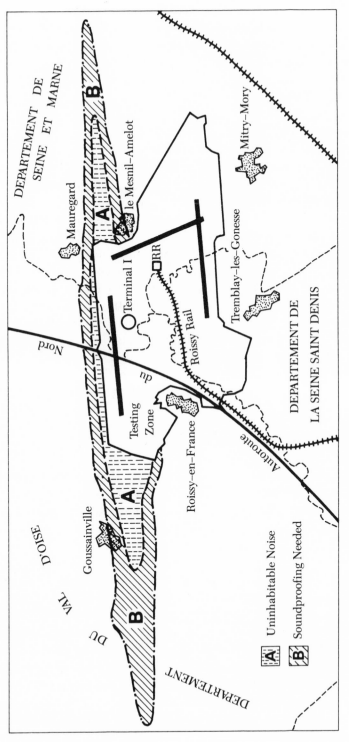

Charles de Gaulle Airport: Environs, Access, and Noise "Footprint" for First Runway

early. Dallas County residents who rejected a proposal for a bi-county public authority because they found Love Field more convenient for their needs did not persuade Dallas–Fort Worth planners that the colossal scale of the new airport would be excessive. Rational planning requires the achievement of narrow objectives; it does not require the participation or accommodation of competing concerns.

Absence of dissent was the product of insistence upon the development of airports strictly as transportation facilities planned by experts. It was the product of belief that success would be measured by the ability to accomplish narrowly defined objectives and that there is an inextricable tie between the goal of anticipating and satisfying demand and the objective of building new facilities.

However much these facilities may fail the test of efficiency, they have been hailed as evidence of successful planning and government performance. The international contracts that have flowed to their developers bear witness to this concept of success. Yet, success and failure obviously must be reconsidered, for the public interest seems sometimes to be served more by government failure—or by the structures of some political systems that spare governments from unnecessary expense and subsequent operational embarrassment—than by government success.

The Impact of Economic Criteria

Rational planning derives from economic theory. Its most celebrated tools, program budgeting and cost-benefit analysis, are economic. Such theories carry assumptions, the most important of which in the context of the cases here probably is that a "one best way" can be found to solve a problem.

There have been attempts to describe the decision-making process, and to formulate theory about the utility of rational planning, with political tools. However, even these analyses, especially as argued by Cyert and March, derive ultimately from economics.[39] They describe a firm as a pluralist political order, and they reduce the role of the chief executive officer, despite his power to hire and fire, to one of many actors engaged in bargaining and negotiation. This description is not a "theory" of politics,[40] and the idea of competition upon which it is based has its origins in a market analogy.

Reliance on economic theory requires judgments of achievement according to market, and consequently business, criteria. Hence, in the remarkable cost-benefit analysis performed by the Roskill Commission for the selection of a third London airport site, the value of a businessman's travel time from downtown to the airport proved a critical variable.[41] And hence alternatives to growth policies are repudiated. The Canadian Ministry of Transport could not accommodate the preferences for "slow growth" expressed by the Greater Vancouver Regional District because it contradicted the premises upon which national airport policy was founded.[42] It did not matter that a competing national policy was to accommodate local and regional planning.

Even after the setbacks of the 1970s, airport planners cling to the growth commitment that is nurtured by their rational plans. The British Conservative Government in 1979 declared its intention to proceed with major construction and development of Stansted as London's third international airport. Canada's Ministry of Transport has held the expropriated lands in Pickering Township and still expects to build eventually. A plan released by the Ministry in the autumn of 1980 proposed the reopening of an airfield at Boundary Bay, near Vancouver, for general aviation, but the second parallel runway remains on the maps of Vancouver International Airport's master plans for "eventual" construction. New York's Metropolitan Transportation Authority still owns over 8,000 acres at Stewart Airport and expects to build in the distant future. And SEA in Milan has begun to construct additional facilities at Malpensa, although on a scale drastically reduced from the disputed plans of the mid-1970s. These various proposals, blocked in some cases for more than twenty years, remain the preferred strategies of many decision makers.

Public officials, moreover, continue to defend these plans in terms of the public interest. The British frequently call their commitment to construction "getting it right," and Americans and Canadians both talk of "getting things done." The French and Italians regard the rejection of dissent and the commitment to business-oriented plans as "normal." In every instance, business-like values, as defined by the economic criteria underwriting rational planning, have been equated with the public interest. Thus is the commitment to business values elevated to a moral imperative.

The Quest for Alternatives

What technology makes possible is not the same as what it requires. Technological developments in civil aviation during the 1960s and 1970s made possible increased air travel with fewer aircraft movements. This possibility resulted primarily from the introduction of wide-body aircraft. These same aircraft also absorb more cargo, thereby reducing the tendency of planners to develop small airports devoted exclusively to cargo. Improvements in air traffic control, moreover, facilitated a much greater number of aircraft movements on existing runways.

These technological advances enabled the British Airports Authority (BAA) to accommodate demand without new construction, once they learned that the international airport which they desired would not be available in the 1970s. Airports are designed to absorb "peak" demand, which refers to the maximum anticipated traffic at the busiest hour of the busiest day of the year. According to this principle, facilities are utilized below their capacity at all other times. If airport users could be induced to operate during slack periods, the peak could be spread and the life expectancy of the facilities extended.

To encourage airlines to fly before and after rush hours, during weekdays rather than weekends, and during non-holiday periods, BAA introduced a price mechanism of differential charges for runway and terminal use. General aviation was displaced rapidly to other airports and many operators made cost-effective adjustments. This deviation from the accepted method of pricing was not adopted as a serious attempt to alter airline behavior until BAA perceived the elimination of a major construction alternative,* but its discovery did inspire the Association of European Airports to explore more generally how it might be employed system-wide.

The use of differential pricing provides an alternative to construction, but it is an alternative derived from technology and from economics. It does not require governments to consider the relationship of civil aviation to other public goods. The application of rational planning has rejected the dissent of competing interests

---

* The pricing mechanism was introduced earlier as a revenue measure. It was given the strength to influence scheduling choices only after the rejection of the Roskill report.

and alternative values. Even when they have been able to intrude, the absence of mechanisms to compare them has contributed to paralysis. For these reasons, neither the policies fashioned for airport development nor the alternatives conceived to meet demand bear any relationship to concepts of justice.

Rational planning, then, often has yielded the over construction of incoherent facilities and the adoption of alternatives only under duress. Thousands of citizens have lost their homes and communities to public utilities, only to see the land remain vacant for decades. Public treasuries have been raided for billions of dollars to acquire land that goes unused and to build facilities that are underutilized.

Technocracy and Bureaucracy

Concern for the democratic control of impersonal bureaucracies that seem beyond accountability has been expressed for decades.[43] In the 1970s a new theme emerged as government performance appeared in decline. Governments were encouraged to become more "businesslike," to adopt the techniques of the private sector in order to become more efficient and effective.

Bureaucracies populated by careerists began giving way to technocracies populated by specialists. And as we shall see in Chapter 5, where governments could not staff themselves with experts they hired outside consultants. The basic direction, throughout the advanced industrial world, has been to entrust greater decision-making authority to experts who are armed with the techniques of rational planning, or officials who are urged to acquire and use them.

There is no evidence that government performance has improved with this change, especially when concepts of success and failure are reconsidered. There is, however, considerable doubt whether the business mentality can generate reliable standards for justice or entertain the legitimate competing voices of democracy. The solution to the unfortunate consequences of rational planning does not reside in glib proposals for "irrational planning," for these are not opposites. Rational planning is ideological, the product of beliefs in inevitable conflict resolution, "one best" solutions, commercial transaction criteria, growth, and development. The ideology of business, with only market standards for justice and no appreciation of a general, non-commercial public interest, is worn uncomfortably by government.

The distinction between business and government needs to be preserved if appropriate criteria are to be applied to the judgment of performance. Technocracy, with its emphasis on technique and expertise, and rational planning, with its economic criteria and business influence, have muted the differences. Although analysts worry about the preservation of democracy from the influence of bureaucrats,[44] they need to appreciate the extent to which technocracy poses a greater threat. Different political structures have contributed to different outcomes in solving the same problems in different countries, but the decision-making elites of these countries operated within the framework of a common ideology, one that is shaping more and more the way in which the business of government is conducted.

Endnotes

1. Herbert Simon, *Administrative Behavior* (New York: Macmillan, 1947), p. 62.
2. James G. March and Herbert Simon, *Organizations* (New York: Wiley, 1958).
3. David Nachmias and David H. Rosenbloom, *Bureaucratic Government USA* (New York: St. Martin's Press, 1980), p. 24.
4. Warner Schilling, "The Politics of National Defense: Fiscal 1950," in Warner Schilling, Paul T. Hammond, and Glenn H. Snyder, *Strategy, Politics, and Defense Budgets* (New York: Columbia University Press, 1962), pp. 21–22.
5. Graham T. Allison, *Essence of Decision: Explaining the Cuban Missile Crisis* (Boston: Little Brown, 1971), p. 68. Model II refers to the organization process, which is the model most applicable to this discussion.
6. Various observations on bureaucratic conflict resolution may be found in Roger Hilsman, "The Foreign Policy Consensus: An Interim Report," 3 *Journal of Conflict Resolution* (December 1959), pp. 361–382; and Warner Schilling, "The Politics of National Defense," *op. cit.* Discussions of how analysts think conflict ought to be resolved may also be found in David Braybrooke and Charles E. Lindblom, *A Strategy of Decision* (New York: Free Press, 1963); Alan Altshuler and Norman Thomas (ed.), *The Politics of the Federal Bureaucracy* (New York: Harper and Row, 1977); Simon, *Administrative Behavior, op. cit.*; and Allison, *Essence of Decision, op. cit.*
7. This formula is enunciated first in March and Simon, *Organizations, op. cit.*
8. R. M. Cyert and J. G. March, *A Behavioral Theory of the Firm* (Englewood Cliffs, N.J.: Prentice-Hall, 1963).
9. Allison *Essence of Decision, op. cit.*, p. 68.

10. Charles E. Lindblom, "The Science of Muddling Through," 19 *Public Administration Review*. (1959), pp. 79–88, is the first full statement of this position.

11. For example, Arthur Maas, *Muddy Waters* (Cambridge, Mass.: Harvard University Press, 1951); Aaron Wildavsky, *Dixon-Yates: A Study in Power Politics* (New Haven: Yale University Press, 1961).

12. Ezra Suleiman, *Power, Politics and Bureaucracy in France* (Princeton: Princeton University Press, 1974).

13. An assessment of the Canadian experience may be found in Elliot J. Feldman and Jerome Milch, "Organizing Disunity: Rational Planning in Canadian Administration," in Wayne Reilly (ed.), *Encounter with Canada* (Durham, N.C.: Duke University Center for International Studies, 1980).

14. B. Guy Peters, *The Politics of Bureaucracy; A Comparative Perspective* (New York: Longman, 1978), p. 179.

15. Richard Fenno, Jr. *The President's Cabinet* (Cambridge, Mass.: Harvard University Press, 1959).

16. Richard Neustadt, *Presidential Power: The Politics of Leadership from FDR to Carter*, Third Edition (New York: John Wiley and Sons, 1980).

17. This same problem has been identified in Australia. See Martin Painter and Bernard Carey, *Politics between Departments: The Fragmentation of Executive Control in Australian Government* (Queensland: University of Queensland Press, 1979).

18. Similar concerns for the impact of individual bureaucrats on policy can be found in Jeffrey Pressman and Aaron Wildavsky, *Implementation* (Berkeley: University of California Press, 1973). A detailed critique of Allison that seeks to restore the saliency of Model I, the "rational actor," for the analysis of foreign policy, is in Robert J. Art, "Bureaucratic Politics and American Foreign Policy: A Critique," 4 *Policy Sciences* (1973), pp. 467–490.

19. Walter Stewart, *The Paper Juggernaut: Big Government Gone Mad* (Toronto: McClelland and Stewart, 1979).

20. Allison *Essence of Decision, op. cit.*

21. Elliot J. Feldman, "The Parisian White Elephant: The Case of Charles de Gaulle Airport," 2 *The Tocqueville Review* 3 (Autumn 1981).

22. For the full details see Elliot J. Feldman and Jerome Milch, *The Politics of Canadian Airport Development: Lessons for Federalism* (Durham, N.C.: Duke University Press, 1982), Chapter 3.

23. Cyert and March, *A Behavioral Theory of the Firm, op. cit.*, p. 1, demonstrated effectively the impact on all organizations of factors other than the profit motive, and especially the influence of individual as well as institutional goals.

24. John P. Crecine, *Governmental Problem Solving: A Computer Simulation of Municipal Budgeting* (Chicago: Rand McNally, 1969).

25. C. J. Hitch and R. N. McKean, *The Economics of Defense in the Nuclear Age* (Cambridge, Mass.: Harvard University Press, 1960).

26. The shifting electoral fortunes of the Liberal Party in Ottawa contributed to these delays. Details of the Toronto case are in Feldman and Milch, *The Politics of Canadian Airport Development, op. cit.*, Chapter 4.

27. *Ibid.*, Chapters 5 and 6.

28. Details are in Elliot J. Feldman, *Airport Siting as a Problem of Policy and Participation in Technological Societies: The Case of Milano-Malpensa* (Cambridge, Mass. and Torino, Italy: Harvard University Center for International Affairs and Fondazione Luigi Einaudi, 1978).

29. Details are in Elliot J. Feldman, *White Elephants and the Albatross: French and British Planning in the Supersonic Age* (Cambridge, Mass.: MIT Press, 1982), Chapter 3.

30. For background on the Port Authority, see Jameson W. Doig, "Regional Politics and 'Businesslike Efficiency': The Port of New York Authority," in Michael Danielson (ed.), *Metropolitan Politics: A Reader*, Second Edition (Boston: Little Brown, 1971).

31. The discussion may be found in clearest form in James G. March, "The Business Firm as a Political Coalition," 24 *Journal of Politics* 4 (November 1962), pp. 662–678. The fuller discussion appeared subsequently in R. M. Cyert and J. G. March, *A Behavioral Theory of the Firm, op. cit.*

32. A similar argument, focusing on bureaucratic control, has been made for Australia, where interdepartmental committees are ineffective because spokesman adhere rigidly to their departmental positions. Ironically, the authors of the study demonstrating this problem imagine the Canadian cabinet to avoid such paralysis. Painter and Carey, *Politics Between Departments, op. cit.*

33. In the Italian case, a highly politicized contest developed between a manufacturer of helicopters, Agusta S.pa., and SEA. The government, with close personal and political ties to Agusta, overrode civil aviation interests. See Feldman, *Airport Siting, op. cit.*

34. Interview with Jeffrey Durante, International Air Transport Association, Montreal, October 7, 1976.

35. The transcripts of international civil aviation meetings are revealing for the salesmanship of industrial world authorities. See for example the *Seventh International Symposium, Appraisal of the Economic and Social Impact of Civil Aviation* (Paris: Institute of Air Transport, 1978).

36. Ernest W. Dean, *DFW News* (July 2, 1981).

37. Richard de Neufville, *Airport Systems Planning* (London: Macmillan, 1976), p. 38.

38. The Air Transportation Association of Canada denounced a federal proposal to transfer traffic from Dorval to Mirabel to help offset the $25 million loss anticipated for 1981–1982. *Toronto Globe and Mail* (April 23, 1981).

39. Cyert and March, *A Behavioral Theory of the Firm, op. cit.*, and March, "The Business Firm as a Political Coalition," *op. cit.*

40. Theodore J. Lowi argues that it is an ideology. See *The End of Liberalism: Ideology, Policy, and the Crisis of Public Authority* (New York: W. W. Norton, 1968).

41. Commission on the Third London Airport, *Report* (London: HMSO, 1971), p. 123.

42. This policy is enunciated in a major planning document prepared by the Greater Vancouver Regional District, "The Livable Region 1976/1986: Proposals to Manage the Growth of Greater Vancouver," March, 1975.

43. Early examples include Carl J. Friedrich, "Public Policy and the Nature of Administrative Responsibility," in C. J. Friedrich and E. S. Mason (ed.), *Public Policy*, (Cambridge, Mass.: Harvard University Press, 1940), pp. 3–24; Herman Finer, "Administrative Responsibility in Democratic Government," I *Public Administration Review* (1941), 335–350.

44. A lengthy discussion can be found in Nachmias and Rosenbloom, *Bureaucratic Government USA, op. cit.*, pp. 235–251.

Chapter 5

THE TECHNOCRATIC SERVANTS

An increasingly prominent characteristic of the policy process in the advanced industrial world since World War II has been the participation of technical experts in government decision making. Governments everywhere have been subjected to a steady rise in the expectations of citizens for service delivery. In many technical areas the requisite knowledge or skills to overcome problems associated with the provision of services belongs exclusively to a small coterie of experts, and governments have turned increasingly to these experts for assistance in solving problems.

The participation of technical experts in the formulation of government policies has been recognized by observers throughout the advanced industrial world. Some have welcomed the growing influence of "apolitical" technical experts and the problem-solving approach they have brought to bear on government decision making.[1] Others have feared the consequences of an emergent technocratic elite whose values may be substituted for the preferences of democratic authorities.[2] Virtually all observers have assumed that the involvement of experts in government has altered the decision-making process in fundamental ways.

This assumption is correct insofar as it reflects changes in the style of politics. The participation of technical experts has reinforced the existing tendency to define policy questions in technical terms. It has forced citizens whose interests are affected adversely by government policies to engage their own technical experts in order to challenge those policies. But there is little evidence that the involvement of technical experts has altered the substance of decisions. Indeed, the experts employed by governments have

131

buttressed policies set politically and bureaucratically, and the experts engaged by opponents consistently have opposed those policies.

The development of civil aviation infrastructure provides an especially useful example of this phenomenon. Airport development has been perceived everywhere as a complex and technical task, necessitating a central role for experts from a variety of disciplines. Forecasters, systems analysts, statisticians, economists, appraisers, architects, and designers have been engaged by governments at various stages of the policy process, and technical expertise often has been cited as the crucial independent variable determining development decisions.

Citizen groups opposing airport development have responded to the increasing importance of technical evidence in decision making by seeking their own experts to oppose government policies. Acoustical engineers engaged by airport neighbors, for example, have challenged the noise forecasts prepared by other acoustical engineers employed by government agencies. The demand for air travel, the costs of construction, and the environmental impact of development—essential components of the technical case for airports—have become critical issues in the debate over development policies.

These debates among experts have succeeded in transforming the rhetoric of policy discourse from the political to the technical, and they have shed light in some instances on aspects of decisions that might otherwise have been ignored. However, they have not introduced independent analysis to weighty problems of public policy. Nearly all the studies reviewed in this research yielded results consistent with the preferences of sponsors. Technocrats, it appears, function more as servants than as an elite when important economic interests are at stake.

The Locus of Expertise

A technocrat is "a man who exercises authority by virtue of his technical competence."[3] Unlike the classical bureaucrat whose authority rests on his position within the organization, technocrats are not limited by formal status considerations; they may be located within the organization or they may operate from the outside. The influence they wield is based on the perceived need for technical knowledge to resolve problems, and they speak with authority whether they are employees of or consultants to the organization.

Governments, like all large organizations, have sought to apply technical knowledge to the resolution of problems through the aid of these technocrats. They have adopted three strategies in the pursuit of this objective. Experts have been hired by the central agencies of government to provide detailed technical knowledge as a supplement to the managerial skills of departmental personnel. Specialized agencies, staffed almost entirely by personnel trained to fulfill a particular mission, have been created to deal with problems that cut across the traditional sectors of government. And outside experts, or consultants from the private sector, are engaged periodically to cope with problems when agency personnel have neither the necessary time nor training.

Central Agencies

Central agencies have been established throughout the advanced industrial world for both traditional functions such as defense, transportation, and foreign affairs, as well as more recent government activities including environmental protection, housing, and urban affairs. Their mandates ordinarily do not overlap. Rather than duplicate the functions of other agencies, they are expected to rely on each other for the performance of particular tasks required for the fulfillment of their obligations but not central to their mission. Ministries of employment, for example, will refer litigation to justice departments and will rely on public works departments to construct facilities for their personnel; they do not employ elaborate legal or engineering staffs. The experts who work for employment ministries focus more narrowly on the specific mission of the ministry.

Transportation departments are typical of these central agencies and are governed by these rules. Their mandate generally requires them to promote and regulate civil aviation, including necessary infrastructure, and they participate to some extent in airport planning activities. Of the five countries included in this study, only Canada has a ministry of transport that owns, operates and develops air facilities in all the most populated metropolitan areas of the country. Elsewhere, the leading role in development is assumed by a specialized agency, the airport authority.

Specialized Agencies

Specialized agencies operate under a different set of rules than central agencies. Their mandates cut across traditional government sectors, and they employ experts from a variety of disciplines and with a range of specialties. Airport authorities, for example, employ economists, forecasters, and statisticians to participate in the determination of airport requirements, and designers, architects, and meteorologists to plan facilities. Lawyers and appraisers help with land acquisition, engineers with construction, and air controllers with operations.

Airport authorities possess unusual powers, derived from their mandate to search for efficiency, that distinguish them from established government departments. The budgets of line agencies normally are approved only after an elaborate and complex review involving central budget offices and legislatures. Airport authorities, by contrast, often maintain autonomous control over revenues and expenditures. Land acquisition generally is the responsibility of justice or public works departments, but airport authorities often may invoke the state's powers of expropriation, bypassing established departments. Land condemned for a public purpose normally must be utilized as planned within a narrow definition; airport authorities frequently convert land into industrial parks and hotels.

The airport authorities examined in this study vary in the extent to which they are staffed with a full complement of experts. Both the Port Authority of New York and New Jersey and Aéroport de Paris have extensive in-house capacities for technical planning and development. The Port Authority is the older of the two agencies, but both became involved in airport development shortly after World War II. The Società Esercizi Aeroportuali was established at approximately the same time, but only in the 1970s did SEA begin to develop its own full technical capacities. The British Airports Authority, a relatively new agency, has been reluctant to carry the costs of comprehensive expertise on a permanent basis.

Outside Consultants

Although the governments of the advanced industrial world have employed large numbers of technocrats in both central and specialized agencies, they rarely command the requisite knowledge or skill to resolve all the problems with which they are confronted. In many technical areas, help from the private sector often has appeared necessary, and a significant consulting industry has emerged to meet government's demand. The growth of this industry has been helped, moreover, by the increasing disparity between government budgets and government salaries; technical experts often have preferred to hire out their services at better pay than they could receive as government employees.

The use of consultants by government agencies has drawn critical attention in recent years as a result of some obvious abuses,[4] but the rationale for employing outside experts can be persuasive. Some governments are motivated by financial considerations, preferring to seek expertise on an *ad hoc* basis rather than carry the costs permanently on an agency budget. Others have been concerned with the tendency of technological change to outpace bureaucratic adjustment. Government agencies, built everywhere on some tenured civil service scheme, are not always equipped to cope with new problems. Many governments prefer to contract out these problems to non-government personnel.

All governments in the advanced industrial world have employed consultants on at least some occasions, but the role and influence of non-governmental personnel varies systematically across countries. States with "liberal" ideologies which prefer to rely on private enterprise rather than expand the scope of government have been particularly hospitable to consultants. States where official responsibility and initiative are more respected tend more toward internal specialization. Hence, the consulting industry has been more profitable in the United States and Canada than in France, while its development has been more ambiguous in the United Kingdom, which tends toward the liberal approach, and in Italy, which tends to copy the French.

These differences are evident in the use of private consultants in airport planning in the five countries of this study. The Canadian Ministry of Transport not only contracts out most of its planning but relies on outside experts to implement development plans. In the United States, consultants are so important that even specialized agencies such as the Port Authority of New York and New Jersey, already staffed with highly competent and specially trained personnel, seek outside experts in airport planning. By contrast, Aéroport de Paris, whose in-house capacities are not substantially different than those of the Port Authority, rarely seeks outside advice. The Società Esercizi Aeroportuali of Milan began in the

1970s to reduce its dependence on outside consultants, while the British Airports Authority, more cost-conscious than either ADP or SEA, contracts out a sizable portion of technical analysis.

The consultants employed by governments are not always individuals or firms from the private sector. Airport agencies themselves serve occasionally as consultants for other governments. The clearest illustration of this phenomenon is ADP, which has provided expertise on contract to the Canadian government, in connection with the development of Mirabel, and to the Province of Varese in Italy with respect to the proposed expansion of Malpensa. French airport builders, it appears, are not opposed to the concept of private consultants; while they are reluctant to seek advice themselves from the private sector, they are not reluctant to sell their own expertise to other parties.

Experts in the Policy Process

The recruitment of technical experts by the established departments and ministries of government, the creation of specialized agencies staffed with technical personnel, and the employment of private consultants were designed to enhance the application of specialized knowledge to public sector problems. Unfortunately, these efforts have been unsuccessful in improving the quality of government decisions with respect to aviation infrastructure. The failures of government policy noted in the preceding chapters cannot be attributed to the participation of experts in decision making. Political authorities, not technical experts, ultimately were responsible for the irrationalities of policy. However, the experts who prepared the studies used by both supporters and opponents of airport development did not always possess the appropriate credentials with which to pass judgment on technical matters. In many instances, they entered the policy process with disciplinary biases that clouded their judgment. Moreover, they were consistently unable to overcome the inherent limitations of bureaucratic structure in order to bring their collective wisdom to bear on the resolution of problems.

Inappropriate Credentials

Experts who participate in formulating and implementing public policies, whether as government officials or as private consultants, benefit from a public presumption about their expertise. Critics may challenge whether government experts are disinterested, but they rarely challenge their credentials. Experts, to be sure, are knowledgeable in some discipline or problem area, but the premise that they bear appropriate credentials for participating in decisions is not consistently valid. Indeed, in the development of international airports, experts occasionally have provided advice on issues about which they have little training or expertise.

WORDSMITH

There are important examples of this basic lack of expertise. The Canadian Ministry of Transport entrusted the planning of air facilities in the Montreal area to the firm of Kates, Peat, Marwick (KPM) in late 1966. KPM was known for its expertise in operations research and was selected by Transport officals because it had developed a cost-effective solution to a traffic logjam on the Welland Canal. The firm, however, had little experience in aviation matters. When the Cabinet agreed to construct a new airport at Mirabel, the Ministry selected Philip Beinhaker, a systems planner with no particular knowledge of airports, as its primary consultant.[5] Municipal authorities in Dallas and Fort Worth exercised the same kind of judgment in assigning the preparation of an environmental impact statement to their general consultant, Tippets-Abbett-McCarthy-Stratton. TAMS had established a reputation for airport planning and development, but the firm had little experience in environmental assessments.

Opponents of airport development were no less reluctant to rely on experts with little training or background. The City of Toronto contracted the firm of Diamond and Myers to prepare a study of the proposed new airport in Pickering Township for presentation at the Government of Canada's Airport Inquiry Commission hearings in the summer of 1974. Their report, the *Pickering Impact Study*, was criticized by the Commissioners for "lack of professionalism" when it was revealed that a major portion of the study was conducted by a lone graduate student. The Commissioners concluded that:[6]

" . . . *no person who prepared any portion of the study . . . had any knowledge or experience to enable them [sic] to be competent to give an opinion on either forecasts or noise [which were fundamental to the credibility of the entire study]*.

Even when the credentials of experts were not specifically questioned, contradictory behavior often raised doubts about the reliability of advice. In 1972 Aéroport de Paris refused to release noise curves prepared for the new Paris airport on the grounds that it is technically impossible to measure noise properly before an airport becomes operational. This technical problem, however, proved to be no obstacle when ADP was approached by the Province of Varese in Italy to estimate expected noise levels at Malpensa Airport outside Milan, even though the plans for facility expansion there were still on the drawing boards.[7]

Disciplinary Biases

Even when experts are equipped with the proper training and background to conduct relevant technical studies, they often suffer from disciplinary biases. Many economists, for example, treat the market as sacrosanct and avoid solutions that require interference in market operations. Architects and planners prefer new construction to the more effective use of existing structures, and they favor innovative designs to more traditional solutions for design problems. Disagreements within disciplines over the validity of underlying assumptions have not dissuaded experts from utilizing familiar tools to solve problems. Forecasters for the Ministry of Transport in Canada, for example, projected future demand for air travel by extrapolating "established" trends, despite indications that the future might look very different than the past.[8] Economists employed by the Roskill Commission in the United Kingdom recommended sites for a third London airport by applying cost-benefit criteria, even when the validity or comprehensiveness of such measures were attacked by critics and doubted by the economists themselves.[9]

The vision of experts often is limited by disciplinary training, and they cannot gain perspective easily on all the implications of a problem that crosses disciplinary boundaries. Architects are trained to develop designs for facilities, not to assess the need for construction. Economists calculate costs; they do not weigh the political feasibility of projects. Airport development is an inter-disciplinary problem, but experts, working within the limitations of their particular expertise, rarely can reach beyond their specialized competence to evaluate the entire problem.

Policy makers, as well as technical specialists, may be attracted strongly to particular tools, even if they do not understand fully how they operate. Both the Roskill Commission and the British Government that received its report were enamored by cost-benefit analysis; they perceived this economic tool as a substitute for political choice. Cost-benefit criteria did not serve ultimately as the basis for site selection, but they did define the choices. The introduction of other criteria had to await the election of a new government.[10]

Limited Data

The development of airport infrastructure conflicts with other laudable objectives, such as noise limitation or the protection of ecosystems. Airport authorities often must negotiate with minis-tries, departments, and agencies with competing mandates. Compromises certainly are possible, but there is little incentive for airport authorities to accept any limitation on development that diminishes efficiency unless required by political authorities.

When experts comply with the rules and procedures of governments, they contribute to the difficulties of negotiating compromises. All governments channel expertise according to narrow mandates and in compliance with the defined responsibilities of bureaucratic actors. Experts employed by an airport authority, for example, are expected to present the most persuasive case for the authority's objectives. The technical studies they produce reinforce the tendency of airport developers to avoid or delay bargaining and compromise.

It is unlikely that political authorities ever see all relevant data, because experts—conforming to government expectations—channel knowledge within agencies. Even where data are shared, the studies never prove truly comprehensive. Contending pressure groups won a demand for a comprehensive review of the impact of airport development in Vancouver, but no social impact study was developed because no participating government agency perceived the need or felt competent to pursue it.

Experts engaged by citizen groups suffer from similar limitations. Citizen groups, like government agencies, define their objectives narrowly and commission studies in accordance with their objectives. They ignore issues that are of little direct relevance to them. Supporters of airport development in Kent (England) underwrote research on the potential impact of construction on trade and industry in their economically depressed area. In Essex, by contrast, technical analysis sponsored by airport opponents concentrated on the deleterious effect of developments on wildlife and fisheries. The Kent group had no more interest in research on wildlife than the Essex group did in measuring the economic effects of construction. By complying with the rules of the game, experts provided only a partial data set.

Elites or Servants?

Since the time of Francis Bacon, thoughtful observers have recognized that knowledge and power are intimately related.[11] The precise nature of the relationship, however, has never been clear. Changing conditions within the political arena have encouraged students of the knowledge-power relationship to alter their views on several occasions. The debate among science policy analysts in the early 1960s concerning the appropriate function of experts in government, for example, was predicated on the assumption that the critical knowledge possessed by nuclear scientists confers a measure of power on them. Several years later, serious doubts were raised about the extent of this power as the influence of the scientific community appeared to decline.[12]

There are several distinct schools of thought concerning the role of experts in policy making. Some observers envision the development of a technocratic elite based on a monopoly of specialized knowledge. The increasing dependence of political leaders on this information enables experts to influence decisions in ways that are consistent with their own preferences. Others perceive experts as apolitical and disinterested participants in the policy process, dedicated to the pursuit of truth and knowledge. Accordingly, the influence exerted by experts is strictly a product of science. Still others dismiss the notion that experts influence policy makers in any significant way. The function of technical specialists is to justify or legitimize choices rather than to seek solutions to problems.

None of these perspectives provides a complete portrait of the role of experts in airport development, but the image of technocratic servant conveyed by the third perspective clearly is the most accurate. Over one hundred reports were reviewed in connection with this research, and all but one were consistent with the preferences of the study's sponsor. Experts employed by proponents of development produced reports advocating growth and expansion, while experts engaged by public agencies or citizen groups opposing development warned of damage to people, property, and the environment. The conclusions of these studies usually coincided with the personal preferences of the experts, and they were not obviously inconsistent with the canons of scientific inquiry. However, they always satisfied paying customers, whether governments or private citizen groups.

Satisfying Client Interests

The influence of client interests on technical studies was evident throughout this inquiry. "Independent" land appraisers hired by government agencies seeking to expropriate land produced lower estimates of property values than "independent" appraisers selected by homeowners. These results did not require explicit instructions from clients. When the buyer paid for the estimate, the price declined; when the seller commissioned the appraisal, the reverse was true. There were no genuinely independent assessments of land values.

The same principle applied when the object of technical study was the expected noise level in communities surrounding air facilities. Noise studies on behalf of those desiring development minimized potential disturbances; studies commissioned by airport opponents warned of noise "footprints" affecting large populations. Conflicting views on expected noise levels occasionally were produced by the same set of experts employed by the same agency; their perspectives on noise problems shifted as the interests of their employers changed. Experts working for the Canadian Ministry of Transport when it was seeking to expand an existing air facility in Vancouver claimed that aircraft noise would decline in surrounding communities. In Toronto, where MOT sought to build a new airport, the same experts were pessimistic about the prospects for a reduction in noise levels at the existing facility.[13]

When the results of scientific inquiry clearly contradicted the preferences of clients, experts responded with adjustments in the language or character of reports in order to reduce the impact on sponsor interests. A citizen group on the Isle of Sheppey engaged Rupert Taylor to determine noise levels in their community if the third London airport were built at a nearby site. Taylor's estimates were not sufficiently large to satisfy his clients, but they were mollified when he agreed to present his findings as "conservative estimates."[14]

The results of technical studies are consistent with the preferences of sponsors for three main reasons. First, experts chosen to conduct technical studies generally share a common perspective with employers. The selection of consultants never is based solely on technical qualifications; indeed, the credentials of experts may be entirely inappropriate, and even qualified consultants generally have biases or preferences well known in their profession. H. O. Walther, for example, had published several articles expressing his belief that airport development does not affect real estate prices before he was hired by the Port Authority of New York and New Jersey to prepare a study on that subject.[15] When technical reports are developed by government experts employed on a permanent basis, bureaucratic loyalties as well as shared perspectives seem to guarantee outcomes consistent with client preferences. And when the experts recruited by opposition groups reside within the affected community, the resulting technical studies are equally predictable.

A second and no less important explanation for this pattern of outcomes may be found in the terms of reference supplied to experts. When studies are commissioned, the purchaser of services specifies the parameters of inquiry. Consultants are asked where to build an airport, not whether to build it. They are asked whether to expand existing facilities or to construct new ones; they are not invited to assess ways of increasing the capacities of existing facilities without construction. The Società Esercizi Aeroportuali, for example, instructed consultants to propose new ways of making cargo operations more efficient. The task of the analysts was to compare the efficiency of alternative systems; they were not asked to examine cost-benefit trade-offs related to construction. The cost of implementing any new system might have been sufficiently high to preclude long-run improvements in efficiency over existing systems, but the terms of reference made it impossible to discover such information.[16]

Shared perspectives and narrow terms of reference ordinarily are sufficient to guarantee outcomes, so conscious violations of the norms of scientific and technical research, at least in the strictest sense of the term, are rare.[17] Ultimately, however, compliance with client preferences is assured by economic concerns, for experts want to stay in business. Experts employed by government agencies are particularly vulnerable to such subtle and often unspoken pressures, but "independent" consultants also are not immune, especially when sponsors can provide lucrative contracts.

Even the single exception to this pattern of fulfilling sponsor expectations demonstrates the importance of economic considerations. Aéroport de Paris' study of expected noise levels at Malpensa was conducted for the Province of Varese, and provincial authorities expected predictions of significant noise disturbances in order to pursue their campaign of opposition to airport development. But ADP, preferring to collaborate with the Società Esercizi Aeroportuali in preparing the study, produced narrow noise curves that minimized potential problems. This decision was prompted by a recognition that support for SEA was more valuable in soliciting future contracts than the satisfaction of local authorities in Varese.[18]

Unfortunately, there are numerous examples in airport development of this tendency to confuse client preferences with the public interest. Developers, for example, see the acquisition of land as a measurable cost only when the site is in private hands. Yet, opportunity costs associated with the use of land for airport development are always present, regardless of the property owner's identity. Developers have no interest in evaluating the costs of government-owned land, and experts obligingly ignore these costs in their studies.

Exceeding Client Expectations

Results consistent with sponsor preferences have not meant that studies yield only suggestions that sponsors expect. Consultants often propose unusual solutions to problems, but even the most radical approach involves development and construction. In the business of international airports, experts do not recommend alternatives to facility expansion or new construction.

The decision to construct new airports in Montreal and Toronto followed assignments to consultants to prepare plans for the expansion of existing facilities. Long-term planning, the experts argued, justified the development of entirely new airports. Of course, the same experts received the much grander planning contracts once government officials, attracted to bolder solutions, accepted the long-term view. The forecasts that justified the construction of new facilities have proved well off the mark and, in Montreal at least, the construction is a lasting embarrassment to government officials. Nonetheless, the same consultants have been able to claim experience in the development of new airports and have been rewarded accordingly with contracts in the Third World.

In Paris, where new airport plans in the late 1950s carried the imprimatur of the prime minister and, later, the head of state, experts did not need to recommend an escalation in the scope of planning. They did make judgments, however, on what expenses could be spared, and they erred consistently on the side of none. Only shrinking budgets and changing political masters reduced limitless commitments to the most advanced technologies. The most pronounced example surely is the *aérotrain* which, according to Aéroport de Paris planners, would float passengers from the central business district to the two international airports. The *aérotrain* was a sophisticated space age response to the simple requirement of access. Unfortunately, it was also more expensive than any other known surface transportation technology, and its development encountered persistent design problems (including noise, which promised serious political liabilities in the acquisition of rights of way) that could not be overcome entirely. Premier Jacques Chaban-Delmas' decision to scrap it was based on both of these factors, as well as growing doubts over the appropriateness of the technology (designed for high-speed travel, it was expected to make numerous station stops) and about underlying social policy (the finest rapid transit link in the world was to be committed to the exclusive use of elite air passengers). Aéroport de Paris officials have displayed almost as much imagination in explaining away this failure, the product of grandiose planning, as they did in conjuring the *aérotrain* in the first place.[19]

Consultants defending the environment or testifying on behalf of development opponents err with equal consistency on the side of the *status quo*. Consultants paid by opponents always have rejected the possible need for any development. As proponents tend to want more, opponents tend to want less. The experts, indeed, often tend more to the extremes than their sponsors.

The Impact of Expertise

Some experts are employed by government agencies to buttress policies whose origins are political and bureaucratic. The aviation forecasting experience described in Chapter 3 is a telling example. Others are engaged by citizen groups to generate evidence in opposition to government policies. The technical reports produced by these experts do not alter the basic preferences of clients, and they rarely clarify issues or contribute to compromise. However, experts have influenced the political process in three important ways. They have (1) changed the terms of the debate over government policies, (2) generated new and difficult problems for decision makers faced with conflicting advice, and (3) escalated the costs of development. The style of politics has been altered, even if the substance remains the same.

Technical Rhetoric

Conflicts over airport development often are caused by inequalities in distribution. Those individuals who benefit most from the construction and operation of air facilities rarely are the same as those who suffer most of the costs. Political debate can reveal this underlying issue even when it changes few opinions. The introduction of technical experts, however, converts the process from a political dispute over conflicting values and perspectives to a technical debate over details. Experts argue over the fine points of proposals (for example, the precise impact of a particular runway configuration on drainage systems), but they rarely address the fundamental issues that have stimulated controversy (for example, declining property values around airports and the willingness of governments to compensate for land not actually taken). Inequalities in the distribution of costs and benefits are not conducive to technical analysis and debate.

Both supporters and opponents of airport development may

prefer to direct the debate to technical, rather than political, issues. Developers, of course, are anxious to avoid any discussion of inequalities; any attempt to resolve the conflict would increase project costs by requiring additional compensation. Opposition groups occasionally have adopted a similar strategy in an effort to avoid the accusation of promoting private concerns at the expense of the public interest. In Toronto, for example, People or Planes, a middle-class opposition group that represented a minority of citizens in the immediate vicinity of the proposed new airport, consciously opted to oppose government plans on technical grounds rather than on the basis of equity.[20]

When the policy debate is structured in technical rather than political terms, participation is restricted to actors who are familiar with technical argumentation. The form of the debate no longer discriminates against organized interests; most parties have become sufficiently adept at such matters to engage the appropriate experts. But the focus on technical issues does not serve the public interest. It diverts attention from the competing values to peripheral, and occasionally irrelevant, questions of technique.

Disputes Among Experts

The recourse to expertise does not eliminate the necessity for political decision making, especially when there are serious challenges to technical arguments. When experts disagree, political intervention generally is necessary. But political decision making in such instances is difficult because the standard criteria of politics cannot be applied easily to technical disputes. Questions of fact are not subject to resolution through democratic means. Even "the preponderance of technical opinion" does not provide an adequate guide for decision makers. In technical disputes, it is not necessary to muster equal evidence in order to cast doubt on the expertise provided by opponents.[21]

There are essentially two avenues open to political authorities who must decide between conflicting expert views. They can accept one set of analyses and ignore the other, or they can seek an effective compromise that incorporates technical arguments from both sets of experts. The Canadian government employed both approaches in Toronto, but neither proved effective. The Airport Inquiry Commission, appointed by the Cabinet to review plans for the new airport, concluded that the technical data supplied by the Ministry of Transport were more convincing than the data provided by opponents. The Commission's report, however, was so controversial that the Cabinet was unwilling to implement the recommendations. A second approach, offered by the government as a compromise, was the decision to develop a "minimum international airport" in Pickering Township. The new policy reflected evidence provided by both sides but was neither technically consistent nor logical. Predictably, it proved as controversial as the policy it replaced.[22]

The Price of Expertise

In one respect, at least, the participation of technical experts in the policy process has affected the substance of politics. Project costs have soared because of the recourse to expert advice. The tendency of experts to propose larger and more grandiose development schemes than those envisioned initially by their clients has been one important factor in the escalation of costs. Expert advice, moreover, can be expensive. The Dallas–Fort Worth Regional Airport Board, for example, estimated in 1971 that expenditures for "engineers, architects, and studies" during the construction stage could reach approximately $43 million, more than 8 percent of the total development costs.[23]

Consultants from the private sector have been responsible, in large measure, for this problem. The airline industry, which has become increasingly cost-conscious in recent years, has accused outside experts of advocating "excessive expenditures on airports which are not wanted by airlines and travellers or which are unnecessarily elaborate."[24] According to spokesmen for the industry, consultants have a strong incentive to jack up the development price:[25]

Although there is no doubt of the need for the high professional skills of these consultants, it is clear that they have a vested interest in making the project on as large a scale as possible, and quite frequently unrelated to the real need of the community or traveller. Not only do consultant fees normally relate in direct proportion to the total cost of the project, but also in many cases the consultants are an arm for the export of airport technology and material from their base country. Containing consultants' ambitions and rationalizing their recommendations is therefore becoming a key part of our overall program for containing airport costs.

The Case for Independent Expertise

Technocratic servants may serve their masters well, but failures are not uncommon, at least with respect to the development of international airports, and such failures reflect poorly on masters. More important, technocratic servants have not served the public interest well. Independent criticism, analysis, and review which answers neither to citizen groups with their parochial concerns nor to governments, public authorities, and businesses is indispensable if technical knowledge is to be applied usefully in the public interest.

Technical experts are not always wrong. Indeed, policy failures stem more often from the misuse of technical information than from poor analysis. British politicians, not the experts employed by the Roskill Commission, abused the tools of cost-benefit analysis and opted for sites that were not recommended. Italian politicians, not analysts employed by the Società Esercizi Aeroportuali, made land-use decisions that forced awkward planning in Milan.[26] And the Canadian Minister of Transport, not the experts in his ministry, opted for the construction of a new Toronto airport despite evidence that an additional facility was unnecessary.[27] But distortions and abuses in the political arena were possible only with the complicity or silence of technocratic servants.

The case for independent expertise can also be made in terms of the impermanence of political masters. Government authorities who commission expert studies often are not around to receive the results. Governments change, and policies may change with them. Technical studies whose results prove incompatible with the new policy line may be shelved or twisted out of shape. Such changes offer the most compelling practical reason for experts to refrain from tailoring their studies to the apparent expectations of sponsors. If a technical study is to have a life of its own, it must present a persuasive case of its own.

If independent experts are to be effective, they must appreciate the realities of the political environment. Technical solutions to public policy problems cannot be implemented if experts lack insight into the political process. Philip Beinhaker, the primary consultant for the development of air facilities in Montreal, exhibited such a failure of insight when he proposed a single airport in Eastern Ontario to service both Montreal and Toronto. The costs of his proposed rail access may have proved prohibitive, but it was Beinhaker's apolitical vision of a Montreal airport located in Ontario that drew open ridicule from politicians in Quebec.[28]

Independent experts also must appreciate the sincerity of competing perspectives if they are to operate effectively in a political environment. All plans are value-laden, and the values that underlie technical solutions may not be shared by all members of the community. Experts who believe in "correct" solutions to technical problems fail to provide responsible political authorities with options based on competing values. Without adequate knowledge of alternative solutions and the values upon which they are based, political authorities may be unable to implement any plan.

Above all, independent experts must appreciate that public sector problems are cross-sectoral and do not conform conveniently to bureaucratic divisions. Airports commonly are within the domain of transportation or airport authorities, yet development encounters greatest difficulty when these authorities fail to appreciate that airports are also the legitimate concern of officials responsible for land use, pollution control, housing, surface transit, employment, and noise. The narrowness of the paymaster, when imposed on the technical specialist, serves no one well. The expertise of planners must be sufficiently broad and comprehensive to recognize other concerns.

Independence from political masters does not mean the absence of political oversight. The application of technique is political, and experts must be politically responsible. Politicians, moreover, must appreciate the limitations of their experts. But experts who are comprehensive in their approach to problems can serve the public interest while remaining independent of political masters. The mechanisms for channelling expertise in this manner must be developed; otherwise, the public interest can be served only through the good will of clients and the unlikely and infrequent coincidence of private and public objectives.

Endnotes

1. See for example Robert Wood, "Scientists and Politics: The Rise of an Apolitical Elite," in Robert Gilpin and Christopher Wright (ed.), *Scientists and National Policy-Making* (New York: Columbia, 1964).
2. Jean Meynaud, *Technocracy* (London: Faber and Faber, 1965). Fear of an emerging technocracy has been more prevalent in Europe (particularly in France) than in the United States, but there have been expressions of concern on this side of the Atlantic as well.

3. The definition is from the *Dictionnaire alphabétique et analogique de la langue française* (Paris: Société de nouveau Littre, 1964) and is quoted in Daniel Bell, *The Coming of Post-Industrial Society* (New York: Basic, 1973), p. 348.

4. Daniel Guttman and Barry Willner, *The Shadow Government* (New York: Pantheon, 1976).

5. Elliot J. Feldman and Jerome Milch, *The Politics of Canadian Airport Development: Lessons for Federalism* (Durham, N.C.: Duke University Press, 1982). The solution for airport congestion at Dorval Airport in Montreal, proposed by KPM, was precisely the opposite of the firm's vaunted solution to the logjam on the Welland Canal.

6. Airport Inquiry Commission, *Report* (Ottawa: Information Canada, 1974), p. 12.

7. Elliot J. Feldman, *Airport Siting as a Problem of Policy and Participation in Technological Societies: The Case of Milano-Malpensa* (Cambridge, Mass. and Torino, Italy: Harvard University Center for International Affairs and Fondazione Luigi Einaudi, 1978), pp. 37–40.

8. See for example the *Written Summary* submitted by the Toronto Area Airports Project team of the Ministry of Transport to the Airport Inquiry Commission. Other examples of this behavior among forecasters are reviewed in Chapter 3.

9. Critics of the Roskill Commission report include E. J. Mishan, "What is Wrong with Roskill," *Journal of Transport Economics and Policy* (September 1970), pp. 221–234; M. E. Paul, "Can Aircraft Noise Nuisance Be Measured in Money?" 23 *Oxford Economic Papers* (November 1971), pp. 298–322; V. C. Nwaneri, "Equity in Cost-Benefit Analysis," *Journal of Transport Economics and Policy* (September 1970), pp. 235–248; and John G. U. Adams, "London's Third Airport: From TLA to Airstrip One," *Geographic Journal* (1971), pp. 468–493.

10. Elliot J. Feldman, *White Elephants and the Albatross: British and French Planning in the Supersonic Age* (Cambridge, Mass.: MIT 1982).

11. See for example Sanford Lakoff (ed.), *Knowledge and Power: Essays in Science and Government* (New York: Free Press, 1966); and Lauriston King and Philip Melanson, "Knowledge and Policy: Some Experiences from the 1960s," 20 *Public Policy* 1 (Winter 1972).

12. This debate is reviewed in Jerome Milch, "The Politics of Technical Advice," 23 *Administrative Science Quarterly* 3 (September 1977), pp. 526–528.

13. Feldman and Milch, *The Politics of Canadian Airport Development, op. cit.*

14. Interview with Lord Boston, Organizer of the Isle of Sheppey airport opposition, House of Lords, London, January 19, 1977.

15. The published studies include "The Impact of Municipal Airports on the Market Value of Real Estate in the Adjacent Areas," 22 *The Appraisal Journal* 1 (January 1954), pp. 15–25, and "Effect of Jet Airports on Market Value of Vicinage Real Estate," 27 *The Appraisal Journal* 4 (October 1959), pp. 465–468.

16. Feldman, *Airport Siting, op. cit.*

17. One study that does appear to violate scientific canons is a public opinion survey conducted by the Elliott Research Corporation for the Metropolitan

Toronto Airport Review Committee, a local citizen group opposed to airport development. The consultant claimed that the survey was methodologically sound and the results statistically significant but could provide no evidence to support either contention. Feldman and Milch, *The Politics of Canadian Airport Development, op. cit.*

18. Feldman, *Airport Siting, op. cit.* Public officials in the Province of Varese accepted the results of the ADP study because of their belief in the integrity of outside experts. The planners at Aéroport de Paris undoubtedly knew that their report would be accepted. Caveat emptor!

19. Feldman, *White Elephants, op. cit.*

20. Feldman and Milch, *The Politics of Canadian Airport Development, op. cit.*, Chapter 4.

21. Dorothy Nelkin, "The Political Impact of Technical Expertise," 5 *Social Studies of Science* 1 (January 1975), pp. 53–54.

22. Feldman and Milch, *The Politics of Canadian Airport Development, op. cit.*, Chapter 4.

23. This estimate is derived from a bond prospectus issued by the Dallas–Fort Worth Regional Airport Board in September 1971, p. 10.

24. Knut Hammarskjold, "The State of the Air Transport Industry," address of the Director General of the International Air Transport Association at the 31st Annual Meeting, Oslo, Norway, September 29–October 2, 1975.

25. *Ibid.*

26. The site on which SEA was planning to build was government land. Authorities in Rome decided to transfer this land to a private company rather than let the Milan airport authority acquire it. Feldman, *Airport Siting, op. cit.*, pp. 25–31.

27. Technical experts in the Ministry of Transport, as well as MOT's own consultant, Parkin and Associates, preferred to build additional facilities at Malton Airport. They argued that a new airport could not be justified. Feldman and Milch, *The Politics of Canadian Airport Development, op. cit.*, Chapter 4.

28. This scheme was called the "Kingston Plan." The response from planners in Montreal was noted in an interview with Harry Lash, former Chief Planner in Montreal and former Planning Director for the Greater Vancouver Regional District, Vancouver, December 7, 1976.

Part Four

CITIZENS AND PROTEST

Chapter 6

PROPERTY AND PROTEST

Public controversy arose in all eight cases of this study, but organized citizen protest varied considerably both in visibility and in impact. Protest was most notable where land was scarce and property owners were numerous on and near the site. Citizen opposition to airport development was stimulated everywhere by threats to private property, regardless of the form that protest eventually assumed.

The popular impression of controversies over technological development is that protest centers on ecological issues.[1] Environmentalists appeared in the 1970s to be well-organized, well-funded, and well-intentioned. Their interpretation of the public interest often seemed more legitimate than the emphasis of developers on paving meadows, polluting waters, and pressing the limits of the ecological balance. Often they captured popular imagination, and always they seemed to captivate the public eye. Among the many protesters, they inevitably are remembered best.

This popular impression is misleading, at least with respect to protest over airport development. Environmental interests commonly were drawn into anti-airport activity by the protests of property owners. These local interests often adopted the rhetoric of the environmental movement because they understood the greater public resonance of unselfish demands for the defense of the environment. They knew that public support was more likely for a protest over the public good of environmental protection than over the private good of property rights. Nevertheless, the single most important influence on the public environmental debate was the private concerns of property owners.

155

Airport development stimulated protest among two types of property owners. First, citizens whose land was included within the designated development site often resisted expropriation or, if that were impossible, sought just compensation and fair treatment from government. Second, citizens whose land was adjacent to designated sites resisted development proposals in an effort to protect property values and preserve the quality of life in their communities. The distinction between these two groups of citizens often was blurred. Development sites were not always designated in detail, and citizens often were uncertain of the precise nature of the threat to their property. The protest of property owners faced with expropriation, however, usually triggered the protest of airport neighbors.

There is a direct relationship between the laws and policies in different countries governing the compulsory purchase of private property and public protest over airport development. This relationship reveals the fundamental character of relations between the individual and the state, for liberal democracies everywhere hold as their basic tenet the protection of life, liberty, and property. The seizure of private property is one of the most traumatic activities of any liberal democratic state. The rules that govern such transactions help define the powers of the state and the character of its liberal and democratic values. They also help explain the differences in patterns of protest and participation among industrial states.[2]

The Dilemma of Compulsory Purchase

Although all liberal democracies allow and even encourage the private development and ownership of real estate, governments may require the use of private land for public purposes. Sometimes the temporary use of a land parcel is sufficient and governments may become tenants to private landlords. However, public ownership of land often appears necessary for some general use. The most common example is for national defense, but land may also be set aside for parks and forests or for the protection of natural resources. And land may be required for the construction of a public utility such as power transmission lines, railroads, highways, and airport facilities.

A cardinal principle in all liberal democracies is that land is transacted in the marketplace where a willing buyer deals with a willing seller. The purchase and sale of property must be voluntary, according to the laws of the western industrial world. An owner may be forced to sell only because of a failure to make payments under a contract voluntarily entered. This market principle, however, is violated when the power of the state is employed to obtain private land. Government may be a willing buyer, but "compulsory purchase" (as it is called in Britain), "eminent domain" (United States), "expropriation" (Canada and Italy), or "condemnation" (France) denies the presence of a willing seller. The community, represented by the agents of government, requires individuals to surrender their rights either to retain their property for purposes they choose, or to sell or rent the property in the free market.[3] Had government not come to them, they would not have been selling or abandoning their property. The absence of a willing seller is the liberal democratic dilemma of compulsory purchase.

Consequences of the Dilemma

When the government of a liberal democracy chooses to violate its own basic rules by forcing an individual to surrender property, it assumes a significant burden. The consequence of invoking the dilemma of compulsory purchase is the responsibility to deal justly and equitably with citizens undergoing a fundamental denial of their rights. The relationship between the state and its citizens can be defined by the procedures adopted for the compulsory purchase of land.

Expropriation imposes three tasks on the state. First, it must demonstrate the need for a particular land parcel. Each individual is entitled to know why he or she, not someone else, is expected to surrender property for the public good. This entitlement derives from the premise that the purpose of the state is to protect private property and from the traditional legal commitment in liberal democracies to due process. Second, the state must establish procedures for compulsory land acquisition. These procedures include notification of intent to expropriate, land assessment practices, and the schedule and forms of compensation. Moreover, the state must decide whether challenges to expropriation may be tolerated and whether citizens will be permitted to participate in the determination of property values. Third, the state must determine

the principles of compensation, both for the land itself and for the
dislocation of residences and businesses. The state must decide
whether it will help people relocate and whether it will compensate for the sacrifice involved in the involuntary surrender of
private property.

In a normal market transaction, the buyer would bear no responsibility at any of these three stages. The buyer is not obliged
to demonstrate a need for a particular property. The procedure
of acquisition involves a simple exchange of the property for compensation; the compensation, in turn, need not be "just," only
accepted by the buyer and seller. The norm for justice in the
marketplace is set by each separate transaction, not by any abstract
or general criteria.

Rules of the Game

The procedures adopted by governments in response to the dilemma of compulsory purchase are similar in all five countries.
A declaration of public utility is required everywhere in order to
obtain land that private owners do not wish to sell. "Just compensation" is inscribed in the laws of all five countries, reflecting
the principle that the declaration of public utility is not an entitlement for public seizure without due recognition of value. Governments are obliged to assess the value of property and reimburse
owners for their loss according to the dictates of the market. Values
are to be ascertained as if the transaction took place between a
willing buyer and a willing seller.

The rules everywhere permit owners of property undergoing
expropriation to contest the price set by government. All countries
permit citizens to seek judicial intervention to settle disputes
between owners and government. The government is expected
to have a legitimate public purpose when imposing compulsory
purchase, and there are provisions everywhere for the eventual
restitution of expropriated land that is not used by the state.

Despite these common rules, there are important legal variations from country to country. The determination of just compensation in Canada, for example, permits a citizen to engage an
independent appraiser, at public expense, should a government
assessment be unacceptable. The law does not bind the government to the independent determination, but such evidence is
admissible for court settlements. At an opposite extreme, the
Italian government authorizes an agency of the provinces, the

Ufficio Tecnico Erariale (UTE), to fix prices by using the tax rolls as a guide. If an owner has enjoyed low taxes through an outdated assessment, decades of currency devaluations can be ignored by UTE appraisers in determining compensation. Should an Italian choose to contest the price, all payment is withheld until the court settles the dispute; in the interim, the government can seize the property and remove the owner, thereby temporarily depriving the citizen of all capital associated with the property.

Governments may be required to declare the purpose for which land is taken, but New York State law permits the Metropolitan Transportation Authority (MTA) to acquire land by eminent domain that is not required immediately for airport development.[4] Laws elsewhere are more stringent, but agencies have considerable leeway in declaring a public purpose for the acquisition of real property. Moreover, the French and Italians have no legal right to challenge a declaration of public utility or to dispute a government claim to require a parcel of land; only price may be contested in court. Canadians are permitted since 1970 to object at a public hearing to a government expropriation, but even the new Expropriation Act does not require government agencies to defend or justify the purpose for which land is acquired.

Despite provisions for restitution, there is not a single example of governments returning unused land in any of the cases examined here. In Vancouver Lester Grauer sued the Government of Canada to nullify the expropriation of his farm in 1954. Twenty-six years later, the government had neither taken possession of the farm nor restored it to him. Italian law specifically requires restitution after a decade, but authorities have found many legal devices to evade the spirit, if not the letter, of the law. Land acquired for airport use but still vacant includes most of Sea Island, the first portion seized in 1954 and the rest in 1969–1971; 18,000 acres near Toronto, taken in 1972; 80,000 "peripheral" acres near Montreal, seized in 1969; 8000 acres west of Stewart Airport (northwest of New York), expropriated in 1971; and 3700 acres near Malpensa Airport outside Milan, also expropriated in 1971.

The Airport Cases

Land was acquired for airport development at seven of the eight sites examined in this study. Only in London were authorities unable to obtain sufficient agreement to undertake the acquisition of land. The response of property owners varied systematically across countries; organized public protest was muted in France and the United States but not in Canada or Italy. There were also some differences in the degree and nature of public protest within the United States, where federal structures permit individual states to determine some of the rules of the game, and Canada, where the rules changed dramatically with the passage of the Expropriation Act of 1970.

France

Most of the land parcel designated by Aéroport de Paris (ADP) as the site for the new airport was owned by 53 families. The site was drawn to acquire the maximum amount of land without taking homes and villages. Only one farmhouse stood on the entire 7104 acres that ADP wished to acquire. Property owners formed a union and employed one of France's most prominent agricultural figures, Pierre Dubois, the President of the Technical Institute for Beetroot and a farmer in Tremblay-les-Gonesse, to negotiate in their behalf. They also agreed to negotiate an overall price for the land and to divide the monies proportionately among themselves. The first step put ADP on notice that it was dealing with the rich and powerful; the second step eliminated the government's need to fix prices for each strip of land (of which there were legally 587), and it saved the farmers from disputes among themselves over relative land values.

The Administration des Domaines, the agency of the Finance Ministry responsible for assessing land to be taken by the state, offered an average price of $1214 per acre plus an additional payment of $567 per acre for eviction from agricultural land.* These prices were based on the going rate for farm land bought and sold in the free market on the Plains of France during the period just prior to the planned acquisition. Administration officials claimed that the real value of land in the area was closer to $850 per acre, and they considered the offer generous. After a year of negotiations, less than 5 percent of the land had been secured on the basis of this assessment through a program of voluntary sale.

---

* Article 10 of the Loi Complémentaire to the Loi d'Orientation Agricole guarantees special compensation for displacement from agricultural land.

Table 6–1 Principles of Expropriation

	Canada	France	Italy	United States
Principle of Exchange	Home for home	"Market price"	"Market price"	"Market price" and special compensation
Basis of Assessment	Negotiations	Negotiations	Fixed prices	Negotiations
Prevailing Concept of Ownership	Crown possession	Private/Communal	Public	Private
Mandated Public Hearings	Yes	No	No	Yes

NOTE: United Kingdom is excluded because no expropriation took place.

The owners demanded compensation between two and five times the proposed price ($2428 to $6470 per acre) plus twice the proposed eviction indemnification ($1134 per acre). The Administration Fiscale in early 1966 investigated land values throughout the region in an effort to resolve the disagreement. The top price in the region, at 1965 values, matched the original government offer.

The government recognized it could not concede to the demands of property owners without distorting the real estate market in the Paris region. It also understood that market compensation would not yield voluntary sales, and it did not want to impose the weight of the state through formal condemnation. A consultant, the Société de Recherche Economique et Sociologique en Agriculture, was hired by ADP to reassess the basis for eviction compensation. New consideration was given to the cost of involuntary dislocation and inflation. In July 1966 ADP negotiated an agreement with Dubois to pay $1620 per acre (one third more than the top price in the region), an additional 25 percent for replacement, and $890 per acre (nearly the original demand) in eviction compensation. In sum, owners were to be compensated overall at approximately $3000 per acre, nearly four times the average market value for the region. 93 percent of the land was settled in this transaction.

ADP did not have the authority to pay this sum, and the Administration des Domaines was unwilling to grant it. The Minister of Finance, Valéry Giscard d'Estaing, personally intervened to complete the sale. Sixty-nine small parcels remained in litigation, but the owners were unsuccessful in pressing their claims. Indeed, the last holdout—who resisted eviction—was paid the least amount of money for his land. The courts confirmed that cooperation would be rewarded in France and resistance punished, and the principal owners established that the government would pay handsomely to avoid controversy. But it took ADP close to three years to complete the transactions and take possession.

An additional 277 acres were taken in 1969–1970 when a site plan finally had been developed for the airport. Prices offered, including all expenses, exceeded the 1967 transaction by 60 percent. Still more land was acquired after the airport opened, when the village of Roissy-en-France was found to suffer inordinately from noise. ADP had assured villagers that the airport would present financial dividends without environmental penalties, but it also had refused to release noise curves before the airport opened. Neighbors were inclined to accept ADP's expertise until real experience replaced optimistic forecasts.

Once the airport was operational, ADP converted its Office for Expropriation into an "Office to Help Airport Neighbors." Help came in the form of home purchases. Residents could sell their homes to ADP, which in turn demolished the buildings so that no one could move in to renew a claim. Facing unlivable conditions, the villagers were gratified to find a buyer. The funds came from a special tax decreed by the Cabinet on all passengers passing through Charles de Gaulle Airport. The noise tax was imposed, moreover, at a rate three times higher for international than for domestic passengers, and it excluded freight and private aircraft. Hence, ADP had found a way to avoid a confrontation with homeowners even though some 260 were destined to lose their homes and community. Foreign travellers were made to pay most of the bill.[5]

United States

Dallas–Fort Worth. The basic French strategy was to pay handsomely for land and, at least in the early phases, to avoid the acquisition of homes. City fathers in Dallas and Fort Worth shared this perspective on compensation, if not on home acquisition. The site selected for airport development was predominantly agricultural, and the going price was $500–$700 per acre in 1965. Municipal officials in these two Texas cities were authorized by state law to seize the land they wanted for airport development and to pay the market price.[6] They preferred, however, to pay sums closer to the demands of owners, who saw in the government purchase a potential bonanza.

The contract between the cities specified that the task of land acquisition would be divided, with Dallas assuming responsibility for acquiring land in Dallas County and Fort Worth for acquiring it in Tarrant County. Both governments were exceedingly generous, effectively paying whatever they were asked in order to assure voluntary sales and avoid conflict. Although the first 4400 acres went for approximately $1300 per acre (only double the market value), speculation, delays, and a spreading awareness that the municipal governments preferred to pay rather than fight encouraged a price spiral. In the summer of 1967, two years after proceedings were initiated, Fort Worth paid $7000 per acre for a 48-acre tract. Overall, 17,500 acres were acquired for an average of $3500 per acre.

Land acquisition affected considerably more individuals in Dallas–Fort Worth than in Paris. A total of 730 people in 249 family units were displaced, and one whole community (Minters Chapel) was erased from the map. Yet, by paying between five and seven times the market value of land (1965 prices), authorities minimized controversy.

In neither Paris nor Dallas–Fort Worth did significant opposition arise during airport development. Protest groups were organized in both cities, as we shall see in Chapter 7, but their effect was blunted by policies of generous compensation for land. In both cases, authorities exceeded the requirements of the law, and in both cases policy was shaped by a commitment to avoid conflict.

New York. Government officials in New York also were prepared to compensate generously for land, but—unlike their counterparts in Texas or France—they were not concerned about avoiding the expropriation of homes. The task of planning and developing a fourth area jetport was assumed by the Port Authority of New York and New Jersey in 1959, but no site satisfying contending parties had emerged after a decade of efforts. Governor Nelson Rockefeller of New York, committed to the facility, assigned development to the Metropolitan Transportation Authority (MTA), an agency more directly under his control.

In early 1970 the United States Air Force ceased operations at Stewart Air Force Base near Newburgh and offered the facility to the State of New York. Stewart Airport began operations in March 1970 as a general aviation facility, but Rockefeller had grander designs. In early 1971 the Governor introduced a bill in the New York Legislature to expropriate 8657 acres adjacent to the airport, enough to sustain full-scale development. Over $70 million was allocated in June 1971, including $30 million for land acquisition.

The targeted land included 337 owners and approximately 1200 residents scattered through five villages and townships. A month after the Legislature allocated the funds, many of the owners joined a suit filed by the Hudson River Valley Council, an *ad hoc* citizens group organized to resist the conversion of Stewart Airport into an international commercial facility. Several political jurisdictions, including Orange County, joined the suit against the State of New York. The central challenge involved the legality of expropriation in the absence of a detailed plan for land use. However, the inclusion of a provision for land banking in the law of June 1971 gave MTA substantial discretion. The injunction sought by owners was denied in court, and in August the state took title to the entire parcel. Only 581 acres belonging to the bankrupt Pennsylvania Central Railroad were excluded from the planned expropriation.

The laws of eminent domain in New York State provide for compensation based on fair market value. Title is transferred upon the government's initial offer of compensation. Until 1980, modest interest at a rate set by the state was paid on outstanding offers, but a failure to respond to an offer could lead to a loss of interest. Since 1980, failure to respond within ninety days can oblige the owner to petition for compensation. Despite these restrictive rules and despite the sudden and unexpected expropriation for Stewart Airport, resistance melted away when state government proved generous in providing compensation for land. Indeed, the Legislature appropriated an additional $7.5 million to complete the land transactions. Only 75 of the 337 owners continued to press their claims in court, and three cases remained unsettled in 1980; most owners, however, were satisfied. The pattern of generosity suggests that in New York, as in Texas and France, the government prefers to avoid litigation if not controversy.

Canada

The Canadian government acquired land for airport development during the same period in three different locations across the country. In each case acquisition touched off intense disputes with land owners who insisted that they did not receive just compensation for their property and were not treated fairly. Citizens affected directly by expropriation rarely contested the claims of progress and technology advanced by airport builders; those themes were advanced by the prospective neighbors of new facilities in Toronto and Vancouver.

Conflict in Canada stemmed in part from the reluctance of federal officials to exceed legal requirements. Unlike their counterparts in France and the United States, Transport officials were not prepared to buy off property owners through payments beyond those mandated by the law. Protest occurred in all three cases, even though part of the Vancouver and all of the Toronto lands were taken under the terms of a new, and more generous, Expropriation Act approved in 1970. The new law mandated public hearings at which citizens could register grievances; authorized compensation at a level sufficient to permit victims of expropriation to replace their property with something comparable and in geographic proximity; and provided compensation for relocation and inflation.[7] The generosity of the law, however, neither affected the basic inclination of government officials to protect the public purse nor increased their sensitivity to the concerns of the expropriated.

Montreal. The Montreal expropriation involved an initial 88,000 acres of land (10,000 more eventually were added), 3000 families, and 10,000 individuals in and around the village of Ste. Scholastique. Under the terms of the law in effect when the expropriation was announced in March 1969, the government assumed ownership of all the property upon the filing of a single map, designating site boundaries, in the local land registry office. There was no requirement to notify, or even identify, individual landowners. Despite the sudden and absolute nature of the acquisition, the initial reaction in the affected zone was positive. Québécois citizens believed that the government would provide generous compensation for their land and they were prepared to cooperate with Transport officials.

Attitudes began to change as expropriation proceeded. Property owners discovered that the government was not obliged to provide compensation, or even to submit offers for the land, upon assumption of control; payment was delayed for five years or more in some cases. Citizens could not mortgage property for capital because they no longer owned it, and they could not move because the government was in no hurry to pay them. Dissatisfaction increased when offers finally arrived. The government hired three companies of private assessors, all of whom were understaffed and unable to make thorough evaluations of each home. They played neighbors against each other in a deliberate effort to keep prices down. Little distinction was made between abandoned farms and those still prosperous. Prices were set at an average of $210 per acre based on 1969 prices in the free market, even though inflation had eroded the buying power of the money and had made it impossible to purchase comparable homes in the immediate area.

The government was unprepared for such a large expropriation and was unable to manage the process. Property owners could not secure answers to simple questions. There was no timetable for development of the land; homes were abandoned in anticipation of eviction, and crime became a problem in the area for the first time. There were no relocation arrangements for owners as they were expropriated and, at least initially, no fringe benefits to cover the costs of moving.[8]

By 1971 a committee established as an information source for owners had become a strategic center of resistance and protest. The government's acquisition strategy had assumed the passive good will of owners. It was designed to obtain the maximum amount of land at the minimum price, even when that price was below market value. The expropriation for Mirabel evolved, therefore, into a national scandal.

Vancouver. Land acquisition in Vancouver began in September 1967 when Federal Minister of Transport Jack Pickersgill declared his intention to make Sea Island entirely federal property.[9] The declaration of intent, which affected 650 residents, destroyed the real estate market on Sea Island because potential buyers feared the shadow of impending government acquisition. The Ministry of Transport (MOT) proposed to acquire the land through voluntary purchase, but more homes were offered for sale than MOT claimed to have funds to buy. Owners could no longer find buyers in the open market, and MOT officials told them to return in six months when government funds might be available. Compensation for homes MOT did acquire, moreover, was notably lower than elsewhere in the Vancouver area for similar homes. This voluntary purchase plainly was of a different character and intention than the program in Paris.

The Sea Island Ratepayers' Association (SIRA) hired a lawyer to clarify the government's intentions. In fact, the government had no immediate use for the property it was acquiring. The acquisition program had been launched in response to rising real estate values and MOT, operating like any other real estate speculator, was seeking to purchase property before the price might send it out of reach even of an eager government. As in Quebec, homes were vandalized when residents moved out, and crime became a new problem. Under pressure from SIRA, MOT rented homes to relieve the impact of depopulation on the community, but the new tenants shared none of the values or traditions of community maintenance held by the remaining owners. The Municipality of Richmond, where Sea Island legally is located, acceded to federal requests to stop issuing building permits. Land use effectively was frozen, and MOT was the only buyer in the marketplace. Through no clearly deliberate policy, the federal government was blockbusting.

The new Expropriation Act was passed in June 1970, and residents of Sea Island appealed to come under its protection, even though they continued to resist expropriation. The federal government insisted that it was purchasing homes "as they became available." Yet, as early as October 1970 residents in the subdivision of Burkeville, on the opposite side of Sea Island, were notified formally, under provisions of the new law, of possible expropriation. Burkeville was facing expropriation for construction of a new bridge to the mainland, while owners in the veterans' subdivisions were negotiating purchases for unspecified airport development. The government was pursuing inconsistent policies on the same island.

Under pressure from local members of Parliament, the government offered a full-scale expropriation. In the absence of an urgent government need for the land, however, the residents preferred a gradual dissolution of the community through voluntary sale. The government, they thought, should accept responsibility for destroying the real estate market and should maintain fair prices in accordance with the provisions of the Expropriation Act. The Assistant Deputy Attorney General, negotiating for the federal government, agreed to such an arrangement, which was named after him, the "Troop Formula." The Ministers of Justice and Transport, however, vetoed the proposal because they feared that a precedent affecting some 60 remaining families in two subdivisions would complicate proceedings in Toronto.

Expropriation finally was declared in November 1972 for the remaining 53 owners. MOT, responding to pressure from the Prime Minister, had claimed an immediate need for the land. Public hearings, required under the new law, obliged MOT to present its airport plans and converted the process into a forum. The Department of the Environment, the Ministry of State for Urban Affairs, the Greater Vancouver Regional District, and municipal officials all came to testify. With federal elections called, members of Parliament and national party leaders were drawn into the spectacle. The central actors were the Sea Islanders, mostly war veterans favorably disposed toward the government until they concluded that officials acted in bad faith by trying to buy their homes at unfair prices and with undue pressure. It was not long, however, before this group in the path of expropriation was replaced at center stage by the residents of "millionaires' row," Southwest Marine Drive, who would be one mile closer to airport noise if the government built a proposed parallel runway.

By the end of the hearings, plans to expand Vancouver International Airport were a major issue of public policy in the province. Had the federal government agreed to the Troop Formula, expropriation would have been avoided and, with it, the public controversy that helped block development for a decade. The Sea Islanders had to sell their homes, and even with the protection of the new Act they suffered disorientation, destruction of their community, and disillusionment with their government. They were the least affluent of the actors and the only ones the government thought it could manipulate easily. They lost more than anyone else in the Vancouver case, but their plight was forgotten as attention turned to the interests of wealthier and more powerful opponents who feared the impact of government policy on their property values.

Toronto. Expropriation in Toronto came entirely under the terms of the 1970 Act.[10] Property owners in Pickering Township, like the residents of Burkeville, were notified of the government's intention to expropriate under the requirements of the new law. They also were invited to submit written objections and to participate in a public hearing. Although the hearing was to focus on expropriation, opposition groups utilized the forum to challenge construction of the new facility.

A contest between the Ministry of Transport and citizen protest groups for the support of general public opinion took place outside the Toronto hearing room for eight days in November 1972. All issues related to the development decision were opened for scrutiny. The controversy led to a formal government inquiry.

The requirements of the Expropriation Act for proper notification and public hearings created a structured opportunity for citizens to defend their homes. The hearings confirmed the government's authority to expropriate, but procedural requirements guaranteed further conflict. Most of the 717 property owners rejected government purchase offers because they considered them below market value. The Department of Public Works (DPW), responsible under the new act for all government land acquisition, held public meetings that generated almost violent opposition, and the Public Works Minister organized a Compensation Review Committee that promptly recommended a 10 percent increment for outstanding offers, plus $3000 payment for the inconvenience and hardship owners faced.

The law permits owners to accept an offer without prejudice against a subsequent claim. Most of the owners exercised this right, and in early 1975 they worked on their member of Parliament to pressure government for greater compensation. The Cabinet adjusted the valuation dates that determine the moment when prices should be firm, a decision which delivered to some two-thirds of the owners compensation exceeding by 45 percent the government's original offer.

The Expropriation Act encouraged public objection and formal delay. The acquisition of land for the new airport in Toronto therefore became the initial focus of protest. Although expropriation was not the whole story, as we shall see in Chapter 7, the legal requirement for open hearings made it a central issue. Government officials, moreover, were preoccupied with minimizing expenditures for land acquisition. The consequence was dissatisfaction among owners, despite the generosity of the law. Given the opportunity to obtain their demands, landowners used the law in their own behalf with considerable success. But the sale of property was not a voluntary transaction in the marketplace and the owners did lose their homes.

Italy

Land acquisition triggered protest in the communities of Ferno, Somma Lombardo, and Lonate Pozzolo because of the amount of land the Società Esercizi Aeroportuali (SEA) was seeking (3707 acres, effectively doubling the size of the airport) and because of fears that strict zoning to protect the airport would prevent urban development. However, protest originated more with individual citizens than with municipal officials. Many owners in the path of Malpensa's expansion already had lost land for airport construction or national defense. These veterans of expropriation knew that their land would not be surveyed, that compensation would be inadequate, that replacement or relocation subsidies would not be offered, and that many years could pass before government would ever pay them.

Their worst fears were confirmed in the Malpensa expropriation. The Ufficio Tecnico Erariale (UTE), operating as the agent for SEA, neither consulted local realtors in determining "market" prices for land nor conducted a survey of land values in the area. Some officials claimed that all land parcels were inspected, but others admitted that only maps were consulted.[11] Property owners claimed that land was worth between $7700 and $9700 per acre in 1972, but UTE's top price was $1862. No distinctions were made between fallow and cultivated land, and no financial assistance was offered for relocating families and commercial enterprises.

Landowners were aware that they could not prevent expropriation. They also understood that a legal challenge to the prices offered by UTE would be self-defeating because they could not win a court contest with the state and because the law permitted UTE to delay compensation until all judicial decisions were rendered. Despite this knowledge, nearly half the owners chose to defy routine expropriation. In January 1974, sixty-three owners banded together to appeal for common property evaluations and, subsequently, to file a common law suit.

Although UTE was directly responsible for these efforts to limit compensation, SEA selected and paid for the land and could have sought other arrangements for acquisition. SEA did agree to a private deal with the small aircraft manufacturer Caproni and his farmer brother that involved special land use privileges and access to the commercial airport, but this arrangement with the largest landowners discouraged the protest of others who thought themselves too small and weak after their potential leader had been bought off. Similar arrangements with other landowners, therefore, never were contemplated. Instead, SEA accused them of greed and refused to acknowledge any legitimacy to their protest.

Table 6–2 **Expropriation Compensation**

	DFW	Milan	Montreal	New York	Paris	Toronto
Average Price per Acre (in U.S. $)	$3500 (1965–69)	$1862 (1971)	$210 (1969)	$4643 (1971)	$3000 (1967)	$8110 (1973/1975)
Amount of Land Acquired (in acres)	17,500	3707	98,000	8076	7381	18,000

NOTE: Compensation was based on both acreage and homes acquired. Vancouver is excluded from this table because purchase price was based primarily on homes, and figures therefore cannot be compared.

No effort was made in any official quarter, at any time, to pacify or appease the victims of expropriation.

It is clear from interviews with property owners that the main theme of the expropriation challenge was the insult of forced sale without consultation and without courtesy. Owners felt they were being deprived of their patrimony without adequate explanation. The protest concentrated on the injury of price rather than the insult of procedure because of the conviction of property owners that higher prices symbolized an attachment to land owned by families for generations and because the law permitted no other form of protest.[12]

Competing Objectives and Strategies

Government officials in France and Dallas–Fort Worth were prepared to ignore, circumvent, or modify the law to avoid conflict over land acquisition. Their counterparts in New York were not as concerned about conflict avoidance, but they too recognized that the cost of land, even at inflated prices, was an insignificant fraction of their project costs. Officials in Canada and Italy, however, adhered to the law despite the demands of property owners for more generous compensation and more considerate treatment.

The officials whose behavior helped precipitate conflict defended three principles. First, they believed that just compensation was defined by the community in law and that their mandate was to uphold the law. Hence, officials were prepared to be more generous in Ontario than they had been in Quebec because a change in law had authorized compensation for loss and dislocation. They perceived themselves as defenders of the law, not purveyors of largesse, and were unwilling to increase their offers to Quebec landowners, even though the process of evaluation and compensation took place after the new law went into effect. It is notable, however, that officials faced articulate and aggressive landowners in Ontario, whereas the victims of expropriation in Quebec were poorer, more passive, and—at first—more trusting. Officials emphasized that they were upholding the law, but there was for them a happy coincidence of social groups and legal change.

Second, officials believed that individuals should not profit from an increase in property values resulting from government actions. This belief reached an extreme in Quebec where the expropriation of 80,000 peripheral acres was designed, in part, to deny windfall profit to individuals on lands adjacent to the airport. However, officials in other countries, including France and the United States, shared this perspective to some degree and acquired land in excess of immediate needs in order to assure that government alone would profit from development.

Finally, officials believed that their responsibility was to minimize government expenditures and to protect the public purse against the rapacious instincts of individuals. This belief was as present among appraisers of the Administration des Domaines in Paris as among officials of UTE in Milan or the Department of Public Works in Canada. Politicians might overrule civil servants, as they did in authorizing higher prices in Paris and in providing supplementary payments in Quebec and British Columbia. But the inclination of civil servants and independent appraisers hired by government was to spend as little as possible on the purchase of land designated for public utility.

The desire to protect the public purse influenced site selection and, as a result, determined the character of subsequent protest. One of the criteria in site selection everywhere is the availability of cheap land on which to build facilities. The cheapest land almost inevitably belongs to the poorest people, who also are the least capable of sustaining a fight against the state. One need seek no conspiracy against the poor; it is enough to understand the operations of the real estate market and the determination of officials to protect the public purse.

Although citizens who were more affluent were protected inadvertently from expropriation, they nevertheless were confronted with the consequences of development. They owned land adjacent to the designated site that the state did not want to buy, and they feared that airport development would reduce the value of their property. They were not displaced because their land was not taken; they could stay to fight, and they had the human and financial resources to sustain the battle. The objective of protecting the public purse dispersed the least able to fight but often assured that those most willing and able to defend themselves would be airport neighbors.

Property owners obviously did not share state objectives. Their first concern was to persuade the state to move the project. They did not oppose development *per se* but preferred that it take place on someone else's doorstep. The neighbors of Dorval in Montreal, Malton in Toronto, Orly in Paris, Love in Dallas, and

"I said . . . we were one of the lucky ones . . . not expropriated for airport expansion."
© 1973 Norris—Vancouver Sun/Rothco.

JFK in New York were successful in arguing the demerits of their own location and the advantages of building additional facilities elsewhere in the metropolitan area. However, when plans for entirely new facilities were developed, property owners rarely succeeded in forcing governments to seek alternative sites. If they were destined to lose their homes and land, they wanted the best possible price; they wanted to suffer minimal disruption and to receive assistance in relocation; and they wanted to preserve their communities and their basic lifestyles.

In pursuit of their objectives, government officials played neighbors against each other, targeted the elderly for first offers, and threatened the weight of the state on the backs of the recalcitrant. They used convenient devices, such as the Italian tax rolls, to limit payments; they took land in New York and Vancouver before any clear public purpose was enunciated; and they seized land in Milan and Montreal before they were ready to pay for it.

Governments proceeded, in all these cases, on the premise that the selection of sites for development and the assessment of property values for compensation were the tasks of experts. Formal site plans followed expropriation in every case. In Dallas–Fort Worth, Milan, Montreal, Paris, and Vancouver additional land was taken because the initial proceedings did not deliver adequate development sites. Yet, government officials insisted everywhere that specific site selection could not be challenged because the process was scientific and technical and the land had been chosen by experts. And even though recognized appraisers in Toronto and Vancouver disagreed radically with the evaluations of government officials and "independent" consultants, in Canada as elsewhere the appraisal of property was alleged to be a technical process—even a science.[13]

Citizens accepted assertions about technical decisions and appraisals, and they expected governments to make correct offers for their property. They were surprised to discover that government was prepared to negotiate prices and that compensation depended on their ability to bargain strongly and effectively. They were dismayed that government seemed to deny information to them or to impress them with misleading data. Trust in government was shattered, especially in Canada and Italy, when citizens learned that governments perceived no obligation to treat them fairly.

Even when the law permitted a contest strictly over price, the roots of protest went deeper. Property owners complained that their personal futures were being decided by forces beyond their control. They wanted an explanation for the decisions that were disrupting their lives and they wanted to participate in discussions about their fate. They presumed that government would reduce the general anxiety resulting from unexpected and unwelcome change, and they rebelled when they were treated without courtesy.

Citizens learned to organize for collective action, to testify at public hearings, and to engage the media in their cause. They learned to employ appraisers and lawyers with political visibility and technical credentials, and they learned to litigate and petition on their own behalf. These lessons were evident in every country under the impact of expropriation. The strategies were not identical everywhere. Some organized to secure a collective price; others settled early, and still others held out. All groped for ways to defend themselves, their families, and their local communities against the power of the state.

Consumers or Citizens?

The relationship of the individual to the state is reflected, to some
degree, in the laws that govern the seizure of property for public
purposes. Sensitivity to individual rights is developed to a greater
extent in American and Canadian laws than in the equivalent
legislation of Italy and France. The Italian system, where prevailing laws were written under fascism, provides minimal rights
and recourse to citizens whose land is desired by the state. French
law, designed largely by the fascists of Vichy and modified modestly in the Fourth and Fifth Republics, provides compensation
for dislocation at less than generous rates. By contrast, the Uniform
Relocation Assistance and Real Property Acquisition Policies Act
in the United States[14] and the Expropriation Act in Canada provide
for generous settlements and minimal individual hardships resulting from government action. Citizens in both countries are
entitled to explanations, negotiated compensation, and relocation
to comparable homes.

These differences in national legislation are mitigated, to some
extent, by the limited scope of federal expropriation laws in the
North American countries. Land acquisition often takes place under the laws of states and provinces in the United States and
Canada, and these laws are not always as generous as their federal
equivalents. Nevertheless, legislation developed by central governments has a considerable impact on the acquisition of land for
airport development in both countries. The U.S. law, by em-
bracing displacement from any "federally assisted program," cov-
ers expropriation for aviation facilities that are subsidized by the
Federal Aviation Administration.* The Canadian act, limited to
Crown Federal acquisitions, includes airport development because
the task is defined as a responsibility of the federal government.

When government wants to seize the property of citizens, then,
the Americans and the Canadians demonstrate through their laws
greater sensitivity to individual rights than the French or Italians.
These differences help explain the evolution of conflict in the
various cases of airport development, and they illuminate the

---

* The Stewart expropriation was not covered by the law because, state officials
argued, no federal funds were involved. A subsequent court case involving state
obligations with respect to environmental impact statements, however, concluded
that the state must abide by federal regulations because the original facility and
the site were donated to New York by the federal government.

Table 6–3 Political Sensitivity of Expropriation

| | | Terms of Expropriation Laws | |
		Generous	*Pecunious*
Behavior of Officials	*Sensitive*	United States	France
	Insensitive	Canada	Italy

character of governing institutions. Nevertheless, the response of property owners to expropriation also was determined by the behavior of governments above and beyond the terms of the law. French legislation is not sympathetic to individual rights, but the French were politically astute and willing to bend the principles of the law for political convenience. Landowners in the Plains of France were compensated well because they were rich and powerful, and the government did not want conflict. By contrast, Canadian bureaucrats were determined to apply the law as written, and even the generous terms of the 1970 Act could not prevent conflict in Toronto and Vancouver. Generous bureaucrats in New York, more than a generous law, prevented a sustained battle over expropriation, while Italian officials, legally and politically insensitive to individual claims, provoked bitter conflict with landowners outside Milan.

Differences in the terms of the law and the sensitivity of bureaucrats are important, but they should not obscure the similarities in the behavior of governments with respect to land acquisition. In every case, governments of the industrial western world treated their citizens as consumers in the marketplace. They haggled and negotiated, cajoled and even cheated. Citizens in every country thought government officials would treat them with special care and attention. Even the more skeptical, who moved quickly to defend themselves, expressed in interviews an underlying positive disposition toward the state. They usually assumed that governments would accept responsibility for the disruption they were caused and would recognize the sacrifices they were asked to make. They usually were inclined to accept claims about the public interest. This perspective on the state knows no national borders and fewer class lines than one might expect. Indeed, those most well off in these societies tended most to distrust the state they seemed to control.

In the end, citizens rebelled because they believed that they were not treated as citizens. The business mentality controlled expropriation, and only citizens who recognized it from the beginning—such as the wealthy farmers of the Plains of France— were able to preserve or improve upon their situation. Citizens inclined to trust the government, such as the war veterans of Sea Island and the small farmers of Quebec and Milan, had to fight harder, and often with less success, to defend their interests. To their own surprise and disappointment, their relations with government were reduced to business transactions.

Endnotes

1. See for example Dorothy Nelkin and Michael Pollak, "The Politics of Participation and the Nuclear Debate in Sweden, The Netherlands, and Austria," 25 *Public Policy* (Summer 1977), pp. 335–357.
2. A wide-ranging philosophical discussion of these issues may be found in J. Roland Pennock and John W. Chapman (ed.), *Nomos XXII: Property* (New York: New York University, 1980). Unfortunately, the articles generally focus on the United States and are influenced more by law and economics than by political analysis and detailed cases.
3. There is considerable debate over exactly what is surrendered, especially between the possibly separable right to dispose of property and rights to exploit consequences of ownership—for example, air rights. See Bruce Ackerman, *Private Property and the Constitution* (New Haven: Yale University, 1977).
4. Laws of New York, 1971, Chapter 473, Section 1. Upon signing the bill into law, Governor Rockefeller stated that the legislation created a "land bank" program for future airport development.
5. Details of this strategy come from confidential interviews with ADP officials and from an interview with M. Oisée, Mayor of Roissy-en-France, in Goussainville, June 10, 1975. A more complete review of the case is available in Elliot J. Feldman, *White Elephants and the Albatross: French and British Planning in the Supersonic Age* (Cambridge, Mass.: MIT Press, 1982), Chapter 2.
6. The Municipal Airports Act, approved by the Legislature of the State of Texas in its fiftieth Regular Session in April 1947, authorizes municipalities to acquire land for the purposes of airport development. The laws of eminent domain were approved by the fifty-second Legislature in 1951.
7. 18–19 Elizabeth II, Chapter 41, "An Act Respecting the Expropriation of Land," Assented to 11th June 1970.

8. Details of this case are available in Elliot J. Feldman and Jerome Milch, *The Politics of Canadian Airport Development: Lessons for Federalism* (Durham, N.C.: Duke University Press, 1982), Chapter 3.
9. *Ibid.*, Chapter 5.
10. *Ibid.*, Chapter 4.
11. An extensive treatment of this case may be found in Elliot J. Feldman, *Airport Siting as a Problem of Policy and Participation in Technological Societies: The Case of Milano-Malpensa* (Cambridge, Mass. and Torino, Italy: Harvard University Center for International Affairs and Fondazione Luigi Einaudi, 1978).
12. The key laws governing expropriation in Italy include Legge 25 Giugno 1865, n. 2359, which defines public utility; Regio Decreto 8–II–1923, n. 422, which defines procedures and compensation; and Legge 23 Giugno 1927, n. 1630, which extends to airports the full status of public utility. Legge 22 Octobre 1971, n. 865, modified the rules but not the principles.
13. A discussion of this principle in land acquisition and compensation may be found in Duncan MacRae Jr., "Scientific Policymaking and Compensation for the Taking of Property," in Pennock and Chapman (ed.), *Nomos XXII: Property, op. cit.*, pp. 327–340.
14. Public Law 91–646, January 2, 1971.

Chapter 7

CITIZEN ACTION

Property owners were not alone in seeking a voice in airport development decisions. Opposition to government projects was led by airport neighbors, often joined by both public and private interest groups and by public officials. In each of the five countries examined in this study, citizens demanded that governments consider a range of perspectives on aviation infrastructure before finalizing development plans.

Citizen action took different forms in different places, but one common phenomenon was the emergence of *ad hoc*, single-interest groups. The objectives, strategies and tactics of these groups differed from place to place, partly as a function of the political system in which they operated and partly as a product of the human and financial resources available to them. Few succeeded in swaying the decisions of public officials. The abandonment of major projects in New York, Toronto, and London, for example, resulted from changes in economic and political conditions, not public opposition. But citizen groups did play an important role in prolonging the decision process until conditions changed. In this sense, their role in decision making often was crucial, and it is by this criterion that we measure their "success."

Two important democratic principles are violated in the cases studied here. The first states that all citizens have an equal opportunity to affect public choices through established institutions. The second states that considerations of equity are fundamental in the distribution of costs and benefits from public activity. However democracy may be defined, equal access to public institutions and equal treatment before the law are essential components. Yet, citizens often struggled unsuccessfully to be heard through established institutional channels, and special compensation was never

181

proposed for airport neighbors by public officials, even when it was apparent that neighbors absorbed more costs than other members of the public. Hence, the technocratic process that favored airport development contradicted democracy by repudiating the layman's role as a citizen in decisions and defied democratic principles by ignoring equity. The protest and controversy in these cases resulted from the confrontation of technocratic inclinations described in earlier chapters and the defense of democratic principles examined here. More will be said at the end of this chapter about the complexity of defining constituency and legitimate participation.

The phenomenon of citizen action groups challenges both elected government officials and the community of scholars concerned with democratic participation. Governments everywhere exacerbated the controversy over airport development by misunderstanding the nature of citizen opposition and by rejecting demands for direct participation. Public officials were wedded to narrow interpretations of representation, constituency, and participation, and they failed to appreciate either the depth of citizen indignation or the legitimacy of competing perspectives. Political scientists who have studied participation in the industrial world have focused primarily on established channels of participation and the cultural bases of citizen action. They traditionally have expected democratic participation to be expressed in orthodox ways, and they have expected political attitudes—which form the bases for concepts of political culture—to predict behavior. Governments were astonished by the extent of spontaneous citizen opposition, and scholars generally were surprised by the forms of citizen action and by the universality of protest in the late 1960s and early 1970s.

The Democratic Challenge

The most vocal opponents of development in this study generally have been citizens residing in the immediate vicinity of major airports. The issues that concern them are not the same as those of other participants such as public officials, environmental groups, and organized economic interests, and airport neighbors have not been the most influential actors in these controversies. Nevertheless the underlying issues that have motivated their opposition and the activities they have undertaken in pursuit of their interests raise important questions for the future of democratic societies.

Equity

The costs and benefits associated with the construction and operation of airports never are distributed among the public in an entirely equitable manner. Those individuals who reap the greatest benefits are not necessarily the ones who pay the costs. Certain costs such as increases in the level of noise, pollution, and road traffic, are imposed principally on airport neighbors. These costs frequently have provoked opposition to development plans.

Airport neighbors contend that the expansion of air facilities affects both the quality of life in their neighborhoods and the value of their property. These two costs are related but not identical, and citizen groups have differed in the extent to which they have emphasized amenities or property values in attacking government policies. Lower middle class citizens in such communities as Newburgh, New York generally have been more inclined to focus on declining resale values than the well-to-do professionals in such places as Morris County, New Jersey. The latter, along with similar groups in Etobicoke, Ontario, and Stansted, England, preferred to concentrate on the loss of amenities. All the groups, however, have been concerned with both the economic and social costs of development.

Governments generally have rejected the contention that airport development has any impact on the real estate market. Research conducted in the 1950s and early 1960s confirmed this view,[1] but a more recent study by the Canadian Ministry of State for Urban Affairs suggested that the relationship is complex. According to the Government's author, residential land values fall when development projects are implemented, yet they eventually return to long-run established patterns when "noise-indifferent people move in and some land is shifted to other uses."[2] Relative land values may not change very much in the long run, but "the type of resident and the pattern of land use (the econoscape) change substantially."[3] Some landowners, then, are harmed economically by airport development.

Governments have been only marginally more sympathetic to the complaints of airport neighbors about the loss of amenities, compared with the decline of property values, due to airport

construction or operation. Airport authorities agreed in many instances to buy additional residential properties in zones heavily
affected by noise, and some were prepared to provide financial
assistance for neighbors seeking to soundproof their homes.* No
government, however, accepted any legal obligation to compensate for a partial expropriation of property rights. All argued that
airports constitute a public purpose and are exempt from such
requirements.

Substance vs. Process

Airport neighbors were motivated by dissatisfaction with government policy, but they came to resent the decision-making procedures of governments as much as the substance of policy itself.
They interpreted participation as the right to influence decisions
directly. They expected to be informed of government plans before
decisions were reached, and they demanded the right to deliberate
over policy choices alongside elected and appointed officials. They
refused to recognize the exclusive right of government agencies
to define the public interest, and they were suspicious that governments would not consider the social and environmental consequences of development without their active involvement.

Governments everywhere rejected these demands and refused
to define participation as sharing in decision making. Citizens
usually were entitled to be kept informed of vital decisions and
to have their views solicited, but public officials were not obliged
to heed those views, adjust decisions, or permit citizens to enter
into negotiations or influence outcomes in any final way. They
regarded airport neighbors as a special interest group. The democratic process, they believed, permits all interest groups to express their views but not to impose them on the public.

By questioning the legitimacy of decision-making procedures,
airport neighbors differentiated themselves from other participants
in these controversies. Environmental groups were concerned
about degradation in the quality of the environment, which the
construction and operation of major air facilities inevitably entails.

---

* A special noise tax is levied on all passengers utilizing the Paris airports,
and the income is devoted principally to purchasing homes (and soundproofing
public buildings) in the vicinity of Charles de Gaulle Airport. The British Airports
Authority offers funds to airport neighbors who request assistance for soundproofing, but there have been few requests so far.

Aircraft manufacturers, airline companies, pilots, and air controllers were interested primarily in maximizing their own profits or ensuring the safety of aircraft operations. Public officials in local governments were concerned with the impact of airports on their tax base and infrastructure, while their counterparts in metropolitan, regional, provincial, and state governments were more interested in the potential contribution of air facilities to the economy. Despite the competing concerns, only the citizen groups questioned the meaning of democratic participation and the legitimacy of decision-making procedures.

Citizen Groups

Government plans for the expansion of aviation infrastructure triggered the formation of *ad hoc* citizen action groups at all eight sites examined in this study. The phenomenon of citizen groups which function only in response to a specific government policy and dissolve when their complaint is settled has not been studied extensively by political scientists.[4] Most students of political participation have recognized that citizens might form *ad hoc* groups in order to influence government decisions, but they have focused their attention more on established political mechanisms such as parties and electoral processes and on traditional, professional lobbying. Challenges to airport development generally were led by citizen groups created specifically to oppose government projects. Consequently, an examination of political participation in airport decisions must concentrate on these *ad hoc* groups.

Twenty-one active groups opposed to government plans were examined in detail in the course of this study (Table 7–1). Several more groups were identified, but insufficient data were available to include them in this analysis. The nucleus of these groups, with but two exceptions, consisted of airport neighbors threatened directly by development plans. Citizens whose property was expropriated for development occasionally participated in the activities of these groups, but they were neither the organizers nor the leading militants anywhere.*

---

* One group, the Centre d'information et d'animation communautaire in Ste. Scholastique, consisted solely of expropriated farmers. They are included because they organized an *ad hoc* citizen group and carried on protest activities like all the other groups.

Table 7–1   Citizen Action Groups

Group	Location
Dallas–Fort Worth:	
Citizens Aviation Association (CAA)	Dallas, Texas
Control Aircraft Noise (CAN)	Irving, Texas
London:	
North West Essex and East Herts Preservation Association (NWEEHPA)	Stansted, England
Wing Airport Resistance Association (WARA)	Cublington, England
The Sheppey Group	Isle of Sheppey, England
Defenders of Essex (DOE)	Foulness, England
Milan:	
Comitato d'Agitazione di Case Nuove (CACN)	Somma Lombardo, Italy
Comitato Popolare di Lonate Pozzolo (CPLP)	Lonate Pozzolo, Italy
Montreal:	
Centre d'information et d'animation communautaire (CIAC)	Ste. Scholastique, Quebec
New York:	
Jersey Jetport Site Association (JJSA)	Morris County, New Jersey
Citizens Jetport Committee (CJC)	Hunterdown County, New Jersey
Hudson River Valley Council (HRVC)	Newburgh, New York
Stop the Jetport Action Committee (SJAC)	Newburgh, New York
Paris:	
Comité de défense des riverains de Roissy (CDRR)	Roissy-en-France
Toronto:	
Society for Aircraft Noise Abatement (SANA)	Etobicoke, Ontario
New Airport Now (NON)	Etobicoke, Ontario
People or Planes (POP)	Pickering, Ontario
Metropolitan Toronto Airport Review Committee (MTARC)	Orangeville, Ontario
Vancouver:	
Community Forum (CF)	Vancouver, British Columbia
Greater Vancouver Citizens Committee for Noise Abatement (GVCCNA)	Vancouver, British Columbia

Most of the groups examined were middle class in origin and membership. Only the Centre d'information et d'animation communautaire, which represented the farmers of Ste. Scholastique (Montreal), and the Comitato Popolare di Lonate Pozzolo, which consisted of a handful of urban industrial workers near Milan, constituted exceptions to this pattern. The abundance of middle-class groups in this sample was not a statistical quirk. The policy of expropriating cheap or uninhabited land by definition made neighbors middle class. Nevertheless, subtle differences between upper middle, middle, and lower middle class groups proved important in determining the resources on which they could rely and the strategies they would pursue.*

The extent of citizen group activity varied from place to place even within the same country. The Canadian government encountered little opposition to its development plans for Montreal, but a similar project in Toronto generated fierce resistance from *ad hoc* citizen groups. Every site proposed by the Port Authority of New York and New Jersey was contested by local citizenry, but city fathers in Dallas and Fort Worth had no difficulty in finding a site for their new airport. Variations in citizen activity across countries was equally great, but differences were not a function of political culture. Citizen groups organized spontaneously to protest airport expansion plans even in an "alienated" culture like Italy, whereas the more "civic" culture in the United States did not prove to be consistently fertile ground for citizen activity.[5]

No single factor can account for these differences across sites. Opposition to airport development in Morris County (New Jersey), Stansted (England), Vancouver, Milan, and Roissy-en-France was led by long-time residents with strong ties to their land and communities; yet the most vocal and active critics of government plans in Pickering Township (Ontario), Hunterdon County (New Jersey), and Cublington (England) were ex-urbanites who had settled only recently in the area. Neither Ste. Scholastique (Quebec) nor the north Texas plains were inhabited by upper middle class professionals who could provide financial, technical, and political assistance for opposition efforts, but the shortage of such individuals in the Province of Varese (Milan) and in Roissy-en-France did not prevent the emergence and active opposition of local "committees of defense." The small farmers of Ste. Scholastique possessed a different concept of the "general will" from anglophone Canadians and were more prepared to accept the legitimacy of government plans; residents of Roissy-en-France and surrounding communi-

---

* We propose no rigid distinctions for defining socioeconomic class. Community profiles were assembled at most sites, but judgment is required everywhere to distinguish class. The characterization of "upper middle class" refers to substantial affluence and professional employment for affected citizens; "middle-class" refers to a range of whitecollar occupations and modest but comfortable living conditions; "lower middle class" refers to a mixed community of less prestigious white collar and working class occupations with limited or no marginal resources.

ties, however, were more divided in their interpretation, and many resisted development despite sharing a similar view of the state with their Québécois cousins.

Objectives

The overwhelming majority of *ad hoc* citizen groups that organized at these eight sites were dedicated to blocking government plans for the expansion of existing facilities or the construction of new airports on virgin territory. For strategic reasons, some groups chose to concentrate their efforts on preventing the construction of additional facilities anywhere in the metropolitan area; others preferred—again for strategic reasons—to promote alternative sites for a new air facility. All airport opponents, however, were concerned primarily with protecting their own communities from the consequences of development.

Most of the groups organized after a formal announcement of government plans. The Citizens Committee Against the Airport, however, was established by residents of Orangeville (Ontario) on the strength of a rumor that their community was high on the list of the Ministry of Transport's preferred sites; and Lord Boston formed the Sheppey Group in order to discourage the Roskill Commission from including the island on its short list. The instinct for self-preservation was sufficiently strong that Hunterdon County (New Jersey) residents organized the Citizens Jetport Committee to prevent the expansion of Solberg Airport into a fourth New York facility, even though the Port Authority already had indicated its intention to build elsewhere.

Although opposition to development of any kind was the dominant theme among the citizen groups, a few adopted more modest goals. The Society for Aircraft Noise Abatement objected to the plans of the Canadian Ministry of Transport for a major expansion of Malton Airport but was prepared to accept limited development in conjunction with a new airport elsewhere in the metropolitan area. Control Aircraft Noise in Irving, Texas sought merely to alter flight paths in and out of the nearby Dallas–Fort Worth Regional Airport, and the Centre d'information et d'animation communautaire in Montreal was organized to obtain more equitable compensation for residents. Stop the Jetport Action Committee in Newburgh recognized the inevitability of development but hoped to persuade authorities to scale down the scope of the project. And the Comité de défense des riverains de Roissy, unable to persuade Aéroport de Paris that a more remote site would be preferable for the new airport, sought to obtain compensation for the inconveniences of development.

Ad hoc citizen groups rarely are formed to support development, but a few such groups were established. In every instance, pro-airport groups arose in response to the activities of anti-airport forces. People Over Welfare (POW) challenged People or Planes (POP), the Cublington Area Supporters Committee opposed the Wing Airport Resistance Association, and the Hunterdon-Somerset Association for Progress confronted the Citizens Jetport Committee. Pro-airport groups had few members and were short-lived, but they were not merely fronts for airport builders, despite the frequent accusation by opponents. They represented an alternative perspective on the issues and reflected a genuine sentiment within their communities. Usually they favored construction to stimulate economic development. Had airport builders provided them with the degree of financial and technical assistance they were reputed to have obtained, they in some instances might have been more successful.

Structures

Each of the effective opposition groups contained a disciplined core of activists, ranging from four to twenty-five people. These individuals contributed their time, effort, and in many instances money. Not all remained deeply committed to the group throughout its existence, particularly when the battle was prolonged, but a large number were prepared to continue the fight even at the expense of family or jobs. The existence of this core of activists was a prerequisite for effective action; long lists of sympathizers may impress decision makers, but a hard core of activists is required to implement most strategies.

Citizen activists came from a variety of political backgrounds. Some had been active in local politics, while others had no previous political experience. Political party affiliations varied within groups as well as among them, and familiarity with the political process was uneven. The common theme repeated by these activists was shock and dismay that governments would ignore their interests. They were not used to this kind of treatment; few could relate any prior experience with government that had not turned out favorably. Even citizens without previous exposure to politics were convinced that they could reverse decisions by calling attention to their plight. Many were disillusioned by the experience and emerged with reduced esteem for government.

Leadership in these citizen groups generally was collegial. Activists shared both the responsibility for decision making and the burden of implementing policies. Collegiality, however, did not prevent the emergence of particularly visible individuals who came to symbolize the objectives and dedication of group members. In many instances, these figures emerged in the confrontation with airport builders. James Tyhurst in Vancouver and Charles Godfrey in Toronto gained the respect and admiration of their protesting colleagues in direct proportion to their success in antagonizing government officials, and James Donovan in Dallas achieved notoriety from his incessant legal battles in behalf of the Citizens Aviation Association. Similarly, Derrick Wood of the Defenders of Essex developed a national reputation in the United Kingdom following his spirited attack, broadcast by the BBC, on the government's plans for Foulness. These individuals played important roles in determining group strategies and tactics, but their views generally were subject to ratification by other activists.

The citizen groups themselves were organized in two basic ways. Some were created as umbrellas, joining together existing homeowners, ratepayers, and neighborhood associations.* Most umbrella groups were organized with formal structures, such as steering committees and executive boards, and virtually all maintained extensive membership lists based on constituent organizations. Alternatively, citizen groups were established independently of existing organizations; these groups generally had informal structures and were little more than loose coalitions of activists.

There is no discernible pattern in the distribution of these two types of groups across sites; only in London was there a marked predominance of one form (umbrella) over the other (Table 7–2). There is also no relationship between group structure and the ability to survive for extended periods of time. Some of the strongest and most durable groups, such as the Jersey Jetport Site

---

* The Sheppey group was an umbrella group of local authorities rather than homeowner or taxpayer associations. The structure and operations of the group were similar to those of other umbrella associations, and participants included chambers of commerce, trade unions, and amenity societies, as well as local councils.

Table 7–2   Citizen Group Organizational Structure by Site

Umbrella	*Independent*
Dallas–Ft. Worth:	
Control Aircraft Noise	Citizens Aviation Association
London:	
North West Essex and East Herts Preservation Assn.	
Wing Airport Resistance Assn.	
Sheppey Group	
Defenders of Essex	
Milan:	
Comitato d'agitazione di Case Nuove	Comitato Popolare di Lonate Pozzolo
Montreal:	
	Centre d'information et d'animation communautaire
New York:	
Jersey Jetport Site Assn.	Citizen Jetport Committee
Stop the Jetport Action Comm.	Hudson River Valley Council
Paris:	
Comité de défense des riverains de Roissy	
Toronto:	
Society for Aircraft Noise Abatement	People or Planes
New Airport Now	Metropolitan Toronto Airport Review Committee
	Citizens Committee Against the Airport
Vancouver:	
Community Forum	Greater Vancouver Citizens Committee for Noise Abatement

Association, the North West Essex and East Herts Preservation Association (Stansted), and Community Forum were organized as umbrellas, but several independent groups, including People or Planes and the Hudson River Valley Council (Newburgh), also proved durable. The key to survival lies more in the active attention to organizational maintenance than in the formal structural arrangements. People or Planes, for example, met weekly for years, even when there was no agenda of significance and fund raising activities such as bake sales served the dual purpose of financing group activities and maintaining an *esprit de corps*. Despite their formal structures and detailed organizational charts, umbrella groups that did not pursue cohesion were no more capable than independent groups of maintaining visibility throughout prolonged conflicts.

Resources

Citizen groups need tangible resources to be effective. A substantial treasury can finance public relations and purchase legal advice. A working knowledge of the technical aspects of airport development helps but must be purchased as technical advice or donated by experts within the group. Powerful allies also can be helpful. None of these resources is indispensable; successful protest was sustained, at least in some cases, with little more than a nucleus of committed members. Nevertheless, those groups that were adequately financed, well advised, and assisted by external forces were more likely to attain their objectives.

Some citizen groups amassed genuine war chests. The Jersey Jetport Site Association raised more than $200,000, and the budgets of People or Planes and the Wing Airport Resistance Association exceeded $100,000. At the other end of the spectrum, the Comitato Popolare di Lonate Pozzolo had no budget at all (Table 7–3). Absolute sums, however, can be misleading. People or Planes exhausted its treasury in the lengthy battle with the Ministry of Transport, yet a rival group fighting against expansion of the existing facility, the Society for Aircraft Noise Abatement, experienced no financial difficulties with a budget of only $1500. Control Aircraft Noise in Dallas was able to operate on a limited budget because vital services (for example, technical advice) and supplies (for example, photocopying and postage) were donated by members or sympathizers. By contrast, the Centre d'information et d'animation communautaire in Ste. Scholastique had to expend vital resources on salaries for professional organizers, an expense encountered by no other group. Financial resources can be important, but the impact of citizen groups cannot be predicted solely on the basis of available funds.

The major source of financial support for all these groups was private contributions from members and supporters. Most groups were successful in collecting small sums of money from large numbers of people; a few benefited from the large donations of wealthy supporters. Fund-raising activities included bake sales, charity marches, and direct mail campaigns. Some groups attempted to collect dues, but none succeeded in obtaining more than a small fraction of their funding from this effort. Governments occasionally supported the activities of citizen groups. Seven received direct subsidies and an eighth, People or Planes, was subsidized indirectly when the City of Toronto employed the group's

Table 7-3 Citizen Group Funding: Amount and Source

	Private	*Government**
More than $100,000	Wing Airport Resistance Assn.	Jersey Jetport Site Assn. People or Planes Community Forum
Between $10,000 and $100,000	Hudson River Valley Council Metro. Toronto Airport Review Committee	Centre d'information et d'animation communautaire North West Essex and East Herts Preservation Assn. The Sheppey Group Defenders of Essex
Between $1000 and $10,000	Citizens Jetport Committee Society for Aircraft Noise Abatement Greater Vancouver Citizens Comm. for Noise Abatement	Comitato d'agitazione di Case Nuove Comité de défense des riverains de Roissy
Less than $1000	Stop the Jetport Action Comm. Control Aircraft Noise New Airport Now Citizens Committee Against the Airport Comitato Popolare di Lonate Pozzolo	

* Includes private sources as well as government

193

attorney as its own representative at the Airport Inquiry Commission hearings. Local governments were the primary source of subsidies, but the Centre d'information et d'animation communautaire was funded by the Province of Quebec, and Community Forum in Vancouver was supported by the Greater Vancouver Regional District through a grant from the federal Ministry of State for Urban Affairs.

Approximately half of the groups developed sufficient expertise to attack government plans on their technical merit; the others never attained sufficient competence to pose a serious challenge. Citizen groups without access to technical information generally represented lower-middle-class communities like Newburgh or Roissy-en-France. But expertise was not perceived uniformly as a prerequisite for successful opposition, and several citizen groups from wealthy communities demonstrated little interest in technical knowledge. The Hudson River Valley Council, the Citizens Aviation Association, and the Metropolitan Toronto Airport Review Committee chose opposition strategies that did not require knowledge of the technical aspects of airport development. They devoted their resources mostly to legal advice, public relations, and opinion surveys.

Expertise came from paid professional consultants and contributions by members and sympathizers (Table 7–4). The Jersey Jetport Site Association commissioned three studies by consultant firms, and the four citizen groups in the London dispute all sought the services of outside experts. Community Forum had access to professional consultants through participation in the Airport Planning Committee. Five other groups developed their expertise internally. The quality of expertise varied from group to group, but the critical variable was not the source of information. Outside experts provided greater legitimacy to the arguments of citizen groups, but they did not necessarily offer greater insight or knowledge. People or Planes, for example, developed a stronger and more persuasive technical case than the Jersey Jetport Site Association, even though POP did not contract out any studies.

Airport opponents everywhere looked for powerful allies to assist in the battle with developers, and almost all were successful in obtaining some support. Public interest groups, particularly those concerned with the protection of the environment, were natural allies for airport neighbors. Anti-noise groups, such as the National Organization to Insure a Sound-Controlled Environment

Table 7–4   Sources of Expertise

Paid Professional Consultants	Contributions	No Expertise
Jersey Jetport Site Assn.	Citizens Jetport Comm.	Hudson River Valley Council
North West Essex and East Herts Preservation Association	Control Aircraft Noise	Stop the Jetport Action Comm.
	Society for Aircraft Noise Abatement	Citizens Aviation Assn.
Wing Airport Resistance Association	People or Planes	New Airport Now
The Sheppey Group	Citizens Committee Against the Airport	Metro. Toronto Airport Review Committee
Defenders of Essex		Centre d'information et d'animation communautaire
Community Forum*		Greater Vancouver Citizens Committee for Noise Abatement
		Comité de défense des riverains de Roissy
		Comitato Popolare di Lonate Pozzolo
		Comitato d'Agitazione di Case Nuove

* Did not employ or pay experts directly.

(NOISE) in the United States, the British Association for the Control of Aircraft Noise (BACAN) in the United Kingdom, and the Fédération contre la nuissance des avions in France, expressed their support for airport neighbors, as did environmental groups such as the Sierra Club in the United States and Canada and the World Wildlife Federation and Italia Nostra in Italy. But these groups rarely provided much concrete assistance to airport neighbors. Only in Vancouver did a major public interest group commit even the full-time energies of a single staff member, and no significant financial resources were committed by these groups anywhere.

Local government officials also were natural allies for airport neighbors, and citizen groups were successful in enlisting at least some of them in their battles with developers. Resolutions of support for airport neighbors were common, particularly in areas

like Morris County where development was viewed as an unwelcome intrusion into the tranquil lifestyle of affluent communities. However, not all local officials perceived airports in this
manner; some viewed development as an important generator of
employment and income in depressed economic areas. Supporters
of airport development balanced or outweighed opponents in areas
such as eastern Ontario, thereby limiting the importance of local
government support.

The most important allies of airport neighbors were private
interest groups, particularly within the aviation community, and
public officials at higher levels of government. Some citizen groups
were successful in developing contacts with these allies, and others
benefited from a favorable conjunction of circumstances. The Jersey Jetport Site Association enlisted the aid of powerful friends
in the New Jersey state government, and People or Planes received open support from De Havilland Aircraft Corporation and
covert support from Air Canada.[6] Other groups, however, experienced more difficulty in cultivating powerful friends. The least
successful group was the Comité de défense des riverains de
Roissy, which was unable to recruit any allies; even the local
militants of the French Communist Party who opposed airport
development were unable to obtain assistance from their own
party apparatus.[7]

Channels of Participation

The resources available to citizen groups helped determine their
strategies and tactics. Even the best organized and financed opposition, however, can make little progress if the opportunities
for participation in the political process are limited. Initial decisions were made everywhere without the direct participation of
citizens, and opposition groups needed access to decision makers
if they were to alter policies.

The availability of institutional channels for participation is the
single most important factor in determining the influence of citizen
groups. Where channels were absolutely closed, as in France, or
effectively closed, as in Italy, the groups had least impact. Only
where some institutional mechanisms promised access to officials
and to the public did citizen action matter.

The timing of access also was important. Vancouver and Toronto protesters gained an audience before land had been taken; Québécois enjoined public debate too late to influence central issues. Affluent residents of the Vallée de Montmorency, denied information on noise levels expected at Roissy, did not protest until operations were imminent. Their efforts, therefore, were inconsequential, unlike those of New Jersey residents, whose early entrance into the process assured continuing delays in policy execution.

Access could be sought through both formal and informal channels. Parliamentary debate, judicial review, and public hearings constitute some of the more important formal channels available in some political systems. Private access to decision makers is the most effective informal channel for airport opponents, but public demonstrations, protest marches, and media "events" provide other informal ways of gaining the attention of government authorities.

Formal Participation

The widest range of formal access routes is in the United States, where airport development decisions are both fragmented and decentralized. Decisions made by one level of government can be challenged at another. The Port Authority of New York and New Jersey, for example, was required to obtain the approval of the governors and legislatures of both New York and New Jersey for its airport development plans, and municipal authorities in Dallas and Fort Worth were unable to create a bi-county public authority to administer their new airport without the consent of the Texas legislature and a positive vote in a state-wide referendum.

Legal intervention in decision making is also feasible in the United States. The Hudson River Valley Council in New York and the Citizens Aviation Association in Dallas filed numerous suits in state and federal courts in an effort to prevent runway construction at Stewart and Love Airports. Public hearings, which provide an excellent opportunity for opponents to air their grievances, are required in all cases of airport expansion involving federal funds. Moreover, enterprising citizen groups such as Control Aircraft Noise in Dallas can persuade friendly congressmen to hold additional public hearings in order to put pressure on administrative agencies. Dale Milford satisfied his Dallas constituents this way.*

Although Canada, too, is a federal system, formal access routes for citizen groups are more limited. Centralized decision making in the Ministry of Transport limits the utility of formal intervention at other levels, and the courts have not been sympathetic to citizen groups protesting administrative decisions. People or Planes tried reaching both the provincial government and the courts but had little success with either. The Ontario government claimed insufficient authority to intervene in the decision,[8] and the courts refused to consider an injunction against the release of a government report unless the group was prepared to supply a $25,000 bond. Since 1970, however, public hearings have been mandatory when the government seeks to expropriate private property, and citizen groups in both Toronto and Vancouver took advantage of this requirement to publicize their objections. Royal commissions and public inquiries provide other opportunities to influence decision makers. The establishment of these mechanisms is an optional decision of the federal Cabinet, but citizen groups may succeed in focusing sufficient attention on the problem to force the hand of government.

The United Kingdom, with a unitary political system and a tradition of judicial non-intervention in administrative matters, offers few access routes to airport opponents seeking to reverse policy decisions. Parliamentary debate ordinarily is perfunctory and the outcome predetermined by disciplined majorities. Inquiries and commissions, however, are not uncommon. Both the Public Inquiry on Stansted in 1965 and the public hearings of the Roskill Commission several years later provided disgruntled citizens with an opportunity to present their views on government policy. Moreover, loopholes in parliamentary procedures may transform that body into a genuine forum for citizen groups. By introducing a "hybrid bill" to develop the Maplin site as the third London airport, the British government opened the door for citizen participation in a parliamentary debate. Any British citizen

---

* The hearing was held in Irving City Hall on November 22, 1974. The Federal Aviation Administration agreed, as a result of the hearing, to establish a formal task force with representatives from the Dallas–Fort Worth Regional Airport Board, Irving city government, and Control Aircraft Noise, in order to consider the problems raised by the citizen group.

can petition against a hybrid bill, and the Defenders of Essex quickly took advantage of the opportunity.

In France and Italy there are no institutionalized mechanisms for citizen participation beyond the electoral process. Both political systems are unitary in structure, and judges are forbidden from interfering in administrative matters. Public inquiries refer to inquiries held in public rather than proceedings that are open to citizen participation. Citizen advisory committees, common in the United States, Canada, and the United Kingdom, are unknown in France and in national government matters in Italy, and neither national system regards activist citizens with any respect.

Informal Participation

Variations in the use of informal channels are more a function of socioeconomic class than of political system. Private access to key decision makers is the most effective mechanism available, and wealthy citizens in all five countries invoked personal ties to gain the ear of political authorities. Morris County residents, the Caproni brothers in Italy, and John Creery in Vancouver responded immediately to airport development proposals by contacting personal acquaintances in important political positions.[9] Success with this approach was uneven, but all were able to express their reservations about government plans to the highest authorities.

Enterprising citizen groups lacking personal connections usually turned to the media. Carefully orchestrated "events" designed to gain media exposure can be effective in bringing opposition to the attention of decision makers. These events sometimes bordered on illegality and organizers were not always successful in maintaining discipline, but excesses often precipitated still greater exposure.

There are abundant examples of the use of this mechanism in all political systems. Derrick Wood led an entourage of one thousand cars from Foulness Island to London in order to demonstrate the traffic burden that airport development would impose on the metropolitan area. People or Planes militants clung to deserted buildings while government bulldozers attempted to clear the land in preparation for airport construction. The Comitato d'Agitazione di Case Nuove in Milan helped organize a public demonstration at Malpensa Airport in July 1972 that provoked clashes with the police. The New York State legislature was picketed by activists from Stop the Jetport Action Committee in Newburgh as it was voting on legislation authorizing the development of Stewart Airport. And four thousand sympathizers, under the direction of the Comité de défense des riverains de Roissy, protested the opening of Charles de Gaulle Airport on March 9, 1974 by demonstrating against the Prime Minister in front of the new facility.

Strategies and Tactics

Of Citizen Groups

Citizen groups opposing development sought to persuade government authorities that plans devised by airport builders were either irrational or unfeasible. The first approach implied a campaign of rational argumentation designed to demonstrate planning mistakes. The second suggested a more overt political demonstration of the extent of opposition and the political costs of implementation.*

A campaign based on rational argumentation was a logical choice for citizen groups. Airport builders justified the expansion of aviation facilities on technical grounds; consequently, an effective response might be to undermine the credibility of the technical case. Some citizen groups raised questions about the necessity for additional aviation facilities, whereas others challenged the site selection process. The specific strategy was dictated, in some instances, by government. The Roskill Commission, for example, was instructed by the British Cabinet to recommend a site for the third London airport; citizen groups opposing development were not permitted to raise questions about the need for additional infrastructure. The leadership of People or Planes, by contrast, hoped to gather support from Toronto residents concerned with uncontrolled growth by opposing the construction of a new airport anywhere in the metropolitan area.

A technical campaign obviously requires access to technical resources, but citizen groups also need an opportunity to present their case to decision makers. The Airport Inquiry Commission in Toronto, the Airport Planning Committee in Vancouver, the

---

* A third approach, limited to the United States, was to seek relief from the courts.

Public Inquiry conducted in Stansted, public meetings in Milan, and the open hearings of the Roskill Commission provided opportunities for citizen groups to present their briefs. Airport opponents often claimed that the hearings were controlled by supporters of development, but they benefitted from media attention.

In the absence of these formal mechanisms, citizen groups had to rely on ingenuity or good fortune to pursue a strategy of rational argumentation. People or Planes exploited the expropriation hearings in Toronto to publicize its contention that a new airport was unnecessary.* The Hearings Officer was instructed to record only objections to expropriation, but the report he issued reflected the impact of the technical arguments presented by opponents. The expropriation hearings produced a similar strategy and a similar result in Vancouver. Elsewhere citizen groups were unsuccessful in obtaining a hearing for technical studies. Even the Jersey Jetport Site Association, the most influential group examined here, was unable to persuade the Port Authority of New York and New Jersey to consider the three studies it had commissioned from consultants.

Efforts to persuade governments of the political costs of implementing development plans were hampered everywhere by the minority status of airport opponents. Public opinion within affected zones was not always unsympathetic to development; People or Planes, for example, apparently reflected a minority opinion in Pickering Township when plans for the new facility were first announced.† Spokesmen in Richmond, whose community depended on airport employment, publicly opposed Community Forum in Vancouver. Even when airport neighbors were united in opposition to development, relevant governments encompassed broader constituencies within which opponents inevitably constituted a minority. The use of political muscle, of course, is not limited to majorities; many special interest groups operate suc-

---

* The Airport Inquiry Commision in Toronto was not authorized until 1973 and did not begin formal hearings until 1974. In the interim, citizen groups were forced to seek other mechanisms for presenting their technical arguments.

† A mail survey conducted by the local M. P., Norman Cafik, in the Spring of 1972 revealed that most of his constituents favored airport development in Pickering Township. A second survey conducted by the Elliott Research Corporation on behalf of the Metropolitan Toronto Airport Review Committee suggested that opinion had changed. Neither survey, however, was methodologically sound.

cessfully in this environment. But minority status created special problems for airport opponents. They had to persuade decision makers that they were capable of creating political problems while demonstrating, simultaneously, that their concerns were not incompatible with a broader public interest.

Demonstrations of political influence were easier for some groups than for others. A resolution to prohibit the development of a major metropolitan airport in northern New Jersey was approved by an almost unanimous vote of the state legislature in 1960. New Jersey politicians were aware of the problems that powerful Morris County residents could create. By contrast New York authorities never believed that airport opponents in Newburgh constituted a serious threat. Urban neighbors of Milan's Linate Airport could limit development and lobby changes in flight paths; less affluent and politically inexperienced neighbors of Malpensa had no such credibility with Italian officials. In some cases external events provided citizen groups with greater credibility. Opponents of airport development in Pickering Township posed little threat to the federal Liberal Party until the elections of November 1972 returned a minority government to Ottawa. The political costs of ignoring local opposition seemed much more serious when power was balanced.

Three tactics utilized by nearly all citizen groups in an effort to impress government authorities were mass public meetings, petition drives, and resolutions of support from local governments. Most groups engaged in some form of lobbying and several organized concerted campaigns to influence legislative decisions. More radical tactics, such as public demonstrations, protest marches, and the picketing of government offices, were avoided by some groups, but most were prepared to engage in these activities in order to draw attention to their cause. Openly illegal actions, such as obstructing airport traffic, were advocated by many militants and undertaken by a few, even though opposition leaders everywhere were concerned that violations of the law might be counterproductive. Several citizen group leaders reported that the most difficult task they faced in the lengthy disputes over airport development was to control the militants within their own organizations.

Airport opponents everywhere were accused of selfishness and a desire to protect their own interests at the expense of the public. Upper middle class professionals who had settled in the country-

To publicize their opposition to development, some groups turned to art. This poster could be found in the villages of Varese after the land acquisition for the Malpensa expansion. Signed by the Comitato d'Agitazione di Case Nuove, the Comitato di Agitazione di Ferno, and the Comitato Popolare di Lonate Pozzolo in August 1974, the poster declared, "No to the SEA project for the expansion of Malpensa!"

side but continued to commute to the city were particularly susceptible to these charges. Some groups, like the Jersey Jetport Site Association, justified their opposition to development on environmental grounds, even though the only environment that concerned them was their own. People or Planes opposed airport development by arguing that Pickering Township was a prime agricultural zone, even though the soaring costs of land had made farming an unprofitable venture.[10] Lawyers masqueraded as environmentalists and physicians as farmers in an effort to dispel the image of wealthy landowners protecting selfish interests.[11]

The effectiveness of opposition strategies was limited, in some cases, by competition among citizen groups. Competitive situations can arise whenever there are options available for locating air facilities. People or Planes opposed the construction of an airport in Pickering Township and supported the expansion of Malton; the Society for Aircraft Noise Abatement opposed development at Malton and favored a new air field elsewhere in the metropolitan area. This difference of opinion, which appeared openly at the Airport Inquiry Commission hearings in 1974, enabled the Ministry of Transport to justify its development plans for Pickering as a concession to Malton neighbors. In the United Kingdom the Wing Airport Resistance Association was unable to form a coalition with airport opponents in Thurleigh and Nuthampstead, the two other inland sites on Roskill's short list.[12] In both cases, conflicting interests prevented cooperation and weakened the arguments of airport opponents. Those groups which overcame the conflict of interest, such as the Jersey Jetport Site Association and the Citizens Jetport Committee in suburban New Jersey, succeeded because the prospective sites were sufficiently close that both communities believed they would be affected by development, regardless of the location.

Of Governments

The response of airport builders to local opposition also varied considerably from place to place. Some failed to appreciate the importance of opposition or the influence of citizen groups; others took opposition more seriously and devised careful strategies in response to the activities of airport neighbors. These counterattacks rarely mollified opponents of development, even when they were accompanied by concessions on substantive matters, but they were successful in many instances in blunting the effectiveness of citizen groups.

Airport builders who failed to respond to local opposition generally overestimated their own influence with higher level decision makers or underestimated the capacity of citizen groups to be creative or to sustain protest. The Port Authority of New York and New Jersey was guilty of both errors in dealing with the varied activities of the Jersey Jetport Site Association. Initial opposition to development plans was discounted on the grounds that the Port Authority's reputation for "businesslike efficiency" as well as the extensive contacts that had been cultivated in the legislatures of New York and New Jersey were sufficient to guarantee success.[13] They were astonished when airport neighbors persuaded the New Jersey legislature to prevent development in Morris County. This defeat, however, was viewed by the Port Authority as a temporary setback, and as late as 1968 they harbored illusions of eventual victory. The Jersey Jetport Site Association, nevertheless, endured. Joining with local conservation organizations, they bought some targeted land for use as a park. A 1941 New Jersey statute protects conservation lands from acquisition through eminent domain, and the internal revenue code even made their contributions to the purchasing fund tax-deductible.

Developers elsewhere may have been surprised by the scope and magnitude of opposition, but they were quick to respond to the threat. The Società Esercizi Aeroportuali was unprepared for opposition in Milan; SEA officials were embarrassed and shouted down at chaotic and unruly public meetings in 1972. Similarly, the Ministry of Transport in Canada did not expect significant opposition to development plans in rural Pickering Township, especially since a similar project in Ste. Scholastique had elicited little public response. Both SEA and MOT, however, devised elaborate counterattacks in response to opposition.

The principal strategy of airport builders was to extol the virtues of development through public relations campaigns. The campaigns involved sleek brochures, radio and television interviews, information kits, and travelling slide shows. SEA published an elaborate "White Book" reviewing the history of contention and proving that the airport authority was innocent of all popular charges and complaints. Aéroport de Paris developed a sophisticated campaign that emphasized the Authority's efforts on behalf of local citizens, including the publication of a newspaper entitled

Entre Voisins ("Among Neighbors"). The campaign organized by
the Ministry of Transport in Toronto emphasized the rationality
of airport planning. Toronto planners distributed a thick kit of
materials designed to "inform the general public as to the rationale
behind the decision to not expand Malton and the choice of Pickering as the site for the second airport for Toronto."[14] These
campaigns were organized in response to specific criticisms, and
they were attacked as misleading or insufficient. Residents of
Roissy-en-France countered ADP's publication with their own,
entitled *Entre Riverains* ("Among the Bordering Communities"),
Malpensa neighbors organized more public meetings, and POP
complained bitterly of the absence of substantive detail in the
material released by MOT. Nevertheless, the official campaigns
were aimed at the general public rather than airport neighbors,
and they succeeded in conveying an image of concern for the local
citizenry and a willingness to share information.

Airport developers were conscious of the importance of the
media in the battle for public support. They, too, were prepared
to create media "events" to strengthen their case vis-à-vis opponents. Don Jamieson, the Canadian Minister of Transport,
proved a master at this game when he organized a joint press
conference with airport opponents in May 1972 following a well-
publicized four-hour meeting. By demonstrating his concern and
good will and by appearing unruffled and conciliatory in the face
of hostility, he provided his Canadian audience with the image
of a loyal public servant fending off the attacks of a special interest
group. Airport opponents freely admitted that the press conference was a public relations *coup* for the Minister.

In addition to using the media themselves, developers sought
to keep opponents out of the public eye. Aéroport de Paris managed to retain control over the electronic media, largely because
radio and television in France are a monopoly of the state; neighbors of Charles de Gaulle Airport never succeeded in voicing their
objections over the air. Elsewhere, developers relied on sympathetic editors and news directors, and sometimes they succeeded.
Control Aircraft Noise in Irving, Texas was denied attention by
the Dallas press as much as the Comité de défense des riverains
de Roissy was by the ORTF. More frequently, however, developers were unable to ensure total support from the media.

The effectiveness of government strategies for dealing with opposition was hampered in some cases by inconsistent behavior.

The Canadian Ministry of Transport, engaged in an effort to develop three major air facilities simultaneously, was particularly guilty of contradictions. Generous compensation for expropriated landowners in Pickering Township incensed the farmers of Ste. Scholastique who had received much less for their land; opposition was generated where none had existed before. The development of an entirely new facility in Toronto was justified as a response to an expanding noise problem, which disturbed Vancouver residents who were informed by the same Ministry that technological developments would reduce the level of aircraft noise. The Canadians, however, were not alone in their contradictions. The Milan authorities argued that Malpensa was destined to become the region's principal airport, thereby requiring immediate development. At the same time, the authority's headquarters was expanded at Linate, the airport allegedly destined for gradual retirement. Paris authorities compensated Charles de Gaulle Airport neighbors through a special passenger tax for noise, but they refused any such compensation for longer-suffering and more numerous neighbors of Orly. They built Charles de Gaulle to replace Le Bourget, and then continued the latter's operations.

Outcomes

Efforts to construct major air facilities were successful in only three of the eight cities examined in this study. Elsewhere development proposals were either abandoned after lengthy battles or delayed indefinitely. Citizen groups often took credit for these policy reversals. Spokesmen for People Or Planes were convinced that the Canadian government had shelved plans for the new Toronto airport because of strong and persistent opposition in Pickering Township, and some analysts still credit them with a direct victory.[15] Similarly, the North West Essex and East Herts Preservation Association, the Wing Airport Resistance Association, and the Defenders of Essex claimed responsibility for the successive shifts of policy that had spared Stansted, Cublington, and Foulness.

The tendency to take credit for defeating the government juggernaut is understandable. Airport opponents who had resisted development plans were bound to assume that their efforts had been decisive in altering policies. Moreover, government authorities often place the blame on citizen groups for obstructing the implementation of policy. But the claims of citizen group spokesmen and the analysts who endorse them are exaggerated. Local opposition was never more than one of several factors precipitating postponement of development, and the significance of citizen action varied considerably from site to site.

Construction of a fourth New York area jetport clearly was delayed by the activities of the Jersey Jetport Site Association and the Hudson River Valley Council. Opposition in the New Jersey legislature in 1960, which forced the Port Authority to commission new and more thorough studies of aviation requirements, was the product of intensive lobbying by airport neighbors. Similarly, legal action by the Hudson River Valley Council forced a postponement in the MTA plans to develop Stewart Airport. But the failure to locate an acceptable site for the facility was also the product of conflict between state officials in New York and New Jersey, and the Stewart project never was economically viable.

Citizen groups were even less influential in Canada than in New York. Construction in Pickering Township was delayed for two years pending review by the Airport Inquiry Commission. People or Planes had demanded a formal reassessment of policy, but the Cabinet decision was precipitated more by the November 1972 election results. POP's existence, more than its activities, affected policy reassessment, and only because of events outside its influence. In Vancouver the Community Forum harrassed public officials and attacked development plans from within the Airport Planning Committee. Completion of the Committee's report certainly was delayed by these activities. Nevertheless, the Committee itself was created as a result of pressure from federal agencies (the Ministry of State for Urban Affairs and Environment Canada) and local authorities (the Greater Vancouver Regional District), not from airport neighbors. The outcome of the Airport Planning Committee process was above all the product of divisions among Ottawa bureaucracies. Although People or Planes and Community Forum were actively involved, neither group was the primary agent in delaying development.

Construction of a third London airport was postponed several times by British governments, and citizen groups consistently took credit for these delays. The North West Essex and East Herts Preservation Association demanded a formal review of the Interdepartmental Committee report in 1964 and of the White Paper in 1967–1968, both of which recommended development at Stansted. The Wing Airport Resistance Association demanded that the government set aside the Roskill Commission Report in 1971, and the Defenders of Essex insisted in 1974 that government drop plans for development at Maplin. In each of these cases, governments appeared to comply with local requests. However, the demands were coincidental with political and bureaucratic change. Officials reported in private interviews a commitment not to be influenced by "special interests" and, therefore, to decide issues on their "merits." In the decision process, this commitment contributed to a bias against responsiveness to citizen action.[16]

Citizen groups were only marginally effective in delaying development in Milan. The Società Esercizi Aeroportuali lacked the resources to finance the expansion of Malpensa, and the critical delays often were self-imposed. Conflict with national authorities in Rome and provincial officials in Varese created additional difficulties. Angry neighbors may have been a nuisance to SEA and they did stall land acquisition, but their overall contribution to policy delay was modest.

The importance of citizen action cannot be judged solely by delays in policy implementation. The Jersey Jetport Site Association did not prevent construction of a fourth New York jetport, but it did preclude development in Morris County by persuading the federal Department of the Interior to declare the Great Swamp a Wildlife Preserve. No other citizen group was as effective as the JJSA in dictating government decisions, but several contributed in important ways to policy reassessments. People or Planes, for example, helped persuade the Ontario government to withdraw from the Pickering project in 1975, and the Defenders of Essex gained considerable support for their cause by fighting the Conservative government's Maplin Development Bill in Parliament. Neither action was decisive in its own right; Ontario officials were already skeptical of the viability of the project before they met with POP, and the Maplin Development bill was approved by the House of Commons, albeit with a reduced majority. Nevertheless, the activities of citizen groups were instrumental in the eventual decision to scrap some development plans. Citizen groups may have exaggerated their influence on policy and casual observers may have credited them too willingly, but activists were relevant actors of some consequence in the lengthy battles over airport development.

International Protest

Two questions initiated this inquiry into citizen action: Was the proliferation of *ad hoc* groups the product of new actors entering the political arena? Did the simultaneous appearance of *ad hoc* protest in so many different countries reflect an international movement?

Some of the activists were new to politics. Most of the leaders were not. The form of participation was changing for citizens accustomed to political choices conforming to their preferences. Their influence in the past had been quiet, even subterranean. When the old mechanisms of influence did not work, they became more aggressive.

The presence of old actors in new activities requires further explanation. Why did the old mechanisms fail? There seem to be two answers. First, some of these actors had been engaged in *ad hoc* groups before. They had been less visible because the issues were less prominent. The failure of old mechanisms, therefore, was not an entirely new phenomenon. Second, the people affected personally by these projects constituted whole communities. Highway programs, for example, had generated their share of protest in the United States in the past, but they cut only a swathe through a community while leaving a great deal behind. In the construction of single large facilities, whether airports or nuclear plants, the whole life of a region can be obliterated. In the United States there had not been state-motivated development on this scale since the Tennessee Valley Authority, and no other country had experienced a comparable program of state-sponsored development. The accustomed individual appeals could not now be heard because so many people were affected simultaneously by the same project. For government to listen to any individuals would be to jeopardize the project. Canadian officials frequently worried aloud about precedent as they denied 53 homeowners in Vancouver what they agreed might be more reasonable treatment; thousands in Toronto and Montreal might have noticed.

The simultaneity of this protest activity in different countries suggested an international movement. There were three hypotheses. One, easily discarded, said international agitators were fomenting protest to disrupt democratic systems. No evidence emerged of any activists in airport protest crossing national boundaries. A second hypothesis said there was something inherent in the technology of aviation that guaranteed protest activity everywhere. Although in the parameters of noise and pollution this hypothesis appeared more plausible than the first, the roots of protest—the expropriation of property—were not peculiar to aviation. The third hypothesis suggested that protesters copied each other through the international media. Although clear evidence did emerge of cross-fertilization among groups within Canada, trans-national influence was not present. Italian protesters were more conscious of their own national labor movements; activists in Britain made no foreign references in explaining their protest; and the movements in New York and New Jersey predated the others.

The data here offer no explanation, then, for simultaneous citizen action in different countries. The international atmosphere of the late 1960s and early 1970s plainly recognized street protest, whether against the War in Vietnam, educational policies in France, or limitations on freedom in Czechoslovakia. Whether that international atmosphere could motivate individuals of different socioeconomic, cultural, ethnic, and national backgrounds to sacrifice quantities of time and money for narrow and local causes must remain an unanswered question.

Challenges

To Government

The activities of the citizen groups described in this chapter irritated elected public officials and civil servants. Airport neighbors and their allies employed many strategies and tactics to draw attention to their cause and to force governments to reconsider expansion projects. Governments, however, were unreceptive to their demands and unwilling to grant them any special status in the decision-making process.

The desire of governments to ignore citizen groups does not diminish the significance of the challenge the latter posed. Two issues they raised are particularly troublesome. Airport neighbors argued that development projects imposed an unfair burden on a small proportion of the population. They also contended that the process of decision making was undemocratic because it limited the participation of affected citizens. Both charges deserve serious consideration by democratic governments.

The Problem of Equity. Airport development is only one example of a government initiative that confers costs and benefits in an inequitable manner. Many public facilities, such as highways, power plants, and waste disposal sites, generate benefits that are broad and diffuse but impose costs that are localized and intense. The techniques of cost-benefit analysis and related tools of decision making generally are unsatisfactory for resolving such problems because they assume that the same individuals receive both benefits and costs.[17] Indeed, airport neighbors criticized vehemently all attempts to justify decisions on the basis of these economic tools.

Aviation infrastructure and other public facilities are required for the economic health of advanced industrial states, even if costs exceed benefits for some segments of the population. Authoritative decisions in the public interest must be made. But democratic governments face two additional problems in connection with these choices. What is the proper constituency for determining the public interest in these cases? What efforts, if any, should governments undertake to redistribute costs and benefits in a more equitable manner?

The problem of constituency derives from the national, or even international, benefits of aviation and the local costs of development. Airport builders insist that such policies must be set in the broadest constituency possible because citizens who benefit from development are widely scattered and unorganized. Airport neighbors contend that a narrow constituency is more appropriate because residents in the immediate vicinity of air facilities must bear a disproportionate share of the costs. The locus of decision making is critical because the criteria that determine the public interest vary as a function of constituency. National governments place considerable weight on the needs of the air traveller in determining the public interest; regional or metropolitan governments are more concerned with the economic benefits of aviation; and local governments focus on the social and environmental consequences of development. There is no consensus whether airports are primarily of national, regional, or local importance.

Airport builders everywhere denied any legal or moral obligation to redistribute costs and benefits. Although they agreed in some instances to compensate the victims of development, they were prepared only in France to finance these obligations by penalizing the beneficiaries—and then in minimal ways. The reluctance to engage in redistributive measures was justified as a fear that air travel, highly sensitive to price fluctuations, would be affected adversely by the imposition of additional costs. But other factors make compensation difficult. The precise impact of development on land values varies over time and across geographic areas. The loss of amenities is difficult to determine under any circumstances. If government compensates an adjacent land owner for a decline in the value of his property, should it also demand reimbursement from other property owners if land values soar?

There are no simple answers. Governments ignored the equity issue by invoking the public interest, and citizen groups were unable to stimulate consideration of the distribution of costs and benefits. But the problem of equity in government policy will not disappear. Citizens who continue to live near airports, as well as those who have organized in opposition to highways, power plants, and waste disposal sites, may yet be more successful in forcing governments to confront the issue of equity.

The Problem of Participation. What constitutes legitimate participation in decision making? Both of the main contestants in these controversies offered their own interpretations. Public officials defined participation as consultation, or the right to receive information. They agreed that critical groups should be consulted on matters of importance to them and that citizens were entitled to information on government plans, but they were not prepared to accord any special status to airport neighbors. Citizen groups, by contrast, defined participation as influence. Some argued that genuine participation implied a veto for critical groups, while others were prepared to characterize successful participation as the ability to negotiate with decision makers.

The conflicting views of public officials and airport neighbors concerning the meaning of democratic participation reflect different theories about the design, purpose, and organization of government. Public officials defended their interpretation of participation by asserting a monopoly on the right to define the public interest. Politicians argued that their electoral mandate provided them with the exclusive right to represent their constituents. Civil servants justified their role by pointing to the instructions under which they operate and the special knowledge they possess. Both insisted that they represented the general will and that other interests necessarily were limited or particular.

Civil servants felt trapped by participatory demands. They were required to defend policies they often believed they had not authored, and they were thrust into public arenas they thought to be the domain of politicians. They were ridiculed when they

proved poor debaters or public speakers, and they insisted that
their expertise need not be exposed to public insult. Civil servants
complained of such humiliating experiences in every case but
Paris, where they were never subjected to public inquiry. They
blamed politicians even as they defended them.

Airport neighbors rejected the notion that governments are
capable of defending the public interest without the direct intervention of affected groups. They argued that governments were
not disinterested actors in these decisions, that their commitment
to the expansion of aviation infrastructure and their tendency to
ignore the social and environmental consequences of development
reflected a specific interest rather than the general will. Indeed,
the public interest could be gauged only if airport neighbors, who
represent a set of interests different from those of airport builders,
are permitted an equal role in decision making.

Public officials were persuaded that the direct participation
demanded by citizen groups not only was contrary to their interpretation of democracy but also was a formula for paralysis and
indecision. This view apparently was confirmed in Vancouver,
where the Canadian Ministry of Transport acceded reluctantly to
the request of other agencies that airport neighbors be included
directly in a review of airport development plans. The result of
the exercise was stalemate, attributed by most participants to the
involvement of the Community Forum. The Ministry of Transport
vowed never to repeat that "mistake," and no other government
agency in any country ever permitted a direct role in decision
making by airport opponents.*

The Vancouver experience suggests that participatory democracy is inconsistent with rapid and authoritative decision making.
The Airport Planning Committee produced irate civil servants,
skeptical citizens, and an outcome that satisfied no one. But the
conflicting perspectives on airport development were revealed
more openly and in more detail in Vancouver than in any of the
other sites. Airport builders, like airport neighbors, defend narrow
interests, and the open confrontation that the APC process facilitated enabled the public to appreciate the issues at stake. The
instrument may have been imperfect, but the mechanisms em-

---

* The Federal Aviation Administration established a task force to consider the
noise problem at the Dallas–Fort Worth Regional Airport and agreed to permit
a local citizen group to participate. After one brief meeting, however, the FAA
took unilateral action to resolve the controversy.

ployed elsewhere permitted public officials to ignore crucial issues and to implement policies not necessarily in the public interest.

The challenge for democratic governments is to develop authoritative mechanisms for decision making that promote a fair and thorough evaluation of all the issues but that are not susceptible to the exercise of a veto by any affected party. There is no assurance that such mechanisms are possible. Nevertheless, a recognition that citizen participation in decision making can be valuable and productive would constitute an important step in the right direction.

To Political Science

Definitions of political participation in the literature of political science consist generally of efforts to delimit a very broad concept in an acceptable and operationally useful manner. Some scholars define participation in behavioral terms, excluding the more subjective dimensions of attitudes and orientations toward politics. Others include only voluntary, or "autonomous," activities of private citizens under the rubric of participation, and every scholar begins by introducing his or her own definition.[18]

Democratic political systems provide mechanisms and channels through which citizens can participate in politics, and those who choose to utilize those channels can be deemed participants. As early as 1950 Woodward and Roper constructed an index of participation based on five established channels of influence. They limited the definition of political activity to "these five ways of behaving."[19] Subsequent scholars such as Lester Milbrath refined and adjusted this hierarchy of political activities,[20] but the lists typically included only legal and conventional actions.

The tendency to limit the study of political participation to legal activities may have been merely an oversight in the early years of the behavioral revolution, but many scholars remained unwilling to modify their interpretation when events in the political arena suggested the framework was too rigid.[21] As late as 1968, when protest in the United States seemed to peak, Michael Lipsky pointed out that "protest activity as it has been adopted by elements of the civil rights movement and others has not been studied extensively by social scientists."[22] Protest and other unorthodox forms of participation were seen to be "almost by definition, extraordinary rather than normal,"[23] and Jeffrey Berry, citing Ziegler and Peak, has asserted that letter writing is a more legitimate method of participation than protest.[24]

Some political scientists have recognized the growing importance of protests and demonstrations. Cobb and Elder, for example, apply the concept of "agenda building" to an examination of poverty questions and conclude that mass participation in unorthodox ways—for example, riots—can be critical in drawing the attention of decision makers to grievances.[25] Huntington and Nelson refuse to distinguish between legal and illegal participatory activities and include "protests, riots, demonstrations—even those forms of insurgent violence that are intended to influence public authorities—. . . [as] forms of political participation."[26] The more common view, however, is expressed by Verba and Nie. Their seminal work on participation in America is concerned exclusively with activities "within the system," even though they recognize that the tactics of political protest are important and, in some instances, appropriate.[27]

Participation, then, was treated by political scientists during the great protest period of the 1960s and early 1970s, largely in "establishment" terms. Participants employ the established channel of democratic political systems in their efforts to sway governments; they lobby public officials, assist sympathetic candidates for political office, and seek to gain the support of political parties. Yet, the *ad hoc* single-interest group present thoughout this period is increasingly the hallmark of participation in the industrial world. Confrontation and protest, rather than voting and joining political parties, are the channels of participation that airport neighbors and many other disgruntled citizens in contemporary societies employ. Protest and demonstrations, as Lester Milbrath argues, may be the last resort of deprived minorities, but even John Creery, a well-to-do Vancouver barrister, stood on a runway with a placard, blocking an airplane carrying a government minister, in order to express his grievance with government policy.

The universality of protest—that is, the existence of organized opposition from citizens in all five countries—poses a second challenge to the accepted wisdom in political science. Scholars generally have assumed that political behavior varies as a function of political attitude and that attitudes vary systematically across countries.[28] Participation in politics is more common, it is assumed, where underlying attitudes or cultures are democratic. As a result, one would not expect to find the same type or degree of participation everywhere.

Almond and Verba, in their classic study of political attitudes, describe these cross-national variations and their implications for participatory behavior. Both the United States and the United Kingdom are characterized as civic cultures, although attitudes in the United States are more participatory and less deferential than in the United Kingdom. Italy, by contrast, is described as an alienated political culture:[29]

> . . . *low in national pride, in moderate and open partisanship, in the acknowledgement of the obligation to take an active part in local community affairs, in the sense of competence to join with others in situations of political stress, in their choice of social forms of leisure-time activities, and in their confidence in the social environment.*

Italians, presumably, are less capable than British or American citizens of organizing in response to government policies and are not inclined to seek a participatory role in the political process.

Cross-national surveys are expensive and there have been few attempts to replicate Almond and Verba's study, but students of political culture in individual countries have provided support for the notion of distinctive national patterns. In the 1950s Edward Banfield described Italian political culture as alienated, and Joseph LaPalombara's study of interest groups confirmed that view.[30] France was not included in the Almond and Verba survey, but students of France have noted a reluctance to join in voluntary associations and a fear of face-to-face relationships.[31] Surveys conducted in Great Britain support the notion of a civic culture in which citizens are entitled to participate in politics but only in orthodox ways.[32] And students of American society and politics since Tocqueville have pointed to the legitimacy of citizen participation in politics and the distrust of authority. The implicit assumption behind these studies is that attitudes determine behavior; hence, one should find systematic differences in citizen participation from one country to another.

The behavior of citizens in the five countries examined here does not support a cultural theory of participation. Protest occurred at all eight sites, and variations in intensity and timing did not depend on culture. Airport neighbors in New York organized more readily than those in Dallas and Fort Worth; neighbors of Roissy-en-France opposed development early while French-speaking residents of Ste. Scholastique at first accepted government plans. And Italians in Somma Lombardo and Lonate Pozzolo felt sufficiently competent to organize a sustained protest against the proposed expansion of Malpensa. Moreover, more than groups anywhere else, the Italians made the right to participate their most important demand. Interviews suggested they were more sensitive to the process than to the outcome, whereas the theory of the civic culture would require the reverse priorities.

Cross-national differences in the level and form of citizen participation did appear. Citizen groups in Britain, Canada, and the United States were more active and more visible than their counterparts in France and Italy, as students of political culture would have predicted. But these variations can be attributed more to the channels of participation available in different political systems and to the success of government in containing protest.

The debate in political science over the relative importance of cultural and structural determinants of behavior is unlikely to be settled by the evidence from this study. The absence of systematic differences in the participatory impulses of citizens from country to country can be explained without abandoning cultural theories of political behavior. Students of political culture might argue, for example, that there are two Italys, and that Milan, in the north, is not part of the alienated culture described by Banfield and Almond and Verba.[33] Nevertheless, there is evidence from other studies to suggest that participation in Italy is not confined to the north.[34] A somewhat different and more powerful argument offered by many contemporary students of political culture is that cross-national differences in attitudes are declining and that similar behavior in the five countries reflects the impact of converging political cultures.[35] Giacomo Sani, for example, points to the emergence of new forms of participation in Italian political life and argues that political culture in Italy has been changing over the past decade.[36] Even those who accept this argument, however, must agree that cultural explanations cannot account for the variations in the level and form of citizen participation from country to country. With respect to these variations, at least, political institutions have more impact on participation than does political culture.

Conclusion

Democratic governments must be concerned about protest movements that do not wait politely for elections to register their grievances. Many citizens have learned that the ballot embraces all issues in a single choice; *ad hoc* groups, therefore, can be more effective by direct action than by the ballot in focusing attention on single issues. These groups operate on the fringe of traditional and established politics. They impose a constant pressure on public officials, and in the controversies studied here they question the legitimacy of the traditional democratic process.

The single-issue orientation of citizen groups poses an institutional challenge for democracy. Complex societies cannot conduct elections repeatedly on single issues, even though there is no obvious legitimate alternative to elections. Yet, the issues raised by many single-interest groups are legitimate. They demand a consideration for equity that traditional politics in these five countries has tried to avoid. They seek a fundamental reexamination of the concepts of constituency and jurisdiction. They sometimes question central values such as growth. The more government seeks to ignore or suppress these controversies and the groups themselves, the more these movements seem to gain strength.

Sooner or later elected officials must deal with the fundamental questions raised by *ad hoc* groups. The answers these groups prefer often are not acceptable for liberal democratic polities, but they are entitled to serious consideration. The airport protestors were among the first groups of the *genre*. Their successors have learned many lessons and probably will not be defeated as easily or as often. If elected officials hope to protect themselves and the public interest from these single-minded single interests, they will have to confront the fundamental questions—equity, constituency, growth—that have stimulated protest. The alternative for many elected officials may be defeat at the polls, and the alternative for democracy may be the loss of democratic procedures for controversial public choices.

Endnotes

1. Herman O. Walther, "The Impact of Municipal Airports on the Market Value of Real Estate in the Adjacent Areas," 22 *The Appraisal Journal* 1 (January 1954), pp. 15–25. An update by the same author five years later confirmed these results. See Herman O. Walther, "Effect of Jet Airports on Market Value of Vicinage Real Estate," 27 *The Appraisal Journal* 4 (October 1959), pp. 465–468.
2. Roland W. Crowley, *The Effects of an Airport on Land Values* (Ottawa: Ministry of State for Urban Affairs, 1972).
3. *Ibid.*, p. 19.

4. Citizen group activity, however, has not escaped the attention of all scholars. See for example the various works of Dorothy Nelkin, particularly *Jetport: The Boston Airport Controversy* (New Brunswick, N.J.: Transaction Books, 1974). Journalists who have covered the activities of these groups and several of the participants in group activities also have written about the phenomenon.

5. These terms are adapted from Gabriel Almond and Sidney Verba, *The Civic Culture* (Boston: Little Brown, 1965).

6. Elliot J. Feldman and Jerome Milch. *The Politics of Canadian Airport Development: Lessons in Federalism* (Durham, N.C.: Duke University Press, 1982), Chapter 4. Air Canada feared paying the final bill for overconstruction.

7. The French Communist Party supported construction because of the new jobs the project would create. Elliot J. Feldman, *White Elephants and the Albatross: British and French Planning in the Supersonic Age* (Cambridge, Mass.: MIT, 1982).

8. Despite their demurrer, Ontario officials were very influential in determining the site for the new airport, and their withdrawal from the project three and a half years after its inception was instrumental in the abandonment of development plans. Nevertheless, formal authority for decision making rested with the federal government. For a detailed analysis of federal-provincial relations with respect to airport development, see Feldman and Milch, *The Politics of Canadian Airport Development, op. cit.*

9. On the activities of the Caproni brothers see Elliot J. Feldman, *Airport Siting as a Problem of Policy and Participation in Technological Societies: The Case of Milano-Malpensa* (Cambridge, Mass. and Torino, Italy: Harvard University Center for International Affairs and Fondazione Luigi Einaudi, 1978). John Creery's behavior is discussed in Feldman and Milch, *The Politics of Canadian Airport Development, op. cit.*, Chapter 5.

10. According to Erven MacIntosh, professor of geography at the University of Guelph, land in the Pickering area was selling in 1974 at six times its value for agricultural purposes. MacIntosh, testifying at the Airport Inquiry Commission hearings, suggested that price inflation was the result of movement into the area by ex-urbanites, such as the militants of People or Planes. *Toronto Globe and Mail* (April 19, 1974).

11. Charles Godfrey, a Toronto physician whose home is on the outskirts of the airport site in Pickering Township, and Hector Massey, a professor of political science at York University, wrote a book in 1972 attacking government development plans. Both identified themselves as farmers. *People or Planes* (Toronto: Copp Clark, 1972).

12. David Perman, *Cublington: A Blueprint for Resistance* (London: Bodley Head, 1973).

13. The term is from Jameson Doig, "Regional Politics and 'Businesslike Efficiency': The Port of New York Authority," in Michael Danielson (ed.), *Metropolitan Politics: A Reader*, Second Edition (Boston: Little Brown, 1971). In 1972 the Port of New York Authority became the Port Authority of New York and New Jersey.

14. The statement is by G. E. McDowell, General Manager of the Toronto Area Airports Project. The kit contained materials on a range of topics including the impact of the proposed airport on the Metropolitan Toronto Zoo and on nearby cemeteries.

15. See the story by Sandford F. Borins, "An Update for Toronto Airport," in the *Toronto Globe and Mail* (April 29, 1981).

16. For more details, see Chapter 4, and Feldman, *White Elephants and the Albatross, op. cit.*

17. Classical economics would reject any public improvement violating the criterion of Pareto-efficiency, and airport development, which imposes measurable costs on some individuals, cannot be Pareto-optimal. In order to get around this limitation, the welfare economists introduced the "Kaldor-Hicks" criterion, which regards change as favorable as long as the gainers could compensate the losers while still generating a net gain. However, the criterion does not require that compensation actually take place. It is the latter provision to which airport neighbors are opposed. See Laurence H. Tribe, "Policy Science: Analysis or Ideology?" 2 *Philosophy and Public Affairs* 1 (Fall 1972), pp. 66–110.

18. Samuel P. Huntington and Joan M. Nelson review the range of definitions of political participation in *No Easy Choice: Political Participation in Developing Countries* (Cambridge, Mass.: Harvard, 1976), pp. 4–7.

19. Julian L. Woodward and Elmo Roper, "Political Activity of American Citizens," 44 *American Political Science Review* (December 1950), pp. 872–885.

20. Lester Milbrath, *Political Participation: How and Why People Get Involved in Politics* (Chicago: Rand McNally, 1965).

21. The definition of political participation as 'legal activities' can be found in Norman H. Nie and Sidney Verba, "Political Participation" in Fred Greenstein and Nelson Polsby (ed.), *Handbook of Political Science*, Volume 4 (Reading, Mass.: Addison-Wesley, 1975), p. 1.

22. Michael Lipsky, "Protest as a Political Resource," 62 *American Political Science Review* (December 1968), pp. 1144–45.

23. Milbrath, *Political Participation, op. cit.*, pp. 27–29.

24. Jeffrey M. Berry, *Lobbying for the People: The Political Behavior of Public Interest Groups* (Princeton, N.J.: Princeton, 1977), p. 266. The reference is to L. Harmon Zeigler and G. Wayne Peak, *Interest Groups in American Society*, Second Edition (Englewood Cliffs, N.J.: Prentice-Hall, 1972).

25. Roger W. Cobb and Charles D. Elder, *Participation in American Politics: The Dynamics of Agenda-Building* (Boston: Allyn and Bacon, 1972).

26. Huntington and Nelson, *No Easy Choice, op. cit.*, p. 6.

27. Sidney Verba and Norman Nie, *Participation in America: Political Democracy and Social Equality* (New York: Harper and Row, 1972), p. 3.

28. The underlying assumption that attitudes affect the way in which a political system operates is reflected in Almond and Verba, *The Civic Culture, op. cit.*, p. 42.

29. *Ibid.*, p. 308.

30. Edward C. Banfield, *The Moral Basis of a Backward Society* (New York: Free Press, 1958); Joseph LaPalombara, *Interest Groups in Italian Politics* (Princeton, N.J.: Princeton, 1964).

31. Michel Crozier, *The Stalled Society* (New York: Viking, 1973).

32. See for example Alan Marsh, "Protest, Orthodoxy and Repression," in *Protest and Political Consciousness*, Sage Library of Social Research, Volume 49 (Beverly Hills: Sage, 1977).

33. Students of Italian politics have stressed the differences in attitudes and

behavior in the north and south. See for example Sidney Tarrow, *Peasant Communism in Southern Italy* (New Haven: Yale, 1967). This thesis, however, has been attacked largely on the grounds that the Almond and Verba data do not support the notion of dualism in Italy. See Norman Kogan's review of Tarrow's book in the *American Political Science Review* (December 1968), pp. 1282–1283, and Edward N. Muller, "Cross-National Dimensions of Political Competence," 64 *American Political Science Review* 3 (September 1970), p. 800.

34. On the movement of the unemployed in Naples, see commentaries in Fabrizia Ramondino (ed.), *Napoli: I Disoccupati Organizzati* (Milano: Feltrinelli, 1977); on the citizen movement for housing in Palermo, see Judith Chubb, "The Organization of Consensus in a Large Southern Italian City," unpublished Ph.d. dissertation, MIT, 1978.

35. This is the conclusion reached by Ronald Inglehart in his cross-national survey of political attitudes, *Silent Revolution: Changing Values and Political Styles Among Western Publics* (Princeton: Princeton University Press, 1977).

36. Giacomo Sani, "The Political Culture of Italy: Continuity and Change," in Gabriel Almond and Sidney Verba (ed.) *The Civic Culture Revisited* (Boston: Little Brown, 1980), pp. 273–324.

Part Five

LESSONS AND THEORIES

Chapter 8

POLITICIANS AND BUREAUCRATS

We began this study by observing different solutions to an apparently common problem in advanced industrial states during the same time period and under the same technological constraints. Cultural differences could not account for these variations because elites defined problems and outlined preferred solutions by applying the same values. Yet, common definitions and strategies were not produced by a technological imperative because no force drove political processes to "one best way" conclusions.

The common approaches in all five countries derived from a business mentality characterized by a belief in the value of economic growth and development, in the applicability of market criteria to some (but not all) aspects of decision making, and in the construction of public works. Elites everywhere justified the development of civil aviation infrastructure (airports and all related facilities) as a public good but insisted that market criteria should govern the distribution of costs and benefits. The result was a business approach not subject to the discipline of the market.

The business mentality encouraged the use of decision-making techniques in the public sector that appeared successful for private enterprise. The government decision makers responsible for civil aviation infrastructure believed that the quality of decisions could be improved through systematic, sophisticated analysis. Hence, the techniques of rational planning, especially cost-benefit and systems analyses, program budgeting, and management by objective were introduced almost everywhere for the purpose of improving the likelihood that established goals of construction and development would be achieved.

The results of this new sophistication were not the same every-

225

where. Different political structures processed aviation agency objectives and deployed rational planning techniques in different ways. Political systems that insulated line agencies from competing interests and armed those agencies with critical powers to define problems, design strategies, and execute programs witnessed the construction of major new airports. In those political systems, however, where competing objectives of environmental management, alternative land use, local and regional planning, or industrial and community development were considered legitimate, and where government officials and agencies were allowed to participate in projects initiated by a line agency, development normally was delayed many years and occasionally abandoned altogether. In systems of concentrated authority, rational planning contributed to the achievement of designated objectives. In systems of fragmented authority, rational planning helped competing agencies organize objectives that eroded grounds for compromise and paralyzed projects.

The systems of concentrated authority denied the participation of official and unofficial competitors and plaintiffs. New airports, developed with little recourse to informed criticism, proved to be overbuilt, underutilized, irrationally planned, incoherent for their airport network, and/or ill-placed for satellite economic development. They also disturbed neighbors, even when planned at great distances from populated areas. By contrast, in political systems of fragmented authority where development schemes failed, existing airport facilities continued to meet travel demand, and revised forecasts, when matched with revised capacity assessments, projected long-term efficient operations. Hence, the successes of rational planning often meant the expenditure of public funds for the fulfillment of businesslike values. The failures of rational planning and the concomitant paralysis of government often meant the successful accomplishment of the principal goal of satisfying air travel demand.

The belief of elites everywhere that long-term growth in civil aviation is inevitable provided the basis for systematic errors in forecasting the future. However, the consequences of poor forecasting usually were limited by the failure of officials to employ the results for decision making. Forecasts served as a principal rationale justifying development decisions, but they usually were prepared after decisions had been taken. The commitment to development was greater than the commitment to sophisticated rational planning. The impact of planning, therefore, generally was confined to the process of fulfilling the defined objectives of civil aviation elites.

The popular view that increased public participation leads to political paralysis suggests that too much democracy is positively harmful to economic progress. In the eight cases of this study, however, participation proved either insufficient to reduce the scale and impact of poorly conceived projects or secondary to the influence of official agencies with competing agendas. Citizen groups acted in defense of their interest, but in some instances they served a public purpose. Their activities encouraged officials to consider policy alternatives and their pressure frequently contributed to an increase in the perceived range of choice.

The principal victims of airport development were the owners of land chosen for construction. They always lost their homes, regardless of formal procedures to hear their objections. The business mentality governed land acquisition and property owners were treated as consumers in a market transaction, not as citizens required to surrender their property for the public good. Those who recognized the reality of expropriation generally were educated and upper middle class; they tended to profit financially from land acquisition. Property owners of modest circumstances trusted in government and finished poorer for the public good. Bureaucratic defense of the public purse in site selection, however, usually meant the expropriation of the less affluent; potential neighbors escaping expropriation tended to be more affluent and more able to defend themselves. Projects free of potential neighbors were more likely to be realized, but only when public authorities deflected official, as well as unofficial, objections.

In cases of conflict all parties resorted to the essential weapon of technocracy, the expert. Experts proved, with rare exception, to be hired guns, irrespective of the identity of their employers or their area of expertise. Their results rarely deviated from the preferences of their clients. They added immeasurably to the cost of analysis and development, but their technical contributions are suspect, at best, given their ability to serve all sides of all disputes. Technique and expertise have altered the style of politics but have neither clarified issues nor contributed to compromise.

Subjects and Objects

The *subject* of this study has been the apparent contradictions of democratic political systems engaged in complex technical decisions. Civil aviation infrastructure, a single technology defined commonly in different countries during the same period of time, has constituted the *object* of our inquiry. We have investigated systematically and in detail the development experience in decision making and public participation for airports in five countries in order to formulate general observations, and perhaps theories, about our subject—the relationship between technocracy and democracy.

Two kinds of final observations now are possible. Because we have had to study the development of civil aviation infrastructure very closely, our analyses lead to certain lessons for the community most involved in this public sector activity. Our perspective is impartial: We have never served as consultants to the aviation industry or to government agencies responsible for civil aviation. We travel often enough that less efficient facilities would not be in our own personal interest. In these respects, we are not unlike much of the public in advanced industrial states. We also are political scientists studying a sector commonly reserved for economists and engineers, giving our observations a different orientation.

In addition to specific conclusions related to the object of this study, there are broader observations possible regarding the relationship between technocracy and democracy. In each of our chapters we have offered some theories of intermediate range, but there remain certain patterns which, at the potential cost of abstraction, may also permit greater generalization. The forces that shape behavior in the aviation sector may be understood in these broader, and more theoretical, terms.

Lessons for Civil Aviation

Authorities responsible for civil aviation, in government and private enterprise, have perceived their task exclusively in terms of public transportation. Even as they have debated the differences between a regulated industry dominated by the marketplace and a public service organized as a public utility, they have never accepted the cross-sectoral character of civil aviation. Airport development necessarily involves land use, noise, and air pollution. Civil aviation will develop in the future only when the limitations, as well as the opportunities, of technology are acknowledged by its proponents as an integral part of the problem and confronted in the earliest stages of decision making.

An Uncertain Future

Civil aviation has enjoyed priority for investment in public transportation for three decades. This dominant era, during which a fascination with technology has worked to aviation's advantage, is coming to a close. Civil aviation cannot expect to grow in the next decade as it did in the last, and one important reason is the evolution of technologically sophisticated competitors for public investment within the sector of transportation. The development of high-speed rail (TGV) between Paris and Lyon, which will compete with air service between France's newest and largest airports (Charles de Gaulle and Lyon-Satolas), illustrates the potential of alternative transportation systems to command public commitment. The TGV will cost more than $1.5 billion, but its operational costs will be lower and its passenger-carrying capacity on a major route far greater than its aviation competitor.

The future of civil aviation also has become clouded by the impact of airline deregulation in the United States, which has generated unintended consequences both for domestic and international airports.[1] Although airlines have consolidated routes, they have learned too that wide-body aircraft can be an operational burden. Deregulation, combined with soaring fuel prices and technological innovation, has made short- and medium-haul flights on smaller aircraft increasingly efficient. As a result, long-haul nonstop transport is giving way to feeder systems through aviation hubs. These developments suggest that pressure on runway systems, reduced in the mid-1970s by the development of wide-body aircraft, may grow once again. Growth in demand, however, will not be uniform across the airport system because the locus of demand for airport utilization is shifting. Some airports will lose traffic, while others will be under much greater pressure than in the past. There is no way to predict how long these effects will last or whether airlines will generate alternative responses to deregulation. Airport authorities must be cautious not to respond to this initial impact of deregulation by assuming, yet again, that they need to build. It is much easier to change aircraft or alter routes than to restore a village or tear down a terminal.

Proponents of civil aviation know they can accomplish narrow objectives when full resources are committed to the task. They must also realize, however, that narrow objectives may yield short-term victories at very high long-term costs. Moreover, the systematic exclusion of criticism or the effective narrowing of objectives can encourage ill-informed decisions and produce dramatic errors. One of these errors appears to emerge from the business mentality governing decision making. The goal of responsible officials, to meet travel demand, frequently has been translated into the objective of construction. However, construction as a goal does not necessarily meet travel demand efficiently or with cost-effective results.

No technological imperative demands construction. Wide-body aircraft and improved air traffic control systems actually discourage runway construction, and the discovery of political and economic alternatives often requires little more than imagination. But pressure groups supporting the élite corps of private aircraft, and a reluctance to regulate schedules to achieve greater efficiency, have limited the vision of public officials responsible for civil aviation.

There are alternatives to construction. Perhaps the most prominent and promising approach is embodied in the British pricing mechanism described in Chapter 4. The Finance Economics Division of the British Airports Authority reported in July 1976 that "in many traffic categories there does appear to be a switch from the peak charging period to the hours immediately before and immediately after."[2] The effects of the pricing mechanism were more modest than expected in the mid-1970s because fuel surcharges and the rapid purchase of wide-body aircraft encouraged airlines to reduce the total number of flights and consolidate activities in the peak hours. Airport fees, after all, represent a very small airline cost when compared with fuel and other operating requirements.[3] Nevertheless, the steep increase in charges at the end of the decade did have desired effects, and pricing had long since discouraged general aviation from using a busy international facility. The capacity of airports plainly can be increased through more efficient utilization during all hours of the day and all seasons of the year. Peak surcharges, moreover, increase airport revenues and help pay for development when genuinely needed.

The key to survival in an uncertain future is flexibility. Even when construction proves necessary, designs must be sufficiently flexible to allow for modification or expansion. The circular terminals of Toronto's Malton and Paris' Charles de Gaulle, for example, cannot be expanded and are wholly inappropriate for the requirements of the 1980s. The Dallas–Fort Worth Regional Airport was designed for flexibility, but the seizure of 18,000 acres reflects assumptions about static, rather than dynamic, technology.

Flexibility does not require land banking. Chicago's O'Hare Airport, the world's busiest, operates on 4900 acres, and both New York's LaGuardia and Washington's National require less than 1000. The new standard of 18,000 acres is based on a desire to capture the economic benefits of airport development, not on the requirements of civil aviation, and it should not be confused with flexible planning.

It is altogether possible that airports in Dallas–Fort Worth, Montreal, and Paris one day will enjoy patronage that will seem to justify the expense. Edmonton Airport in Alberta, built to service a polar route just as propeller aircraft were becoming obsolete, has experienced congestion in the late 1970s as a result of the economic boom induced in Western Canada by oil. The Volpe International Terminal at Boston's Logan Airport, grossly underutilized during its first four years following construction, has become crowded because of deregulation. There are many other examples, for overconstruction has been common and demand sometimes has caught up. Nevertheless, the long wait for the utilization of facilities constitutes an incalculable opportunity cost for the land and for the investment. Underutilized facilities built with the aid of subsidies and low-interest loans provided by national governments may not create an excessive financial burden for airport operators, but the public interest suffers when resources are spent in this manner. Construction well ahead of demand can never be vindicated fully by later use. Demand, moreover, may be induced to justify expenditures; officials in Dallas–Fort Worth, for example, have attracted transfer traffic to keep the airport in the black, but they confuse the public interest with their own when they justify the scale of the airport this way.

Cross-National Experiences

The international character of civil aviation might lead the casual observer to assume that experiments in one airport inevitably must be known to authorities at another. Airlines are certainly conscious of experiments introduced by their competitors because they confront each other directly at numerous ports of call. Airport authorities, however, do not communicate as well, in part because competition is less obvious and they are more attuned to their own political systems and pressure groups. The International Civil Airports Association encourages members to employ similar criteria when judging performance and deciding on development, but international organizations do not guarantee mutual awareness of experience. Thus, the British pricing mechanism was unknown to the American and Canadian authorities in this study. Even the Europeans learned of it through the Western European Airports Association only after the mechanism had been operating for several years.

The British experiment is only one example of the lessons that can be drawn from the cross-national observation of experience dealing with common problems. Political systems and cultures tend to define few choices. The examination of responses to a common problem beyond these boundaries can reveal additional choices. The Malpensa experience proves that it is not necessary to anticipate demand through construction, and Malpensa, Mirabel, and Dallas–Fort Worth demonstrate that economic growth does not necessarily accompany airport development. The absence of a policy for multiple airport systems in Milan, Montreal, and Paris warns against the hasty commitment to new facilities. The Kingston Plan for Canada discussed in Chapter 5 illustrates the importance of political sensitivity when proposing "technical" solutions to problems. And the incoherent network of road and rail transportation developed in Paris forcefully demonstrates that comprehensive planning must go beyond the mandate of airport authorities and include other government agencies.

It is important for governments to be consistent in statements and policies. SEA was penalized for developing two sets of noise curves, and Canada's Ministry of Transport paid for its inconsistent treatment of landowners in Quebec, Ontario, and British Columbia. SEA did not enhance its case for Malpensa by permitting traffic to grow at Linate, any more than ADP's credibility was strengthened by supporting a noise tax at Charles de Gaulle Airport while ignoring the neighbors of Orly.

Still another lesson that can be learned from systematic observations of cross-national experiences is that the cost of land represents a fraction of development costs. Those unwilling to pay generously for land (the Canadians and the Italians) should learn from the French and the Americans. The Canadians proved they could make generous laws stingy, and the French proved that pecunious laws can be made generous. The consequences in each case were consistent with official behavior.

National experiences are not always transferable. When SEA

could not find money to proceed with the Malpensa project, it hired the American financial firm of Dillon-Read to recommend a solution. Utterly ignorant of Italian politics, the consultants proposed the floating of revenue bonds to finance construction. Revenue bonds are the lifeblood of American airport authorities but were inappropriate in the context of SEA's intricate relations with various agencies and the state. The Americans might have offered a fresh perspective on the Italian problem if they had understood the constraints on their clients.

Dealing with the Public

The most important lesson that civil aviation can draw from the experiences of these five countries is the importance of establishing new and healthier relationships with the public. Aviation enthusiasts have demanded public support for unlimited growth on the basis of a technological mystique and the knowledge of experts. The controversies of the 1970s demonstrated that there is no monopoly on expertise because experts frequently disagree. Support for development will have to be won in the future more through public debate and persuasion than through technological mystique.

A major step toward this new relationship would be recognition that the claims of airport neighbors are not necessarily illegitimate. Spokesmen for aviation sometimes have blamed airport neighbors for their problems. Sir Peter Masefield, for example, argues that property owners were aware of the existence of airports before purchasing homes and that claims lodged against airport authorities are based on greed.[4] Many airports were built far from residential areas only to succumb to urban encroachment. Most urban development near airports in the industrial world, however, preceded the commercial introduction of jet aircraft, which is the undeniable source of complaint. Literally millions of people exposed to undesirable and often inescapable noise purchased their homes without any forewarning that the problem would expand with technological development in the aircraft industry. Neighbors absorb the costs of civil aviation disproportionately and they have a legitimate claim to compensation, whether from the general treasury because of the public service involved or from the industry that profits from the provision of this service as a business. Acknowledgement of the plight of neighbors and a commitment to work with them effectively and honestly will certainly be in the interests of civil aviation.

The desire of aviation proponents to accomplish narrow objectives often appeared thwarted in the 1970s by public participants. Participation can delay development until costs exceed budgets and public officials begin to doubt a plan's wisdom. The experience of the Vancouver International Airport Planning Committee suggests some of the potential problems of citizen participation. However, some efforts to include citizens in decision making have been more successful. The British established citizen advisory councils that integrate neighbors into the basic decision structure of the airport. They have helped diffuse protest, not only through cooptation but also through genuine adjustments in flight paths and operating procedures. The Port Authority of New York and New Jersey also has invited citizens to participate on advisory councils. These experiences suggest that compromises can be reached, competing interests can be accommodated, and aviation objectives can be served. The rejection of participation seems, on balance, more costly than its active solicitation.

The success of invited participation in New York and London might signal airport operators to a more general requirement in the 1980s. It is possible that the future of airport operations will depend above all on friendly relations with neighbors. Airport authorities probably will have to acknowledge that, after those who lose their land and homes, the greatest price for civil aviation is paid by neighbors bearing the burdens of noise and pollution. A confidential study for the United States Environmental Protection Agency in 1980 recommended assisting 100,000 people to move from their homes where they suffered from excessive noise.[5] An additional 2.5 million homes, the report revealed, require soundproofing because noise abatement efforts in the next twenty years will not relieve them. Spokesmen for civil aviation concur with this judgment. As Boeing's Vice-President for Engineering has declared, "in the noise area it is going to be exceedingly difficult to achieve significant further reduction."[6] Community noise damage claims in the United States alone exceed $1 billion. And the Environmental Protection Agency estimates a bill of $10 billion, coupled with the prohibition of further production for the noisiest aircraft (including the popular Boeing 727) to remedy the situation.

The costs of civil aviation infrastructure have not been borne easily in the industrial world. Controversies have not been without reason and financial struggles have not been for petty sums. Airports have not proved themselves magnets for economic development, as demonstrated by disappointments in Milan, Dallas–Fort Worth, and Montreal. Nor are they the obvious symbols of prestige that their developers consider them. Yet buyers and sellers both seem to believe that the control tower has supplanted the cathedral spire. Airport authorities are eager to sell their expertise and technology, and officials in the Third World often appear eager to buy. The sellers promise economic development around the polar attraction of airports and they pretend that industrial countries have absorbed the costs easily. They promise prestige. But the vigorous selling of airport development to the Third World is no more than a further colonial exploitation. If the profit motive is greater than the moral constraints, then this lesson may be lost on aviation interests in the industrial world. Perhaps it will not be lost, however, on the Third World.

Technocracy vs. Democracy

Airport development has been the focus of sustained public controversy throughout the industrial world. Narita Airport, 41 miles northeast of Tokyo, opened eleven years late because of protesting farmers and students: 13,000 protestors manned barricades for the May 1978 opening; a year later 10,000 people gathered to threaten airport operations; and even two years after the opening 5,000 people rallied against the $2.6 billion enterprise. Various conflicts delayed other airports in this study more than two decades.

Public authorities are concerned above all with avoiding conflict. Preferences for the acquisition of essentially vacant land or the use of land already owned by government, and strategies for developing new airports instead of expanding existing facilities in urban areas, generally result from efforts to avert conflict. Authorities everywhere believe that it is possible to establish policies that can be executed efficiently and without public objection.

Conflict in the cases discussed in this book probably could not be avoided. The French and the Americans reduced conflict by compensating handsomely for land, but even in these cases neighbors still protest and competing agencies remain hostile. For conflict is inevitable when the central values of affected actors are irreconcilable, and contests over airport development involve such value conflicts. This study has revealed similar controversies everywhere, with similar actors, despite gross systemic and cultural differences. The outcomes differed from place to place, but patterns emerged from the criteria for choice exercised by élites everywhere.

Inevitable Conflicts

The dilemma of compulsory purchase may serve as a paradigm for conflicts over values inevitable in all liberal democracies. The individual asserts the right to use and dispose of private property, including the freedom to sell voluntarily in a free market. The community asserts the right to seize private property for the public good without a market transaction. The individual compromises by acknowledging the community's right to take the property; the community compromises by compensating as if the transaction were in the free market.

In compulsory purchase, the individual invokes the values of liberalism. Each individual in the ideal liberal state is free to transact business with other individuals without interference from the state. Minimal government serves primarily to guarantee the integrity of private transactions and the freedom of individuals. In contests between the judgment of the individual and the judgment of the community, the individual should prevail. Such a state was proposed for economic reasons by Adam Smith and in political revolt against tyranny by John Locke.

The values of democracy, invoked by the community in compulsory purchase, reverse these priorities. In the ideal democratic state, property is for public use; the community may permit individuals to use property, but it also may revoke that privilege at any time. In disputes between individuals and the community, the collective judgment prevails. The state, created by the community, defines the public good to which all particular interests are subordinated. This philosophy guided Jean-Jacques Rousseau, both as he shaped a government in the *Social Contract* and as he repudiated aristocracy in the *Discourse on the Origin of Inequality*.

Locke was the philosopher of England's "Glorious Revolution" of 1688 and Rousseau was the philosopher most associated with the French Revolution a century later. Both Locke and Rousseau conjured states governed of and by the people in reaction to tyrannical monarchies. Locke's solution to the problem of excessive state power was to reduce it; Rousseau's solution was to transfer the authority to new hands.

Modern England is no more an ideal liberal state than modern France is ideally democratic. They, like all liberal democracies, tend toward one philosophy or the other depending on their origins, but their histories and institutions represent compromises. Liberalism and democracy each represents a different world view,[7] and during the nineteenth and twentieth centuries many philosophers have tried to explain, defend, or reconcile them. They remain, nevertheless, contradictory. Both the individual and the state cannot prevail under all circumstances; what is good for the collective is not always good for the individual. If it were otherwise, society would never have to impose taxes on citizens, because they would contribute voluntarily from their own estates; society would never have to seize property from citizens, because they readily would surrender it for the public good; and society would never have to conscript soldiers, for citizens would rise to defend their own collective interests.

Elements of liberalism and democracy, present in all western states, guarantee conflict over the most fundamental issues of life, liberty, and property. Hence, the most challenging debates in western political systems, the ones least susceptible to consensus or simple solution, concern capital punishment and military conscription (the community's claim on the lives of individuals), incarceration and civil rights (the denial of individual liberties), and taxation and expropriation (the seizure of private property). The most difficult problems thus involve an ideological confrontation between liberal and democratic values.

This dual ideological heritage is an important dynamic element in all modern western states. The contradiction between liberal and democratic values demands sustained attention and compromise, and the shifting relationships between rights and responsibilities, freedom and order, and faith and reason assure perpetual creativity and ingenuity. However, the negative consequence of the dual heritage is the guarantee of conflict. Issues that focus attention on these contradictions inevitably invite furious debate.

The politics of technology implicitly rejects democratic processes in favor of transferring power into the hands of a narrow élite. When these politics require choices on traditional issues, such as expropriation or restriction on the use and enjoyment of private property, the contest is joined. As long as technological development requires expert decision making and as long as projects will require land or affect the use or value of adjacent property, there will be serious public controversy. And as long as society is ambivalent whether the public good is served by the development of facilities that require personal sacrifices from many individuals, controversies will be protracted and their resolutions will dissatisfy most parties involved.

Resolving Conflict

The commitment to rational planning began with the belief that good decision making could eliminate these public controversies. Various reasons were offered in Chapter 4 for the failure of rational planning, but one additional explanation—more fundamental—is appropriate here. The controversies associated with technology are inescapable because their causes are embedded in the very heritage that defines the modern liberal democratic state.

Debates over the seizure of private land for public use, or over degradation of the environment for an alternative public good, or over the commitment of public resources to specific tasks servicing narrow populations* cannot be avoided through "better," wiser, or more "rational" decisions or implementation. The effort to reduce conflict is noble, for these conflicts erode democracy by effectively disenfranchising citizens. They drain the public purse and they lead often to decisions that favor the few over the many. The inevitability of conflict, however, does not mean that liberal democratic states must suffer all these consequences. As James Madison most ably explained in another context, where causes cannot be changed, the most useful strategy is to control effects.[8]

Several avenues to the reduction of these effects have been suggested. More open decision processes protect democratic principles, reduce the anxiety of affected parties, and avoid a sense of betrayal. Flexible plans reduce reliance on forecasting. Separation of the business mentality from the concept of the public good would reduce the grandiose scale of plans and much of the

---

* Aviation is a common mode of transportation for a very small public. Americans fly more frequently than any other nationality, but only 7 percent of Americans fly more than once a year. In Europe the figures are considerably lower.

public expense. Full knowledge of the interests and objectives of all parties may not make reconciliation easier, but with a clearer sense of respective agendas, universal dissatisfaction may be displaced by a keener appreciation for compromise. The contest between liberal and democratic principles will, of course, remain, but it may not encourage so many apparent attempts at mutual annihilation.

There does not appear to us to be a basic alternative to this approach without a fundamental restructuring of liberal democracy. A decisive triumph of either liberal or democratic values might permit the emergence of a consensus, but the result would be a system far different from the one we presently know; the socialist ideal, for example, favors such an outcome. But if any balance between liberalism and democracy is to survive—and hence the simultaneous and sometimes contradictory defense of civil liberties and collective will—then policies reducing the effects of conflict are more promising than the general approaches that have dominated decision making until now.

The experiences of countries having similar values and facing similar problems are a vital resource in the search for policies that will limit the harmful effects of inevitable conflict. Mistakes will be made, but their elevation to symbols of achievement can only frustrate the public good. The experiences of five countries with airport development was replete not only with mistakes and problems but also with wise and sound policies. Countries that pay attention to the experiences of their neighbors can learn from each other how to deal equitably and honestly with the interminable dilemma of liberal democracy.

Endnotes

1. See especially John R. Meyer, et al., *Airline Deregulation: The Early Experience* (Boston: Auburn House, 1981).
2. "Peak Movement Surcharge at Heathrow," Internal Memorandum of British Airports Authority, July 1976.
3. In 1975–1976, overall airport charges, including landing fees, rent, handling and other services, represented only 10.6 percent of the operating costs of British Airways. Fuel represented 21.2 percent of costs, and that percentage has risen sharply since 1978. Statistics provided by H. E. Marking, Deputy Chairman of British Airways, in private correspondence with authors, January 28, 1977.
4. Masefield presented this argument in detail in an interview in London, January 10, 1977, and more vociferously and publicly in Paris at the Seventh

International Symposium of the Institute of Air Transport, May 1978. Mase-field is former Chief Executive of British European Airways and was the first Director of the British Airports Authority.

5. Reported by Peter J. Bernstein of the Newhouse News Service in *The Boston Globe*, July 12, 1980. The estimate is in a report, "Aviation Noise—The Next 20 Years," which was circulated internally in the Carter Administration.

6. H. W. Withington, *Commercial Air Transportation Developments in the Next Three Decades* (Delft, The Netherlands: University of Technology, 1977), p. 42.

7. Elliot J. Feldman plans a separate volume that will examine the liberal-democratic dilemma in a longer historical perspective, relating classical theory to contemporary policy problems with reference to Plato and Aristotle, Augustine and Aquinas, Machiavelli and Mill. We limit the argument here, however, to the eighteenth and nineteenth century philosophical origins of modern western states.

8. Alexander Hamilton, James Madison, and John Jay, *The Federalist Papers* (New York: New American Library of World Literature, 1961). Federalist Number 10, by Madison, argues that, "There are methods of curing the mischiefs of faction: the one, by removing its causes; the other, by controlling its effects. . . . Liberty is to faction what air is to fire . . . liberty . . . is essential to political life. . . The latent causes of faction are thus sown in the nature of man." The causes, then, could not be cured. See pp. 77–84.

A METHODOLOGICAL APPROACH TO COMPARATIVE POLICY

The basic approach to this study, the definition of subjects and objects and the rationale for strategic methodological choices, is described in Chapter 1. However, social scientists and political scientists, in particular, tend to be uncomfortable with studies that do not depend on fixed interview schedules from which numerical assessments can be made. Hence, it is important to explain in more detail what we did to gather the evidence supporting our analysis.

Selection of Respondents

The portion of our study concerned with technocracy required the collection of information from decision makers. In order to determine whether technocrats indeed made essential political choices, we spoke with the top and middle-ranking officials responsible for civil aviation in general and airport development in particular in each country. Their specific identities are not listed here because the few requesting confidentiality might be recognized even by exclusion from a select group.

Officials

We divided these official actors into two broad categories, representatives of private enterprise and public officials, with the latter category subdivided among political appointees and career civil servants. We interviewed the incumbent presidents and/or vice-presidents of ten major airlines, including the national flag-carriers in Canada, France, Britain, and Italy. Sometimes we interviewed former top airline officials if critical decisions were made affecting airport development during an earlier period. In all, we met with twenty-three airline officials, plus a spokesman from the International Air Transport Association (IATA).

Our choice of respondents among public officials depended more on the peculiarities of each political system. In the United States, for example, essential development authority resides locally. The Federal Aviation Administration (FAA) and the Civil Aeronautics Board (CAB) do make decisions with lasting effects, but the Dallas–Fort Worth experience testifies to the ability of local officials to determine the location and character of facilities. By contrast, the Ministry of Transport owns and operates the major airports in Canada and exercises all final authority. And although independent public authorities in France, Italy, and the United Kingdom control airports in major cities, each must answer directly to a government minister.

In the United States, then, we concentrated on officials in the states of New York and Texas and in the respective airport authorities. We interviewed officials in the Department of Transportation in both New York State and New York City. We spoke with past and present directors of aviation in the MTA and top officials and planners in the Port Authority of New York and New Jersey. In Texas we interviewed the Deputy Executive Director of the Joint Regional Airport as well as members of his staff and of the Airport Board. We also interviewed planners and public officials in both city and county governments in Dallas, Fort Worth, and Irving as well as the North Central Texas Council of Governments.

In Canada we worked at the federal, provincial, and local governmental levels. We interviewed past and present ministers of transport, a senior assistant deputy minister, past and present deputy ministers for air, and past and present ministerial directors-general. We also interviewed officials in the Transport Ministry responsible for forecasting and policy planning, and regional administrators assigned to different areas of the country. We interviewed two top-ranking aides to the Prime Minister, and a half-dozen former Cabinet members who shared in critical airport decisions. Finally, we interviewed middle-level officials responsible for activities in Quebec, Ontario, and British Columbia and in the Ministry of State for Urban Affairs, the Department of the Environment, the Ministry of Justice, and the Department of Regional Economic Expansion.

At the provincial and local levels, we interviewed two former premiers, three former ministers responsible for transportation, former mayors of Toronto and Vancouver, policy planners on the staffs of all three cities (for Toronto and Vancouver, including the regional districts), and officials of the federal teams assigned to local development in Montreal and Toronto. We also attended public meetings where testimony was given by a wide range of officials concerned about airport development.

The work in France involved a variety of transportation agencies, the Airport Authority, and the Ministry of Transport and Civil Aviation. In addition to the Director-General for Civil Aviation, we interviewed six other top and middle-ranking ministerial officials, including present and former directors for civilian air bases. We also interviewed three former ministers of transport and civil aviation.

At Aéroport de Paris we met with three present and former directors-general and chief executive officers, plus the directors of three operating departments. We met with middle-level officials in the RATP and the SNCF, and with top officials in two regional districts, Paris and O.R.E.A.P. (at Amiens). Testimony was collected, too, from the mayors of Roissy-en-France and Goussainville. A high-ranking member of the prime minister's cabinet answered questions regarding final deliberations for Charles de Gaulle Airport.

In Italy, we interviewed in the central government in Rome, in the provincial government of Varese, in the regional government in Lombardy, and in all the small communes whose property lay in or near Malpensa. We also interviewed extensively within the Airport Authority where the terms of our grant provided access to officials and documents.

In Rome we interviewed present and past directors-general for civil aviation in the Ministry of Transport and Civil Aviation, the former minister, the past and present directors-general for land in the Finance Ministry, and air officials in the Defense Ministry. We met with the president of the region, several officials assigned there to the airport portfolio, and the past and present presidents of the provincial government. Past and present mayors of a half-dozen communes testified for us, plus two members of the Milan City Council. We further checked related issues with officials in the Parco del Ticino, in the ATM, MM, and FS, and in Bergamo where a competing airport was politically entangled. In Italy, it must also be noted, a variety of official bodies formed, met, and disappeared at various times. We think we reached spokesmen for all of them through 1977. At SEA we worked directly through the office of the Director-General to interview a host of officials as well as members of the Governing Board and a past president of SEA.

Our British interviews included two former ministers responsible for the aviation portfolio, present and former directors of the British Airports Authority, and top-ranking civil servants in the Departments of Environment and Trade and in the Civil Aviation Authority. Three top staff members of the Roskill Commission testified for us, plus key advisers to two ministers. In Britain, Italy, and Canada we also interviewed members of parliament representing both the government and the opposition on key committees concerned with transportation in general and airport development in particular.

Non-officials

For the democracy part of our study, we concentrated on expropriated property owners and on the leaders and spokesmen of most of the citizen groups we were able to identify. In some instances, such as Vancouver, we were able to meet with most of the members of the group's nucleus. In other cases, such as London, we relied more on the extensive documentation available about the many amenity groups. We also interviewed lawyers and consultants serving these groups, and we interviewed officials in the larger and more established organizations when they became involved in the airport controversies including, for example, the World Wildlife Federation in Italy and Canada.

We made preliminary inquiries into the role of labor and unions, but we found that their influence, when it existed at all, was confined to operational, not developmental issues. Similarly, we attempted to trace the impact of the largest development contractors, but because this issue was not our primary focus, we found it too difficult to pursue. It is certainly appropriate for another, perhaps different, study that concentrates less on government *decision making* and more on decisions themselves.

Interview Objectives

We sought to interview as many people in each of our categories as we could, based on both our time and their accessibility. Because these interviews averaged some two and a half hours in length, we had to choose actors whom we believed were decisive in processing airport choices. We followed leads from documentation and from respondents as they identified other key actors.

Our primary objective in interviews was the collection of essentially factual information. Despite volumes of documents on each case, there is little information available about the process of choice and the roles of different actors. Most of the documentation is technical and generally oriented around the preferences of those who paid for it. Hence, the documents in themselves testified to one aspect of our inquiry but left many of our questions unanswered.

There were, of course, many private or confidential and official files that were invaluable. In every country we managed to gain access to such materials, although more in Italy, Canada, and France than in the United States and the United Kingdom. Despite the length and quality of our interviews, we could not have managed this analysis without these documents.

Our interviews also concentrated on how respondents perceived their own role, power, and responsibility in the process. We relied heavily on story-telling techniques to secure this attitudinal information rather than on a fixed formula that would lack subtlety and be unable to follow up effectively on testimony peculiar to the particular respondent. A fuller discussion of the interview procedures can be found in *A Practical Guide to the Conduct of Field Research in the Social Sciences* (Boulder: Westview Press, 1981).

Data Collection

Three strategies were available to us for data collection. We could collect the data together; we could divide the subject matter and each work at all eight sites; or we could each do all the work at roughly half the sites. The first strategy would have been ideal but was impractical. Nevertheless, we did do most of our work in Ottawa together, and often we felt these interviews were our most successful. The second strategy would have been our best alternative because it would have enabled each of us to specialize on a set of problems across all eight sites. This approach, unfortunately, far exceeded our modest budgets because it required each of us to spend considerable time at each site. It also had the disadvantage of requiring equal knowledge of each site, which would have been more time-consuming. Hence, we each worked all the subject areas of four sites; Feldman in London, Milan, Paris, and Vancouver; Milch in Dallas–Fort Worth, Montreal, New York, and Toronto.

We coordinated our activities and data in three ways. First, we agreed on a list of forty-four questions to be answered at every site. These questions obliged us to interview parallel actors everywhere, but because the political systems and settings were different we did not confine ourselves to certain actors at the expense of acquiring information. This document, entitled "Pertinent Considerations for the Maintenance of Comparability," was prepared in the autumn of 1973 and guided all our research. We believed that we would be able to address the broader issues of our study if we could answer these forty-four questions at all eight sites.

The "Pertinent Considerations" divided the information we required into six categories: statutes, land, citizen action, the decision process, technical facilities, and outside expertise. The following questions are examples indicative of the overall guide:

Statutes:
What are the statutes governing the expropriation of land?
Who has legal powers governing airport development?
What are the nearby zoning and construction codes? Who controls them?
What laws govern the airport authority?

Land:
Who owns the land on which the airport is located?
Who paid for the land? Who would pay for additional land?
Who owns the land on which a new airport or an expansion of old facilities may take place?
Has there been speculation on land in the area?

Citizen Action:

What citizen action groups are there? What is the precise nature of their complaint?

What have they done, and what do they plan to do, in pursuit of their objectives? How do they express their complaints?

Do governments or authorities meet with protest groups?

The Decision Process:

What criteria have been employed in the decision to build anything new?

What criteria have been used for site selection?

What decisions are taken at which levels of government?

Technical Facilities:

Who pays for different services, and who provides the services, at the airport?

Who determines flight paths, how constrained are the facilities to alter them, and what are the means of enforcement?

Outside Expertise:

Have the authorities responsible for the airport called in outside analysts? Who?

Exactly what special studies have been done? By whom? For what purpose? What do they say? Who paid for them?

A corollary document we developed for "general considerations" served to remind us of the basic purpose behind our list. This document signalled us to watch for the role of certain actors, to explore the informal as well as formal rules of the game, to comprehend the distribution of power over airport decision making. It also reminded us of potential sources at different sites. Air-traffic controllers, for example, provided us with vital technical information.

The second coordinating device was a frequent correspondence (when Feldman was in Europe, Milch in America), and an expensive telephone exchange. A great deal of work was done by telephone, whose companies certainly have been the principal financial beneficiaries of this study.

Finally, we developed two kinds of reports. For every interview we prepared a lengthy report organized by subject. These reports ranged from two to twenty pages and became our principal source of data. We sent each other copies as soon as they were ready, usually within a week of conducting the interviews. Unlike data summaries from surveys, these reports explained the identity and role of each respondent, our own impressions, the information provided, and the questions asked. The interviews permitted considerable probing and follow-up and occasionally tips and insights for another site. We have some 2,000 pages in detailed interview reports. The second report was a periodic summary, either of our findings on a particular subject or a chronological account of a particular site. These reports helped us both stay knowledgeable of all eight sites, so that each could think comparatively beyond his own four as we proceeded.

At our own expense, we arranged to meet at least twice for lengthy discussions and data exchange during each year of the study, beginning in 1973. The final six months writing this book took place in Cambridge when Milch was named a Visiting Scholar to the University Consortium for Research on North America and to Harvard University's Center for International Affairs.

Movement Among Sites

It is not practical in a multi-national comparative study to do all the work at one site and then travel to the next one, unless the study is historical. This method would destroy the control of chronology. The alternative, however—to travel continuously from site to site—is expensive.

Based in Ithaca, New York, Milch made frequent trips to Montreal, Toronto, and New York City collecting parallel data simultaneously to keep the sites in phase. Only when the basic story was known at these sites did he travel to Dallas–Fort Worth, and it is regrettable that time and money did not permit a subsequent visit there to complete some missing details. Feldman, based in Bologna, Italy, travelled frequently to Rome, Milan, Paris, and London. Subsequently based in Vancouver, he worked the Vancouver site and met Milch in Ottawa. Finally, during a grant year at Harvard's Center for International Affairs, he travelled over a four-month period to Vancouver, Ottawa, London, Paris, Montreal, Milan, and Rome, bringing each story up to date and completing all details. In Milan he also employed two waves of trained graduate students so that Milan was the most thoroughly researched site. More than one third of all the interviews in the study were conducted in Italy, a measure justified by the absence of any prior studies of this kind there and the exceptional difficulty of securing basic information.

Only Dallas–Fort Worth was not visited several times, and the other seven sites were all visited during the final twelve months of data collection. Thus, data were matched constantly from site to site, notes were compared and choices were made about subsequent sets of respondents to complete the answers to outstanding questions.

Writing the Book

With extensive data collected systematically, we pondered possibilities for aggregation. We had asked essentially the same questions of numerous actors in their categories (for example, the airline presidents, government ministers, property owners, citizen activists). Here, however, we suffered from an embarrassment of riches. Our data were so detailed (the product of the in-depth interviewing techniques) that subtleties and nuances differentiated testimony in significant ways. Despite the detailed information on citizen groups, for example, we found that many generalizations had to be confined to a small number of them. Aggregation would have yielded a garland of asterisks that promised more confusion than enlightenment.

We were pleased to be able to aggregate at the level of the sites themselves. The data did lend themselves to general statements about processes and procedures, criteria, and the general behavior of actors in their discrete categories. We were able to generalize about the citizen groups, or the technocrats, or property owners, or politicians, but not with statistical precision. There were simply too many subtle differences to prevent such statistical statements from frequently misleading the reader.

Before we began this study, we had never written anything together. Two books and a half-dozen articles later, we have developed several methods. For this book we have employed them all. One of us generally has taken first crack at a chapter with the other correcting, adding, and mostly filling in from the cases he knows best. The manuscript for each chapter, drafted this way, has changed hands at least four times, and it is now almost impossible to identify who was responsible for which idea or example or assessment. We have also written shorter pieces, each taking some part, with one of us stitching it together and the other revising. Lastly, we have each taken an independent hand to a chapter, compared versions, and invited one or the other to try the second version based on which first version we preferred.

It takes longer to write a book this way than by yourself, for you are perpetually dependent on someone else's response before you can proceed. It is also more terrifying because you are constantly awaiting the scathing criticism reserved only for someone claiming co-authorship of an idea. It is, lastly, more satisfying, we think, when the final product represents consensus without compromise.

Appendix 2

CASE SYNOPSES

Dallas–Fort Worth

Chronological Synopsis

1940—Civil Aviation Authority urges Dallas and Fort Worth to build a joint airport.

1962—Civil Aeronautics Board orders investigation of existing service in the Dallas–Fort Worth area.

1965—In May, Dallas and Fort Worth sign contract to develop joint airport.

—In September, site on county line selected for facility.

1967—Dallas County voters reject referendum to create a bi-county Regional Airport Authority.

1968—Site preparation work begins.

1970—Eight airlines sign agreement pledging to move their operations to the new airport upon its completion and to accept a fee structure designed to meet all obligations of the Board.

1972—Environmental impact statement prepared.

1974—In January, airport opens for business.

—In November, Irving residents protest noise at the airport.

1980—Traffic at the new airport reaches 21.6 million passengers; fewer than 50% of passengers originate or terminate their trip in Dallas–Fort Worth area.

The Plan and Its Alternatives

A joint airport servicing both Dallas and Fort Worth was proposed initially by the federal government in 1940. Dallas, however, preferred to expand and modernize its own Love Field rather than join Fort Worth in constructing a new airport. Both fiscal incentives and pressures from the Federal Aviation Administration (FAA) and the Civil Aeronautics Board (CAB) were unsuccessful until the mid-1960s, when the threat of competition from Houston and Kansas City, both of which were engaged in building new air facilities, provoked a change of heart in Dallas. The decision to build a joint regional airport was reached in 1965, and a site—on the border of Dallas and Tarrant Counties, midway between the cities—was selected several months after the contract was signed.

No serious alternative to this plan ever was considered. Further expansion at Love Field, surrounded by urban development, would have been difficult, but the Fort Worth Airport could have been expanded to accommodate demand. Neither local authorities nor the federal government, however, was interested in a two airport system. The site of the joint airport was determined by political choice, not technical considerations; any location not on the border of the two counties was excluded by political fiat.

Key Actors

The Dallas–Fort Worth Regional Airport Board was created in 1965 as an interim managerial team pending the establishment of a bi-county public authority. The Board, however, became the permanent builder and operator of the new facility in 1968 following the defeat of the proposed authority in a referendum. The Board represents, and is responsible to, the city councils of Dallas and Fort Worth. Its executive Director, Thomas Sullivan (formerly, First Deputy Director of the Port Authority of New York and New Jersey), developed the plans for the facility with the assistance of the primary consultant, Tippetts-Abbett-McCarthy-Stratton (TAMS).

Construction of the regional airport was subsidized by the FAA, but the facility was financed largely through the sale of revenue bonds backed by the pledge of eight airlines to meet all outstanding debts through the payment of landing fees. The CAB regulated fares and determined route structures until the late 1970s; its intervention in the Dallas–Fort Worth dispute was instrumental, although not decisive, in obtaining agreement on a joint regional facility.

Citizen groups were active in opposing the expansion of Love Field (the Citizens Aviation Association) and in protesting noise at the Regional Airport (Control Aircraft Noise). No group, however, organized to oppose either the development of a joint airport or the specific site selected for the facility.

Studies

No studies appraising the need for a new airport were conducted by any party prior to the May 1965 decision. The CAB investigation, conducted between 1963 and 1965, sought to determine the utility of designating a single air facility to service the region. The study aimed at reducing waste and consolidating services; it provided no justification for a new airport. FAA forecasts were prepared routinely for all major hubs, but neither Dallas nor Fort Worth developed independent forecasts.

Three major studies were conducted by the primary consultant, TAMS, following the decision to build: a site selection study (1965), a master plan (1967), and an environmental impact statement (1972). In addition, TAMS developed forecasts in September 1965, four months after the decision, justifying need. The Joint Regional Board commissioned supplementary studies on such issues as access from the central business districts and transportation between terminals within the airport.

Land

17,500 acres of land were taken for the airport between 1965 and 1969. Nearly $60 million, an average of $3500/acre (5–7 times the going price in 1964), were spent for land acquisition. 730 people, 15 business establishments, and one community were displaced in the process.

London

Chronological Synopsis

1953—Traffic growth for London area studied under Command 8902.

1960—Hole Committee reappraises traffic projections for London area.

1963—Hole Committee recommends development of Stansted as third London international airport.

1964—Labour Government appoints Inspector to reconsider Stansted proposal.

1967—Chelmsford Inquiry concluded with Command 3259 for development of four runway international airport at Stansted; Labour Government repudiates White Paper and Stansted proposal.

1968—Labour Government appoints Royal Commission chaired by Justice Roskill to propose site for third London airport.

1970—Conservative Government receives report of Roskill Commission recommending development of Cublington and naming three other sites; Conservative Government rejects Cublington recommendation but selects coastal alternative from Roskill short-list.

1972—Maplin Development Authority established to build third London airport on Maplin Sands in the Thames River estuary east of London.

1974—Labour Government dissolves Maplin Development Authority and cancels Maplin project.
New interdepartmental study launched to assess London area air traffic requirements.

1978—Command 7084 calls for further development at Heathrow.

1979—New Conservative Government renews plan to develop Stansted.

The Plan and Its Alternatives

Several plans were prepared for a third London airport. First, there has been the possibility of development at Heathrow. Heathrow's Star of David design closes the terminal area within the runways and chokes traffic to the airport through a tunnel under a runway. The only direction available for major development beyond the runway configuration is used by the main sludge works for London, and planners have considered the obstacle immovable. Nevertheless, a fifth terminal has been planned. It is not considered enough.

A second plan called for expansion at Gatwick, which is a one-runway airport. British authorities formally decided to limit Gatwick's development and used land in the potential flight path of a second runway to guarantee that Gatwick would not grow.

London in fact is serviced by several airports, but the most important besides Heathrow and Gatwick, Luton, is owned by a county and is not included in the calculations of the British Airports Authority. Therefore, although it carries substantial charter traffic, it has never been considered formally as an alternative for development.

Stansted has the longest runway in southeast England and repeatedly has been the site favored for development by aviation enthusiasts. The 1967 plan, however, called for repositioning this runway, which effectively negated the site's principal advantage. Other main sites were Thurleigh, Nuthampstead, Foulness, and the Cublington proposal of the Roskill Commission. The main defect of the coastal site has been distance and access, but the inland sites have posed important political liabilities, especially on Conservative constituencies. Except for the 1974–1978 review, British authorities always assumed a third major airport development is required for the London area.

Key Actors

The British Airports Authority has operated and controlled the major airports in the United Kingdom since 1965. Before that time the Ministry of Aviation was directly responsible for airports. The Civil Aviation Authority has full responsibility for safety and navigation, and the Board of Trade, followed by the Department of Trade and Industry and later still the Department of the Environment, have had direct governing responsibility for BAA and the airport system. After 1976 responsibility was moved to the Department of Transport.

In addition to the various ministerial portfolios that have overseen BAA, British Rail has been responsible for rail access, especially to Gatwick and to various proposed sites for a third London airport. The Greater London Council has been responsible for proposals regarding highways. The Port of London Authority was central in the planning of Maplin Sands. The Chancellor of the Exchequer has been responsible for budget proposals concerning project development. Furthermore, there have been independent boards, including the Hole Committee and the Roskill Commission, the Chelmsford Inquiry, the Inspector, and the Interdepartmental Working Group established by Labour in 1974. Key ministers have included Roy Jenkins (Aviation), Michael Heseltine (Aviation), and Antony Crosland (Trade in 1968; Environment in 1974).

Various citizen groups, usually linked to formal amenity groups and local governments and sometimes to members of Parliament, have influenced the site selection process through public hearings. The single most effective voice was of Derrick Wood, who opposed the Maplin site; Terry (later Lord) Boston sustained the group from the Isle of Sheppey and subsequently supported Wood. Other groups formed to fight Stansted and Cublington; the major groups were the North West Essex and East Herts Preservation Association (Stansted), the Wing Airport Resistance Association (Cublington), and the Defenders of Essex (Foulness).

Studies

Each of the citizen groups commissioned or prepared on their own numerous studies, including examination of industrial development on the Isle of Sheppey and noise at Foulness and at Stansted. Each of the government proposals was backed by a separate study, including the Hole Committee, the Inspector's Report, the Chelmsford Inquiry, the Maplin Development Authority, and the Interdepartmental Review. The most comprehensive by far was prepared by the Roskill Commission, which was the most detailed cost-benefit analysis prepared anywhere.

Studies also were prepared by British Rail on access to Foulness, by the Port of London Authority on development at Foulness, and by British Airways on traffic distribution and development. British Airports Authority prepared site plans and detailed aviation forecasts; the Civil Aviation Authority studied navigation and prepared forecasts. Nowhere were more studies prepared for airport development, by more different agencies and actors, than in London.

Land

Despite designation of various sites, no project ever proceeded far enough for land to be taken.

Milan

Chronological Synopsis

1965—First expansion plans for Malpensa.

1967—SEA petition to acquire lands northeast of the airport owned by the government and leased to the helicopter manufacturer Agusta, S. pa.

Meetings of officials in Rome on SEA petition.

Petition denied; land awarded to Agusta, which then builds a golf course.

1968—SEA formulates a new expansion plan southwest of the airport including construction of a third parallel runway.

1969—In January, the Consiglio Superiore dei Lavori Pubblicci in Rome rejects SEA plan.

1970—In January, SEA revises cost estimates for expansion to 92.3 billion lire, and soon thereafter to 111.9 billion lire.

—In December, SEA's operating concession is extended 30 years.

1971—The Ferrovie dello Stato persuades the Ministry of Transport and Civil Aviation not to build a rail link to Malpensa

—In May, SEA's expansion plan is approved under Law 420. The Ufficio Tecnico Erariale of the Provincia di Varese begins evaluating property for expropriation.

—In July, expropriation of land southwest of Malpensa begins.

1972—In January, "explosion" of popular opposition to the expansion of Malpensa.

—In February, public protest meeting at the Cinema Odeon in Somma Lombardo attended by 1200 people.

—In July, major demonstration at entrance of airport led by local mayors and members of Parliament.

1973—In April, roundtable discussion and public meeting at Piccolo Teatro in Milan to protest airport on environmental grounds.

1974—In January, sixty-three property owners file suit to block expropriation; SEA publishes Libro Bianco defending policies of expansion.

1975—SEA's financial incapacity revealed; expansion stalled.

The Plan and Its Alternatives

The expansion plan at Malpensa began as the development of a cargo facility. A small parcel of land was required, and SEA hoped for a direct cost-free transfer of government property. Negotiations for the parcel obliged SEA to prepare more elaborate and more ambitious plans. When the petition for the parcel was denied, SEA had argued that expansion was imperative, and officials in Rome prodded the airport authority to expropriate land southwest of the airport for essential development.

One alternative never seriously contemplated called for the closure of Linate Airport, only seven kilometers from the Duomo in the heart of Milan, and for the transfer of all traffic to a fully developed Malpensa. A second possibility involved the absorption of growing traffic in the Milan airport system at a new airport in Bergamo. Powerful political forces began the construction and development of the airport at Bergamo despite fierce opposition from Milan and SEA.

Malpensa and Linate are both plagued by fog, but there is no apparently superior site in the Milan region. Malpensa's flight operations are constrained also by the Alps, and the airport's efficiency is hampered by its distance from Milan and poor access (no direct rail or highway). Malpensa's expansion became premised on traffic exceeding capacity at Linate, but without any transfer of operations from Linate the needs at Malpensa were difficult to prove. Through the 1970s traffic at Malpensa actually declined.

Key Actors

In addition to the Società Esercizi Aeroportuali (SEA), responsible for the Milan airports directly, SEA's shareholders govern development. They include, principally, the Commune of Milan, the Province of Milan, and the Province of Varese. Construction permits must be issued by the local communes on whose land the airport is located. SEA's financial capacity depends on the unions that influence operations and wages and on the Commune of Milan with direct responsibility for budgets. Project approval must come from the shareholders and from Rome, particularly from the Director General of Civil Aviation and the Supreme Council for Public Works.

The Milan airports must satisfy navigation and safety requirements determined by the Ispettorato Telecommunicazioni e Assistenza al Volo (ITAV), and operations must be approved by the Ministry of Defense. Access is controlled by the Region of Lombardy, the Province of Varese, the Ferrovie Nord Milano (formerly a private railroad acquired by the regional government), and the Milanese tram and subway systems (ATM and MM). Alitalia, as principal user of the Milan airports and a state-owned airline, is exceptionally influential in setting fees and rates that affect SEA's revenues, although the Director-General for Civil Aviation and the Chamber of Deputies are officially responsible. Because many activities are governed by legislation (including subsidies to various airports, planning approvals, construction licenses, fees), the *correnti* (factions) of the Christian Democratic Party can be decisive.

Other central actors in the Milan case include Italia Nostra and the World Wildlife Federation, who joined the opposition to development by defending environmental interests. All the local communes were involved, including especially Lonate Pozzolo, Somma Lombardo, and Ferno. The Comitato d'Agitazione di Case Nuove, which was formed by the government of a neighborhood in Somma Lombardo, was the leading protest group.

Studies

SEA produced a major two-volume study, *Adequamento del Sistema Aeroportuale Milanese—Aeroporto Malpensa Sud-Ovest*, and various smaller studies supporting development. Forecasts were prepared by the Battelle Institute (Geneva) in 1974, by S.O.M.E.A. in 1968, and in the 1970s by the Centro Sviluppo Transporti Aerei, Alitalia, and the Director-General's Office for Civil Aviation.

The Lino report prepared for the Italian Government in 1972 reviewed the national airport system and recommended national subsidies. Dillon-Read reviewed SEA's financial situation in 1975; Aéroport de Paris prepared a noise study for the Province of Varese in 1974, following a similar study by the Commune of Milan in December 1973. The Lombardy Region assessed the overall plan in July 1973. Access studies were done by the Region of Lombardy, by the Commune of Milan (July 1971), by the Castiglione Commission (1972), and by SEA. An assessment financed by Italia Nostra was prepared by Stefano Nespor in 1975.

Land

The southwest site expropriated by SEA covered 3707 acres and involved 139 owners. Top price paid was $1862/acre, although owners claimed land was worth between $7700/acre and $9700/acre. Sixty-three owners organized to sue, but they ultimately lost their case. The evaluations were done in 1971; most of the land was possessed by SEA by 1976.

Montreal

Chronological Synopsis

1966—Kates, Peat, Marwick (KPM) employed by Ministry of Transport to examine air facility requirements in the Montreal area.

1968—Government announces plans to replace Dorval with a new airport.

1969—Ste. Scholastique and surrounding communities selected for airport development over objections of provincial government; 88,000 acres expropriated.

1970—Additional land expropriated when planners discover that they have no adequate site for runways.

1973—Residents of expropriated territory conduct angry marches in Ottawa and Ste. Scholastique to protest compensation procedures.

1975—In April, control over peripheral lands (80,000 acres) transferred from Ministry of Transport to Department of Public Works and Ministry of State for Urban Affairs.

—In October, Mirabel receives first passengers.

1980—Traffic at Mirabel reaches 1.5 million passengers, far below expectations.

The Plan and Its Alternatives

Plans for a major new airport in the Montreal region were generated by consultants in 1968 as an alternative to facility expansion. Although Dorval Airport on the western side of Montreal Island was not congested, government planners sought to develop additional infrastructure in anticipation of growing demand for air services. The consultants argued that economic considerations dictated immediate development of a new airport elsewhere in the metropolitan area rather than the expansion of the existing facility.

The plan was accepted readily by all parties, but site selection proved controversial. Government planners preferred a site west of Montreal because of its proximity to the air travel market; provincial officials favored a location east of Montreal to promote economic development. The "compromise" site, Ste. Scholastiques (north of Montreal), was unacceptable to provincial authorities but the federal government overrode their objections and acted unilaterally to implement development plans.

The original proposal approved by the Cabinet in August 1968 envisioned the closing of Dorval upon completion of the new airport (called Mirabel). The government has been reluctant to close the more convenient Dorval, however, and it has continued to carry the bulk of air travellers from Montreal through 1980. Demand has been so slack that both facilities are operating well below capacity.

Key Actors

The Air Administration of the Ministry of Transport (MOT) owns and operates all important air facilities in Canada. Plans for the new Mirabel Airport were developed ostensibly by a special project team from the Air Administration, the Bureau d'aménagement du nouvel aéroport internationale à Montréal (BANAIM). Outside consultants, however, played a critical role in persuading the Cabinet to build a new air facility, selecting the site, and overseeing development at Mirabel. Kates, Peat, Marwick (KPM) developed preliminary plans, and Philip Beinhaker, the principal consultant to BANAIM, directed the planning team during its early stages and negotiated with the Quebec government for a suitable site.

Provincial officials exercise no formal role in airport development, but their cooperation is valuable in assuring ground access. While MOT was prepared to ignore provincial concerns in site selection, the newly established federal Department of Regional Economic Expansion (DREE) urged them to negotiate. A special task force, headed by Benjamin Higgins, recommended Ste. Scholastique as a compromise.

A Comité des Expropriés was created in Ste. Scholastique in 1969 to assist residents in adjusting to change. The *comité*, however, was transformed into the militant Centre d'information et d'animation communautaire (CIAC) several years later when residents discovered that the government had been far more generous to land owners in Toronto than in Montreal.

Studies

Studies favoring the development of a new air facility in Montreal were prepared by consultants in 1968. No formal report was prepared by MOT in conjunction with site selection, but the special task force, established and financed by DREE, produced a report recommending the selection of Ste. Scholastique. The Quebec government established its own task force that prepared a report challenging the conclusions of the federal study. Still other studies were produced by BANAIM on a number of topics relevant to airport development during the period 1969–1974.

Land

88,000 acres of land, or 135 square miles, were expropriated in April 1969 by MOT (another 10,000 acres were taken later in two separate acquisitions). Over 3000 families and 10,000 individuals were affected. Both the procedures employed in the land taking and the prices offered by the government were resented by local residents. Despite a modest increase in these offers, the government was unwilling to extend the benefits of the new Expropriation Act to Quebec residents. Property owners received, on the average, $210/acre for their land.

New York

Chronological Synopsis

1957—Preliminary studies for a fourth New York jetport initiated by the Port Authority.

1959—Port Authority reveals intention to build a new facility in the Great Swamp of Morris County, New Jersey.

1960—New Jersey Legislature approves a bill prohibiting the development of a major commercial airport in northern New Jersey; governor vetoes legislation.

1961—Port Authority publishes multi-volume study justifying both the need for further development and the choice of the Morris County site.

1966—Port Authority issues report reaffirming the need for a fourth jetport in Morris County.

1969—Election of Governor William Cahill, a confirmed opponent of the proposed Morris County airport, persuades the Port Authority to seek a new site.

1970—Proposed expansion of Kennedy Airport criticized by National Academy of Sciences; Stewart Air Force Base deeded to the State of New York.

1971—New York State legislature authorizes expenditure of $70 million for acquisition of land and airport development at Stewart.

1972—FAA instructs New York to prepare Environmental Impact Statement for Stewart project.

1973—In April, master plan for Stewart Airport, calling for a $1 billion expansion and development project, released.
 —In December, Governor Nelson Rockefeller resigns.

1974—Stewart development plans scaled down by Rockefeller's successor, Malcolm Wilson.

The Plan and Its Alternatives

The Port Authority's plans for aviation infrastructure in the New York metropolitan area called for development of a fourth jetport on a 10,000 acre site in rural Morris County, New Jersey. Numerous sites were identified in the various studies undertaken by the Port Authority, but only the Morris County site was acceptable to Executive Director Austin Tobin. State officials in both New

York and New Jersey preferred other locations within their re-spective states. Their inability to agree on an acceptable site per-mitted the Port Authority to resist pressure for airport develop-ment elsewhere in the metropolitan area.

One alternative to the development of a new airport in the New York area was to restrict use of the three major airports to com-mercial aircraft and to develop general aviation facilities in other parts of the region. This proposal was advanced by the airlines in 1965 but rejected peremptorily by the Port Authority. A version of this plan, nevertheless, was put into effect by the FAA for several months in 1968.

A second alternative proposed by the Port Authority itself in 1970 was to expand Kennedy Airport. This approach, however, was rejected when a study by the National Academy of Sciences suggested that expansion would harm the ecology of the bay.

The final proposal for New York was to develop Stewart Airport in Newburgh. Land was acquired and plans drawn up, but the proposal died when the demand for air services in the New York area slackened in the mid-1970s.

Key Actors

The Port Authority of New York and New Jersey, created in 1921 by a compact between the two states, assumed responsibility in the late 1940s for the operation of Newark and La Guardia Airports and the completion of Idlewild (Kennedy). All three facilities had been built originally by local governments. The Port Authority gained exclusive right to build any additional commercial airports in the New York metropolitan area, but Port Authority programs require the approval of the legislatures and governors of both New York and New Jersey. Bondholders, moreover, exercise consid-erable influence in determining Port Authority policies.

The Metropolitan Transportation Authority (MTA) was estab-lished by the state of New York in 1968 to operate bridges, tunnels, commuter railroads, and other transportation facilities in the New York metropolitan area. Its charter included the operation of gen-eral aviation facilities, and it assumed control of Stewart Airport from the US Air Force in 1970. Unlike the Port Authority, the MTA answered only to Albany. It operated as the personal in-strument of Governor Nelson Rockefeller until his resignation in 1973.

Airport development in U.S. cities is controlled by local governments but is supervised and subsidized by the FAA. Flight operations at civilian air fields also are under the jurisdiction of the FAA. The Department of the Interior, which accepted a donation of land in the Great Swamp to establish a wildlife preserve, was the only other federal agency to become involved directly in the development of air facilities in the New York area. Both federal and state courts, however, participated in the resolution of the conflict at Stewart.

The principal citizen groups involved in controversies over airport development were the Jersey Jetport Site Association (Morris County site) and the Hudson River Valley Council (Stewart site). Many local and county government officials and several environmental groups opposed development, but public officials, particularly in the Stewart area, were not unanimous in their opposition to development.

Studies

The Port Authority issued three major studies during the decade of controversy. The 1959 and 1966 studies were conducted in house; the 1961 study involved both outside consultants and in-house technical studies. In addition, several smaller reports reviewing alternative development sites were prepared by the Port Authority at the request of the governors of New York and New Jersey. The MTA employed Trans-Plan, Inc. and Seelye Stevenson Value and Knecht to prepare a master plan for Stewart airport. The consultants' ambitious proposals never were adopted, and a second and more modest study was commissioned from the Dallas–Fort Worth planners several years later. An Environmental Impact Statement for Stewart was prepared by Landrum and Brown.

Other major studies prepared for New York include: the National Academy of Sciences' report on the expansion of Kennedy; the Metropolitan Airlines Committee report advocating the transfer of general aviation to Teterboro Airport in New Jersey; the report of the Metropolitan Commuter Transportation Authority (the MTA's predecessor) recommending Calverton on Long Island as the site for a fourth jetport; and several studies and forecasts by the FAA and the Regional Plan Association. In addition, the Jersey Jetport Site Association commissioned three studies of air facility requirements and Orange County (N.Y.) contracted with a consultant firm to measure noise levels around Stewart Airport.

Land

The MTA expropriated 8076 acres of land adjacent to Stewart Airport in 1971, displacing 337 home owners and 1200 people. Despite strong opposition, only 75 homeowners went to court to obtain a better price for their land. The rest appeared satisfied by government offers that averaged $4643/acre.

Paris

Chronological Synopsis

1957—District of Paris proposes closing Le Bourget for park land and offers Aéroport de Paris larger land parcel further north of Paris; Aéroport de Paris accepts the proposal.

1959—Plans are leaked and inhabitants of local communities try to organize resistance.

1963—Plans officially announced with designation of Paris-Nord site; Declaration of Public Utility freezes all land within site and acquisition procedures launched.

1965—Less than 1% of land acquired through voluntary sale; expropriation begins.

1967—Land acquisition completed; ground broken for construction of first runway and Terminal I.

1968—Aéroport de Paris meets for the first time with Air France, and with the national railroad (SNCF), concerning terminal design and access, respectively.

1971—Groupe du Travail Paris-Nord, including the SNCF and the Métro authority (RATP), conclude necessity for rail line and foresee possible abandonment of plans for *aérotrain*.

1972—Due date for opening airport passes.

1974—Terminal I opens; Roissy-Rail construction begins.

1976—In May, Roissy-Rail opens.

1978—Due date for Terminal II passes; rescheduled for 1981.

1980—Traffic for whole Paris system less than 50% of original projection justifying construction of Charles de Gaulle Airport.

The Plan and Its Alternatives

The premise for the construction of Charles de Gaulle Airport was that Paris would be served by two international airports, one north and one south of the city. Initially the District of Paris wanted to close Le Bourget, north of the city, to create more green space. Later, Aéroport de Paris developed a rationale about traffic growth to justify construction of a major facility that would exceed in size and capacity Orly Airport (which opened in 1960). Aéroport de Paris also continued to operate at Le Bourget into the 1980s.

No alternative either for development in general or for the site in particular was ever contemplated seriously. Nevertheless, Charles de Gaulle Airport does have problems with fog, and adequate road access will not be in place for more than a decade after the airport's opening. Poor planning prevented construction of a rail line until after the airport opened for business, and Orly and Charles de Gaulle Airports will not be linked by public transportation before the mid-1980s.

Key Actors

The key actor is Aéroport de Paris, an autonomous public agency that controls its own budget and is backed by the powers of the French state, including the power to expropriate land for public utility and the capacity to borrow money at the state's rates of interest. The authority must answer to a *tutelle* in the Ministry of Transport and Civil Aviation, but Aéroport de Paris is far better staffed and financed and therefore is effectively free of supervision. Although support from the District of Paris was required for final site designation, once the land was taken the District (later the Region) had no effective authority over ADP.

Access must be provided by the Minister of Equipment (roads), the SNCF (rail), or the RATP (if the Métro were to be linked to the airport directly). The Ministry of Finance was to control setting prices for land acquisition, but the Minister overruled his bureaucrats for political reasons. Air France has considerable influence over actual airport operations, but influenced almost not at all the airport's development. Other airlines rely on Air France as a spokesman.

The mayors of Goussainville and Roissy-en-France attempted without success to influence development, as did various small local groups of citizens. They did not prove of consequence in the Paris airport story.

Studies

All studies were done in house by Aéroport de Paris.

Land

Expropriation took place in two phases between 1964 and 1967. In the first acquisition, 7104 acres were purchased at an average of $3000/acre. An additional 277 acres were taken at an average of $4800/acre. There were 53 major owners of 587 parcels, with only one home located on the entire site.

Toronto

Chronological Synopsis

1966—Parkin and Associates employed by Ministry of Transport to examine air facility requirements in the Toronto area.

1968—In August, Cabinet endorses plan for Malton expansion.
   —In December, Cabinet reverses policy, approves development of a new airport.

1972—In March, Pickering Township selected as site for new Toronto airport.
   —In November, expropriation hearings held in Toronto.

1973—Cabinet confirms expropriation but announces delay in project implementation pending review.

1974—Airport Inquiry Commission hearings and report.

1975—In February, Cabinet announces intention to develop "minimum international airport" in Pickering.
   —In September, Ontario government withdraws from project; Federal Cabinet votes to shelve development plans.

The Plan and Its Alternatives

Two plans were prepared for airport development in Toronto. One called for the expansion of Malton, including the expropriation of 3000 acres of land near the airport; the other advocated the development of a new facility to supplement Malton. Both plans were approved by the Canadian government: the first in August 1968, and the second four months later. Although the latter choice remained government policy until the project was abandoned in 1975, Malton expansion always was a viable alternative for many technical experts in the Ministry of Transport and for other interested parties in the controversy.

The site for the proposed airport, Pickering Township (east of Toronto), was not selected until March 1972. Indeed, Pickering was not even considered a serious alternative until the summer of 1971. Four other sites were studied exhaustively by government planners and rejected before this compromise site was selected.

One alternative never considered seriously was the "Kingston Plan," proposed in 1967 by a consultant to the Ministry of Transport. That plan called for a single airport to service Toronto and Montreal from a site in Eastern Ontario. The plan had technical flaws but was rejected for political reasons.

Key Actors

Development plans in Toronto, as in Montreal and Vancouver, were the responsibility of the Air Administration of the Ministry of Transport (MOT). Once the political decision to build a new air facility was reached, a special planning group, the Toronto Area Airports Project (TAAP) was established within MOT to develop specific proposals, select an appropriate site, and manage construction. The provincial government appointed a team of civil servants to work with TAAP, and the newly established (federal) Ministry of State for Urban Affairs (MSUA) sought to influence the selection of sites. Three individuals were particularly influential in fashioning plans for the air facility: Paul Hellyer, the Minister of Transport who rejected the expansion of Malton; his successor Don Jamieson, who selected the Pickering site; and Philip Beinhaker, the primary consultant to TAAP.

The expansion of Malton was opposed by several citizen groups, including the Society for Aircraft Noise Abatement (SANA) and New Airport Now (NAN). Opposition to the Pickering project was led by People or Planes (POP) and the Metropolitan Toronto Airport Review Committee (MTARC). Pickering opponents supported the expansion of Malton, while Malton opponents sought development at any other site in the metropolitan area.

The controversy involved two *ad hoc* institutional mechanisms, the Expropriation Hearings in 1972, and the Airport Inquiry Commission in 1974. Neither proved decisive in resolving the conflict. Ontario Premier William Davis was more influential in determining the final result. His decision in September 1975 to end provincial cooperation encouraged Transport Minister Jean Marchand to recommend shelving the project.

Studies

The only study on airport development prepared prior to the December 1968 announcement was the Parkin Plan, which advocated the expansion of Malton. Neither Parkin's forecasts nor those of MOT supported the construction of a new airport. The TAAP team produced numerous small reports, including revised forecasts justifying the decision to build, but MSUA sponsored a study by Llewelyn, Davies (the results of which were suppressed) questioning the utility of additional construction. TAAP forecasts also were questioned in the Hodge Report, a study on the regional impact of airport development sponsored by the Ontario Department of Treasury and Economics.

The selection of the Pickering site was not supported by any formal studies when the announcement was made in March 1972, but the TAAP team prepared subsequently a number of reports justifying the choice. Although citizen groups contested this decision, only one (MTARC) commissioned any outside studies (a public opinion survey). The others utilized expertise from within their own groups or were content to prepare public relations materials. One additional study was prepared by the Airport Inquiry Commission in 1974; its report advocated the development of Pickering as well as the expansion of Malton.

Land

The Department of Public Works (DPW), acting on behalf of MOT, acquired 18,000 acres, principally in Pickering Township. The land belonged to 717 property owners who were compensated well by the federal government. Land owners exploited a new and more generous expropriation law to force the government to increase payments, and approximately two-thirds of the owners received a sum 45% higher than the original government offer. Compensation averaged $8110/acre.

Vancouver

Chronological Synopsis

1953—City of Vancouver prepares report suggesting all of Sea Island become an airport.

1954—Government of Canada expropriates 1102 acres adjacent to city airport, including homes recently built by Veterans Land Administration.

1962—City of Vancouver sells airport to Government of Canada.

1965—Government of Canada acquires additional 550 acres on Sea Island through single purchase.

1967—Transport Minister Jack Pickersgill declares federal intention to buy remaining property on Sea Island for airport; invitation issued for voluntary sales.

1968—Municipality of Richmond, legal jurisdiction for Sea Island, ceases issuing building permits to freeze property, in compliance with federal request.

1970—Expropriation Act passed by Canadian Parliament; Sea Island residents appeal for protection under the Act.

1972—Charles Johnstone, attorney for the Sea Island Ratepayers Association, negotiates land acquisition agreement with Peter Troop, Assistant Deputy Attorney General; "Troop Formula" rejected by federal government.

1973—In January–February, expropriation hearings for land in community of Burkeville (for planned bridge to Sea Island) and remaining veterans' subdivisions for parallel runway construction.

—In March, tri-level meeting in British Columbia postpones decision to build new airport infrastructure six months, pending formation of study; agreement reached to establish Airport Planning Committee (APC) that will include public participation.

—In April, Minister of Transport confirms expropriations.

—In summer, APC formed.

—In November, Citizens Forum (renamed later Community Forum) joins APC; final decision on runway and development plan postponed until completion of report by APC.

1974—Expropriated property possessed by federal government.

1975—Department of the Environment issues independent study calling for freeze on all development activity in Fraser River estuary pending detailed ecological studies.

—Ministry of Transport revises runway proposal, shortening required length from 11,000 feet to 10,600 feet (and later to 9500 and then to 9250); proposal conforms to DOE concern not to breach a dyke in the estuary.

1976—APC issues studies and reports; federal government remands issues to Environmental Assessment Review Panel.

1979—Ministry of Transport issues Master Plan for airport; calls for short parallel runway in the future and immediate study for reopening nearby airport at Boundary Bay for general aviation.

1980—Boundary Bay proposal sent to Environmental Assessment Review Panel; no development takes place on Sea Island.

The Plan and Its Alternatives

The plan for a parallel runway on Sea Island came about from pressure to acquire land. Forecasts and technical justifications followed. Therefore, no site search had taken place and no alternatives to development on Sea Island had been contemplated.

Once the proposal for development was offered, consideration was given to expansion of the airport at Abbottsford (rejected as too distant—65 miles—from Vancouver). Demands were made by some participants in the APC for reconsideration of the entire runway need on the basis of altering forecast assumptions. The main alternative, however, was a proposal for a shortened runway. MOT first held that the 11,000-foot runway was technically essential. When this proposal was criticized on environmental grounds, MOT offered a series of compromises reducing the length, eventually saying there would be no significant technical sacrifice.

The final alternative was for the reopening of a facility at Boundary Bay for general aviation, which sometimes represents more than 50% of the aircraft movements at Vancouver International. MOT does not accept this proposal as a long-term alternative to runway construction on Sea Island, but rather as a temporary measure.

Key Actors

The planning agency for development on Sea Island is the Air Administration of the Ministry of Transport. They have been supported by the Corporate Planning Division responsible for forecasting and by a succession of ministers of transport. The Municipality of Richmond, economically dependent on the airport, and the B. C. Aviation Council, representing general aviation, have supported MOT's expansion proposals, and quieter support was offered most of the time by CP Air as spokesman for the commercial airlines.

Other federal agencies central to the development plans were the Ministry of Justice, responsible for the rules governing expropriation; the Property Services Branch of MOT (the Real Property Division of the Department of Public Works after passage of the 1970 Expropriation Act) for expropriation; the Ministry of State for Urban Affairs that sided with local interests; the Department of the Environment that questioned the ecological safety of the runway plans. Three members of Parliament (Tom Goode, John Fraser, and John Reynolds) were prominent at various stages, as were three ministers in the federal government from British Columbia (Jack Davis in Environment, Ron Basford in MSUA, and Arthur B. Laing in Public Works).

The Greater Vancouver Regional District was the leader in establishing the APC, where their studies and participation were led by Nancy Cooley and Gordon Stead. The Sea Island Ratepayers Association was central to the protest over expropriation; the Noise Abatement League, and later the Community Forum, spearheaded citizen protest over the runway plans. John Creery led the former organization; James Tyhurst was the most prominent member of Community Forum.

Studies

The 1954 study prepared by the City of Vancouver is no longer on record. The Ministry of Transport issued "Vancouver International Airport Capacity-Demand Analysis for Selected Runway Configuration" in November 1971, a report that was contradicted by a second MOT study issued in October 1972, "An Analysis of the Vancouver International Runway System with Reference to the Requirement for a Parallel Runway 08L-26R."

A variety of expert witnesses testified at the expropriations hearings, offering results from numerous small studies. A community study was prepared on the impact of the new bridge on Burkeville. The Department of the Environment assessment begun by Charles

Hutton was the first major evaluation introduced into the decision process, followed by major studies commissioned and performed by the APC. MOT's efforts, apart from forecasts prepared in the Corporate Planning Division, were channelled through the APC until the master plan was issued in 1979.

Land

There are approximately 4000 acres on Sea Island. The federal government bought 450 acres from the City of Vancouver in 1962, including the runways and existing terminal. The federal government expropriated 1102 acres in 1954, purchased 550 acres in 1965 from Webb and Knapp (who had acquired this land in 1956 from Arthur B. Laing and Dal Grauer), and then proceeded through a voluntary purchase program to seek the remaining land outside the community of Burkeville beginning in 1967.

There were 650 residents in the path of voluntary sales and subsequent expropriation after 1967. By November 1976 the federal government had spent $9,515,000 acquiring this land. It is impossible to specify acreage values because most of the land involved homes of different character and value (government compensation ranged from $35,000 to $75,000), and there was also farm land, both working and fallow. All the residents except a holdout farmer, Lester Grauer (who had been expropriated in 1954), had departed by 1978.

INDEX

Abbottsford, British Columbia, 276
Adams, Carolyn Teich, 35n, 63n
Adams, John G. U., 64n, 150n
Administration des Domaines (France), 106, 160, 173
Administration Fiscale (France), 162
ADP (*see* Aeroport de Paris)
Aéroport de Paris (ADP)
  in access planning, xl, 120
  on Aerotrain transit, 144
  aviation forecasts by, 81, 84n
  and Charles de Gaulle Airport, 92, 93
  and citizen opposition, 206
  compensation agreement by, 162
  as consultant, 94, 119, 136, 138, 143, 260
  coordination by, 269
  in decision process, 107t
  development rationale by, 269
  and economic development, xli–xlii
  in expropriation, 160, 162–163
  inconsistency of, 232
  in land acquisition, 106, 108, 269
  objectives of, 59
  powers of, 108, 114, 270
  public relations campaign of, 205
  and role of experts, 134, 135
  state subsidization of, 60
  studies by, 94, 138, 260, 270
Aerotrain, 144
Agusta, S. pa. (Italian helicopter manufacturer), 258
Airbus, 7, 44
Air Administration (*see* Ministry of Transport, Canada)

Air Canada, 196
Air France, 269
Airport authorities, 134
Airport construction (*see also* Airport development) effectiveness of, 230
  forces behind, 230
  land acquisition for, 54–55
  vs. market solutions, 49–50
  objectives in, 114
  vs. other options, 23, 50–51, 230
  site selection for, 51–54
  as universal, 23
Airport development (*see also* Airport construction; Case studies; *specific cases of airport development*)
  and business mentality, 59–62, 225, 226
  causes of, 44
  and consumer demand, 49, 90–92, 114
  controversy over, 44–45, 235
  cross-sectoral problems in, 113
  and democratic rights, 181–182, 211–215
  economic factors in, 58, 61, 90
  as escaping business discipline, 60, 61
  flexibility in, 230–231
  forecasting in, 70–71
  groups supporting, 57–58
  narrow focus of, 122, 229–230
  need for, 48
  popularity of, 44
  and public interest, 61
  and rational planning, 225, 226
  stages in, 46–55

systematic characteristics of, 48–49
technocrats in, 132, 134, 135–136, 137–138
and technological imperative, 225
Airport Inquiry Commission (Toronto), 272, 273
and construction delay, 208
in decision process, 107t
establishment of, 201n
and experts, 137–138, 146–147
as opposition forum, 200
and protestors' divisions, 204
study by, 274
Toronto representation at, 194
Airport Planning Committee (APC) (Vancouver)
and citizen participation, 208, 234
in decision process, 107t
establishment of, 275, 277
and expertise, 194
as opposition forum, 200
participatory democracy in, 214
studies by, 88, 276, 278
Airports
criteria for judging of, xl–xli
and economic growth, xli–xlii
investment in, 7
and property values, xli
size of, 8
urban encroachment on, xlii
Airports, international (*see also* Airport development; Case studies; *specific airports*)
access to, xl
forces behind, xx
impact of, xx–xxi
investment influence of, viii
as public works, viii–ix
and role of experts, xx
symbolism in, viii
technology in, 43
Air travel, growth in, 46, 47t, 48
Alitalia
aviation forecasts by, 77, 87, 260
and SEA revenues, 260
Allison, Graham, 36n, 103, 104
Almond, Gabriel, 24, 35n, 217, 218
American Municipal Association, 48

American Society of Planning Officials, 48
Armstrong, J. Scott, 68
Association of European Airports, and differential pricing, 124
ATM (*see* Aziende Trasporti Milanese)
Autoroute du Nord (Paris), 120
Aviation industry, 7
Aviation infrastructure (*see* Airports)
Aviation technology (*see* Technology)
Aziende Trasporti Milanese (ATM), xl, 111t, 244, 260

BAA (*see* British Airports Authority)
Bacon, Francis, 33n, 140
Banfield, Edward C., 24, 217, 218
Barbados, new airport in, 9, 119
Basford, Ron, 277
Battelle Memorial Institute, 87, 260
Beer, Samuel, 33n, 36n
Beinhaker, Philip, 98n, 137, 148, 263, 273
Bell, Daniel, 4, 23, 150n
Bergamo, Italy, 244, 259
Berry, Jeffrey, 215
Birnbaum, Pierre, 30
Block, Jacques, 83
Board of Trade (U.K.)
in decision process, 107t, 112
responsibility of, 255
Boeing Aircraft, 87, 234
B-1 bomber, 45
Boorer, N. W., 97n
Boston, Terry (Lord Boston), 188, 256
Boundary Bay, B.C., 123, 276
Bourassa, Robert, 94
Britain (*see* United Kingdom)
British Airports Authority (BAA)
in decision process, 107t
demand met by, 124
forecasts by, 75
and improvement in forecasting, 94
in international competition, 44
and Luton Airport, 255
objectives of, 59
pricing mechanism of, 230
responsibility of, 255
role of experts in, 134, 136

and soundproofing of homes, 184*n*
state subsidization of, 60
studies by, 256
British Airways, 256
British Association for the Control of
    Aircraft Noise (BACAN), 195
British Columbia, xl, 110, 277
British Rail, 255, 256
Bureau d'aménagement du nouvel
    aéroport internationale à Montréal
    (BANAIM), 263
Bureaucrats (*see also* Rational plan-
    ning; Technocrats)
    and citizen protest, 172–173,
        174–175, 213–214
    and conflict, 103–104, 114, 226
    and decision making, 30
    and technocracy, 125
    and upholding of law, 172–173
Burkeville, B. C.
    bridge for, 277
    and expropriation, 168, 275
    as land-taking exception, 278
Business mentality
    and absence of market discipline,
        60, 61, 225
    and airport development, 59–62,
        225, 226
    in expropriation, 178, 227
    and justice, 125
    and public interest, 123, 225, 238
    and rational planning, 122–123,
        125–126, 225
    and social costs, 59
    in "technical" choice, xliv
    vs. technological imperative, 60–62

Cafik, Norman, 201*n*
Cahill, William, 265
Calverton, Long Island, 267
Canada
    citizen advisory committees in, 199
    citizen participation in, 218
    citizen protest in, 160
    compensation in, 158, 232
    consulting industry in, 135
    control of air facilities in, 133
    decision making in, 30, 107*t*

expropriation in, 161*t*, 177
land-taking strategy in, 172
law and property in, 176
protest channels in, 198
role of experts in, 31
Canada, government of
    ADP as consultant to, 136
    airport responsibility in, 10–11, 56
    coordination in, 104
    in decision making, 110
    economic promises by, 94, 120
    and experts' conflict, 146–147
    in expropriation, 274
    and Toronto compensation, 170
Canada, Ministry of Transport (*see*
    Ministry of Transport (Canada))
Canadian Pacific Air, 277
Caproni brothers, 171, 199
Carey, Bernard, 127*n*, 128*n*
Case studies (*see also specific cases*)
    choice of, for this book, 9–11
    cross-national, 28–29, 42–43
    Dallas-Fort Worth airport develop-
        ment, 11–12, 251–253
    issues addressed by, 30–33
    London airport development, 12–13,
        254–257
    methodology of, 241–249
    Milan airport development, 13–14,
        258–261
    Montreal airport development,
        14–16, 262–264
    New York airport development,
        16–17, 265–268
    overall summary, 225–227
    Paris airport development, 18,
        269–271
    preparation of, for this book, 29–30,
        34*n*
    rationale for, 28–29
    Toronto airport development, 19,
        272–274
    Vancouver airport development,
        20–21, 274–278
Castiglione Commission (Italy), 260
Central park, xi–xiii
Centre d'information et d'animation
    communautaire (Montreal), 185*n*,

186*t*, 188, 191*t*, 192, 193*t*, 194,
195*t*, 263
Centro Sviluppo Transporti Aerei, 87,
260
C-5A, 45
Chaban-Delmas, Jacques, 144
Chamber of Deputies (Italy), 111*t*, 260
Chambers of Commerce (French), 10
Chancellor of the Exchequer (U.K.),
256
Chapman, John W., 178*n*, 179*n*
Charles de Gaulle Airport (*see also*
Paris airport development)
access to, xl, 120
capacity of, 118*n*
and division of traffic, 118
faults of, xxxix–xl, 108, 120, 230,
270
map of, 18, 121
rail competition for, 229
size of, 8
and transportation costs, xli
virtues of, xxxix
Chelmsford Inquiry (London), 198,
201, 254, 256
Christian Democratic Party (Italy), 260
Ciampino Airport, Rome, xlii
Citizen action groups (*see also* specific
protest groups; Citizen protest)
creation of, 263
and expertise, 142, 194, 195*t*
funding for, 193*t*, 194
membership of, 185*n*
resources of, 192
impact of, 207, 208, 209, 214
organization of, 190–191
and media, 206
strategy of, 194, 197, 198, 199, 200,
201, 204, 205
leadership of, 190, 210
and coalition-building, 204
vs. pro-airport groups, 189, 196
goals of, 189, 204
claims of, 207
studies for, 201*n*, 267, 274
and terminal arguments, 201
complaints of, 206
as minority, 201–202
allies of, 194–196

case summaries of, 22*t*, 186*t*, 191*t*,
193*t*
Citizen participation
cross-country comparison of, 31
determinants of, 23–24
and experts, xix, xx
iucrease in, xix–xx, 31
inviting of, 234
and technology, two views on, 3–4
Citizen protest (*see also specific
protest groups*; Citizen action
groups)
and decision making, 184–185,
213–215
determinants of, 25, 173, 234
and environmental interests, 155
and equity, 183–184, 211–213
expropriation as spur to, 175,
177–178
extent of, 187–188
and forecasting, 88
through formal participation,
197–199
forms of, 181
government responses to, 204–207
impact of, 181, 207–209, 227
through informal participation,
199–200
internal conflict in, 204
international nature of, 210
by landowners, 155–156
makeup of, 185–187, 189, 202
objectives of, 188–189
and political theory, 25, 215–219
rationale for, 233–234
and rational planning, 122
resources of, 192, 193*t*, 194
and role of civil servants, 213–214
strategies of, 197–200
treatment of, in this book, xliii, xliv,
31–32
universality of, 23–24
use of experts by, 132–142, 194
variation in, 155
Citizen protest, response to
misunderstanding in, 182
Citizens Aviation Association (CAA)
(Dallas), 186*t*, 190, 191*t*, 194,
195*t*, 197, 253

Citizens Committee Against the
Airport (Ontario), 188, 191*t*, 193*t*,
195*t*
Citizens Forum (Vancouver), 275 (*see
also* Community Forum)
Citizens Jetport Committee (New
Jersey), 186*t*, 188, 189, 191*t*,
193*t*, 195*t*, 204
Civil Aeronautics Board (CAB)
authority of, 242
and Dallas–Fort Worth airport, 251,
252
investigation by, 253
Civil aviation, 228–235, 238*n*
Civil Aviation Authority (CAA) (U.K.)
forecasts by, 75, 87, 256
responsibility of, 255
Civil Aviation Authority (U.S.), 251
Cobb, Roger W., 216
Comitato d'Agitazione di Case Nuovo
(Milan), 186*t*, 191*t*, 193*t*, 195*t*,
199, 260
Comitato Popolare di Lonate Pozzolo
(CPLI) (Milan), 186*t*, 191*t*, 192,
193*t*, 195*t*
Comité de défense des riverains de
Roissy (Paris), 186*t*, 189, 191*t*,
193*t*, 195*t*, 196, 200, 206
Comite des Expropries (Montreal) (*see*
Centre d'information et
d'animation communautaire)
Communes, Italy, 111*t*
Communist Party (France), 108, 196
Community Forum (Vancouver) (*see
also* Citizens Forum), 186*t*, 191,
191*t*, 193*t*, 194, 195*t*, 201, 208,
214, 277
Comparative politics, 25–26, 28–29, 30
Compensation (*see also* Expropriation)
in Dallas-Fort Worth, 163–164, 171*t*
as expropriation principle, 157–158
in Milan, 171, 171*t*, 232, 261
in Montreal, 166, 171*t*, 172–173,
264
in New York, 165, 171*t*, 268
in Paris, xli, 160–162, 171*t*, 173,
232, 271
for partial expropriation, 184
and technical expertise, 175

in Toronto, 169–170, 171*t*, 172, 207
in Vancouver, 171*n*, 173
Compensation Review Committee
(Toronto), 170
Compulsory purchase (*see*
Expropriation)
Concorde
and international competition, 44
and noise forecasting, 84
Condemnation (*see* Expropriation)
Conflict
avoidance of, 235
and development outcomes,
109–112, 114
and experts, 139, 146–147, 227
and liberal democracy, 236–239
organizational bases of, 103, 109
and rational planning, 103–104, 106,
226, 238
Consiglio Superiore dei Lavori Pubblicci (Italy), 258
Consumer demand, 114
Control Aircraft Noise (CAN)
(Dallas–Fort Worth), 186*t*, 188,
191*t*, 192, 193*t*, 195*t*, 197, 206, 253
Convergence theory, 22, 41–42
Cooley, Nancy, 277
Coordination, 103–104
Cost
of airline operation, 7
of expertise, 147
of government-owned land, 143
Cost-benefit analysis
in airport development, 225
as public works criterion, xix
sectoral approach to, 27
in site selection, 52
Creery, John, 199, 216, 277
Creil, France, 54
Crosland, Antony, 256
Cross fertilization of protest, 211
Cross-sectoral problems, in airport de-
velopment, 113
Crozier, Michel, 34*n*, 221*n*
Cublington (U.K.)
citizen opposition in, 187, 207
as London airport site, 254–255
Cublington Area Supporters Committee (London), 189

Cultural differences, importance of, 22–23
Culture (*see also* Political values), xxii
Cyert, Richard M., 36n, 103, 113, 122

Dallas, Tex. (*see* Dallas–Fort Worth, Tex.)
Dallas County, Tex., 106, 163, 242, 252
Dallas–Fort Worth, Tex.
  air travel growth, 47t
  and benefit from airport, 119
  field work in, 242, 246, 248, 249
  local authority in, 242
  and Regional Airport Board, 252
Dallas–Fort Worth airport development, 11–12, 22t, 251–253 (*see also* Dallas–Fort Worth Regional Airport; Love Field)
  availability of land for, 116
  and citizen participation, 214n
  citizen protest in, 186t, 187, 191t, 197, 217 (*see also* Citizens Aviation Association; Control Aircraft Noise)
  compensation, 163–164, 171t
  cost of, 70, 147
  decision process in, 106, 107t
  expropriation in, 161t, 163–165, 172–173, 175, 253
  and forecasting, 91, 92, 93
  and Greater Southwest Airport, 11
  lack of economic growth from, 235
  legal basis of, 60
  lessons from, 232
  outcomes in, 101, 106, 107t, 108, 117, 119–120
  and overconstruction, 231
  planning in, 105, 114
  and rational planning, 101
  role of experts in, 119, 137, 267
  site selection in, 53
Dallas–Fort Worth Regional Airport, 11–12, 22t
  criticisms of, 108, 230
  map of, 8, 12
  noise protection by, 55
  transfer traffic for, 231

Dallas–Fort Worth Regional Airport Board
  creation of, 251–252
  objectives of, 114
  role of, 105n, 106
  studies by, 253
Danielson, Michael, 128n, 220n
Davis, Jack, 277
Davis, William, 273
Decision making (*see also* Rational planning; *specific cases of airport development, decision making in*), 30–31, 32
  citizen protest over, 184–185, 213–215
  criteria for, 4
  cross-national variation in, 30
  and culture, 62
  definition of problems in, 32
  and democracy, 215
  and forecasting, 67, 90–92, 226
  impact of technocracy on, 145–146
  and institutions, 42, 56, 62, 101–102, 104–105
  political values in, 42
  and rational planning, 101–102, 104–105, 113
  and rise of technocrats, 131–132
  and social costs, 56–57
  and technological imperative, 42–43, 45, 56–57
  theories of, 30
Declaration of Public Utility (1963) (France), 269
Defenders of Essex (London), 186t, 190, 191t, 193t, 195t, 207, 209, 256
De Gaulle, Charles, vii
De Havilland Aircraft Corporation, 196
Democracy
  and conflict, 236–239
  and decision making, 214–215
  and experts, 24
  and expropriation, 236
  and liberalism, 236–237
  and public-interest criteria, xlv
  and rational planning, 238
  and single-interest groups, 219

and technocracy, 126, 228, 237–239
values of, 236–237
Democratic planning, xxii–xxiii
Democratic rights
and airport development, 181–182,
211–215
and technocrats, 181–182, 212
Department of the Environment
(DOE) (Canada)
in decision making, 107*t*, 109, 110
in expropriation hearing, 168
and inter-agency conflict, 115
in Vancouver, 208, 276, 277–278
Department of Environment (U.K.),
255
Department of the Interior (U.S.),
209, 267
Department of Justice (Canada), 110
Department of Public Works (Canada)
in decision process, 107*t*
in land taking, 169–170, 173, 274
transfer of land to, 262
Department of Public Works, Real
Property Division of (Canada), 277
Department of Regional Economic
Expansion (DREE) (Canada), 243
in decision process, 107*t*
and Montreal study, 264
role of, 108
in site selection, 263
Department of Trade (U.K.), 78, 83,
87, 244
Department of Trade and Industry
(U.K.), 255
Department of Transport (DOT)
(Canada) (*see* Ministry of
Transport)
Department of Transportation (New
York State), 242
Detroit airport, 72
Deutsch, Karl, 35*n*, 63*n*
Diamond and Myers, 137
Dillon-Read, 233, 260
Director-General for Civil Aviation
(France), 243
Director-General's Office for Civil
Aviation (Italy)
in decision process, 111*t*, 259

forecasts by, 260
and SEA revenues, 260
Director General's Office for Land
(Italy), 111*t*
District of Paris
in development of Charles de Gaulle
Airport, 92
in site selection, 106, 108
DOE (*see* Department of the
Environment (Canada))
Doig, Jameson W., 128*n*, 220*n*
Donovan, James, 190
Dorval Airport, Montreal, 14–15, 16
and intra-city airport transfer, 118
map of, 15
proposed closing of, 262, 263
saturation forecast for, 90
and urban development, xlii
Douglas Aircraft, 87
Dubois, Pierre, 160

East Africa, airport development in, 9
Edmonton, Alberta, 231
Elder, Charles D., 216, 221*n*
Elliott Research Corporation,
150*n*–151*n*, 201*n*
Eminent domain (*see also* Expropria-
tion), viii, xvii–xviii
Environment Canada (*see* Department
of the Environment, Canada)
Environmental Assessment Review
Panel, 276
Environmental issues
and citizen protest, 155
sectoral approach to, 27
and Vancouver International Airport,
xxxviii
Environmental Impact Statement, 267
Environmental Protection Agency
(U.S.), 234
Equity
and airport development, 211–213
and citizen protest, 183
and democracy, 181, 212
and public interest, 213
and technocracy, 211–213
Etobicoke, Ontario, 183

Experts (*see also* Technocrats), 31–32
  in central agencies, 133
  and citizen protest, 194
  and client interests, 141–145
  and conflict, 227
  costs of, 147
  and cross-sectoral approach, 149
  and democratic rights, xliv, 24
  independent role for, 148–149
  and information flow, 31
  limited focus of, 138–139, 142–143
  as consultants, 134–136, 141, 227
  and public interest, 143
  and rational planning, 113, 115
  in specialized agencies, 134
Expropriation (*see also* Land
    acquisition)
  and business mentality, 178, 227
  and class distinctions, 227
  in Dallas–Fort Worth, 161*t*,
    163–165, 253
  and democratic rights, 156
  dilemma of, 156–157
  irreversibility of, 159
  laws governing, 176–177
  and liberal democracy, 236
  in Milan, 161*t*, 170–172, 174, 177,
    178, 261
  in Montreal, 161*t*, 166–167,
    172–173, 264
  in New York, 161*t*, 164–165, 176*n*,
    268
  in Paris, 160, 161*t*, 162–163, 178,
    270–271
  partial, 184
  principles of, 161*t*
  procedures, 158–159
  as spur to citizen protest, 175,
    177–178
  state responsibility under, 157–158
  in Toronto, 161*t*, 169–170, 177
  in Vancouver, 159, 161*t*, 167–169,
    177, 274
Expropriation Act (1970) (Canada), 275
  and citizen protest, 160
  and defense of land acquisition, 159
  impact of, 177
  protections under, 166, 176
  and public hearings, 109

Expropriation Hearings, 168, 273
Externalities, 26–27, 35*n*

Fear of face-to-face relations (*see Hor-
    reur du face à face*)
Federal Aviation Administration (FAA)
    (U.S.)
  authority of, 242
  and citizen participation, 214*n*
  commercial orientation of, 59
  and Dallas–Fort Worth airport, 252
  forecasts by, 71, 86, 87, 91, 253,
    267
  responsibility of, 267
  and Stewart site, 265
Federation contre la nuissance des
    avions (France), 195
Fenno, Richard, 104
Ferno, Italy
  citizen protest in, 170
  in Milan airport development, 260
Ferrovie dello Stato (FS) (Italian
    national railroad), 107*t*, 111*t*, 244,
    258
Ferrovie Nord Milano (FNM), xl, 260
Finance Ministry (France) (*see also*
    Administration des domaines), 106
Finance Ministry (Italy), 243
FNM (*see* Ferrovie Nord Milano)
Forecasting, xliii, 67–69
  and decision making, 226
  of economic development, 70
  of environmental impact, 70
  of noise, 84, 93–94
  over-optimism in, 68–69, 83
Forecasting, aviation
  and alternative transportation, 95
  assumptions in, 68–69, 71–72,
    82–85, 95
  and citizen protest, 88
  conservative bias in, 85–86
  and consumer demand, 82–83
  and decision making, 90–92
  disparities in, 72
  fashion in, 86
  faults in, 67, 72, 73, 84–85
  and "hired guns," 86–89
  impact of government action on,
    71–72

as legitimation, 89–90, 92–94, 226
need for, 70–71
overestimation in, 67, 73–82
stages in, 71
and technology, 84
use of, 67–68
Fort Worth, Tex. (*see* Dallas–Fort
Worth, Tex.)
Foulness Island (U.K.)
and citizen protest, 190, 199, 207
as London airport site, 255
studies on, 256
Fragmented authority (*see* Conflict)
France
airport control in, 242
citizen participation in, 218
consulting industry in, 135
decision making in, 30
expropriation in, 176–177
ownership of airports in, 10–11
political culture in, 217
protest channels in, 199
role of experts in, 31
France, government of
airport responsibility in, 56
coordination in, 103–104
Fraser, John, 277
Fraser River, xxxvii, 21, 115
FS (*see* Ferrovie dello Stato)

Gabor, Dennis, 36n, 96n
Galtung, Johan, 31
Garonor, France, xli
Gatwick Airport, London, 12, 255
General Electric, 87
Gilpin, Robert, 63n, 149n
Godfrey, Charles, 98n, 190
Goldman, Guido, 33n, 36n
Goode, Tom, 277
Goussainville, France, 243, 270
Government
and aviation forecasting, 70–72
as guarantor of travel availability, 50
promotion of technology by, 41,
43–44
in controlling technology, 45
Grauer, Dal, 278
Grauer, Lester, 159, 278
Great Britain (*see* United Kingdom)

Greater London Council, 255–256
Greater Southwest Airport, Fort
Worth, 11–12
Greater Vancouver Citizens
Committee for Noise Abatement
(GVCCNA), 186t, 191t, 193t,
195t, 277
Greater Vancouver Regional District
and airport expansion, 21
and Airport Planning Committee,
208, 277
in decision process, 107t, 110
in Expropriation Hearing, 168
opposition funding by, 194
and "slow growth," 123
Great Swamp, Morris County, N.J.,
53, 209, 265, 267
Greeley, Horace, xii
Groupe du Travail Paris-Nord, 269
Guth, Herbert J., 96n, 97n

Hammarskjold, Knut, 65n, 151n
Harvard University, Center for
International Affairs, 248
Haussmann, Georges, ix–xi, xiii–xiv,
xx
Heathrow Airport, London
citizen protest over, 12
development of, 254
saturation forecast for, 81
and urban development, xlii
virtues of, xl
Heclo, Hugh, 35n, 63n
Heidenheimer, Arnold J., 35n, 63n
Hellyer, Paul, 273
Heseltine, Michael, 256
Higgins, Benjamin, 263
Hodge Report (Toronto), 273–274
Hole Committee
development decisions by, 90
as independent board, 256
London traffic study by, 254, 256
Holiday Inn, and Charles de Gaulle
Airport, xli
"Honest graft," xi, xvi
Horonjeff, Robert, 35n, 64n
Horreur du face à face, 22, 56
Houston, Tex., 11, 91, 252
Howard, George P., 96n, 97n

Hudson River Valley Council (New
York), 164, 186*t*, 191, 191*t*, 193*t*,
194, 195*t*, 197, 208, 267
Hunterdon County, New Jersey, 187,
188
Hunterdon-Somerset Association for
Progress, 189
Huntington, Samuel P., 33*n*, 35*n*,
37*n*, 63*n*, 216
Hutton, Charles, 277–278
"Hybrid bill" (*see* Maplin
Development Bill)

Idlewild Airport (*see* John F. Kennedy
Airport)
Incrementalism, 115, 123
Infrastructure, aviation (*see* Airports)
Inspector's Report (London), 256
Institutions
and decision making, 42, 56, 62
as determining political choice, 3
and outcomes, 101–102
as discussed in this book, xxii, 4
and methodology of this book,
25–26
and rational planning, 226
in site selection, 52
Interdepartmental Committee
(London), 208
Interdepartmental Working Group
(London) (*see* Hole Committee),
256
International Airline Pilots Association,
120
International Air Transport Association
(IATA), 7, 58, 118, 242
International Civil Airports
Association, 58, 231–232
International Civil Aviation
Organization, 58
"Iron law of oligarchy," 22–23
Irving, Tex., 55, 242, 251
Ispettorato Telecommunicazioni e
Assistenza al Volo (ITAV), 260
Italia Nostra, 195, 260
Italy
airport control in, 242
citizen activity in, 187

consulting industry in, 135
ownership of airports in, 10
political culture in, 217, 218
property law in, 176
protest channels in, 199
role of experts in, 31
Italy, government of
airport responsibility in, 56
and compensation, 158–159
and Milan development, 111*t*

Jamieson, Don, 206, 273
Jenkins, Roy, 256
Jersey Jetport Site Association (JJSA)
(New York), 88, 186*t*, 190–191,
192, 193*t*, 194, 195*t*, 196, 204,
205, 208, 209, 267
John F. Kennedy Airport, New York,
16, 17
citizen protest, 174
proposed expansion of, 266
and urban development, xlii
Johnstone, Charles, 275
Joint Airport Board (Dallas–Fort
Worth) (*see* Dallas–Fort Worth
Regional Airport Board)

Kansas City, Mo., 252
Kates, Peat, Marwick and Company
aviation forecasts by, 77–78
as Montreal consultants, 137, 262,
263
Kennedy Airport (*see* John F.
Kennedy Airport)
Kent (England), 140
Kiernan, Janet D., 96*n*, 97*n*
"Kingston Plan," 148–149, 232, 272

LaGuardia Airport, New York, xlii,
231, 266
Laing, Arthur B., 277, 278
Land acquisition (*see also*
Compensation; Expropriation), xliii
and citizen protest, 32
cross-national similarities in, 54–55
through expropriation, 54–55
government strategies in, 174, 177

principles followed, 172-173
and residents' interests, 173-174
Landrum and Brown, 267
Land-use decisions, xxi
LaPalombara, Joseph, 24, 217
Le Bourget Airport, Paris
and Charles de Gaulle Airport, 54,
92, 93
closure plans for, 18, 269
and urban development, xlii
Liberalism
and democracy, 236-237
values of, 236-237
Linate Airport, Milan, 13-14
closure of, 259
and inconsistency, 232
saturation forecast for, 81
and urban development, xlii
Lindblom, Charles E., 126n, 127n
Lino report (Italy), 260
Lipsky, Michael, 215
Llewelyn, Davies, 273
Locke, John, 236, 237
Lockheed Aircraft, 87
Logan Airport, Boston, 231
Lombardy, Region of, 111t, 115, 260
Lonate Pozzolo, Italy, 170, 217, 260
London, England
airport map of, 13
air travel forecasts for, 76t, 81, 88
air travel growth for, 47t
division of airport function in, 118
research in, 244, 246, 248
London airport development, 10, 12,
21, 22t, 254-257 (*see also* British
Airports Authority; Heathrow
Airport; Hole Committee; Roskill
Commission)
and adequacy of facilities, 119
citizen protest, 186t, 191t, 208-209,
256 (*see also* Defenders of Essex;
North West Essex and East Herts
Preservation Association; Wing
Airport Resistance Association;
Sheppey Group)
conflict in, 115
decision making in, 30, 107t, 110,
112

outcomes in, 57, 101, 117n
planning in, 101, 174
rationale for, 12
site selection in, 53, 116, 123, 188,
254, 255 (*see also specific sites*)
Love Field, Dallas, 11
citizen protest, 174, 197, 253
as Dallas–Fort Worth alternative,
122, 252
and urban development, xlii
Lowi, Theodore J., 36n, 128n
Luton Airport, U.K., 255
Lyon-Satolas Airport, France, 229

Madison, James, 238
Malpensa Airport, Milan
and economic growth, xli–xlii, 235
expansion plans for, 258
noise levels for, 138, 143
Malton Airport, Toronto, 19
faults of, 230
and Mirabel Airport, 118
and urban development, xlii
Maplin Development Authority, 254,
256
Maplin Development Bill, 209
Maplin Sands, 254, 256
March, James G., 36n, 102, 103, 113,
122
Marchand, Jean, 273
Masefield, Sir Peter, 233
Massey, Hector, 98n, 220n
Methodology, of this book, 24-33,
241-249
choice of case studies for, 9-11
as cross-national, 28-29, 42-43, 232
data collection, 245-248
interview objectives, 245
respondents, selection of, 241-245
travel in field, 248-249
Metropolitan Airlines Committee (New
York), 267
Metropolitan Milanese
and airport access, xl, 260
in decision process, 107t, 111t
officials interviewed in, 244
Metropolitan Commuter Transportation
Authority (*see* Metropolitan

Transportation Authority, New
York)
Metropolitan Toronto Airport Review
Committee (MTARC), 186*t*, 191*t*,
193*t*, 195*t*, 201*n*, 273–274
Metropolitan Transportation Authority
(MTA) (New York)
and citizen protest, 208
in decision process, 107*t*, 112
in expropriation, 164, 165
land taking by, 159
objectives of, 114
as Port Authority rival, 87
responsibility of, 266
and Stewart Airport, 16
studies for, 267
Meynaud, Jean, 36*n*, 149*n*
Milan, Italy
and airport access, xl
airport system of, 10, 13–14, 22*t*
air travel forecasts for, 73, 77, 78*t*
air travel growth for, 47*t*
division of airport function in, 118
field work in, 244, 246, 248
as SEA shareholder, 259
studies by, 260
Milan, subway system of (*see*
Metropolitan Milanese)
Milan, tram system of (*see* Aziende
Trasporte Milanese)
Milan airport development, 13–14,
22*t*, 258–261 (*see also* Linate
Airport; Malpensa Airport; Societa
Esercizi Aeroportuali)
and adequacy of facilities, 119
availability of land for, 116
citizen protest in, 25, 160, 170, 175,
186*t*, 187, 191*t*, 196, 202, 218
(*see also* Comitato d'Agitazione di
Case Nuove; Comitato Popolare di
Lonate Pozzolo)
and closing of Linate Airport, 259
compensation in, 171, 171*t*, 232,
261
conflict in, 115
construction in, 123
decision making in, 107*t*, 110, 111*t*
expropriation in, 161*t*, 170–172,
174, 177, 178, 261

and forecasting, 91, 92
inconsistency in, 207
lack of economic growth from, 235
land acquisition in, 118, 159, 175
lessons from, 232
Lombardy government role in, 115*n*
outcomes of, 57, 101, 107*t*, 117*n*
rational planning in, 101, 114–115
site selection for, 54, 116
and use of expertise, 148
Milbrath, Lester, 215, 216
Milford, Dale, 198
Mills, C. Wright, 30
Minister of Equipment (France), xl,
120
Ministero dei Transporti e Aviazione
Civile (*see* Ministry of Transport
and Civil Aviation, Italy)
Ministry for Air Defense (Italy), 111*t*
Ministry of Aviation (U.K.), 107*t*, 112,
255
Ministry of Defense (Italy), 110, 243,
260
Ministry of Finance (France), 270
Ministry of Finance (Italy), 111*t*
Ministry of Justice (Canada), 168, 243,
277
Ministry of Justice (Italy), 111*t*
Ministry of State for Urban Affairs
(MSUA) (Canada)
in decision making, 110
in expropriation hearing, 168
and opposition funding, 194
study by, 183
in Toronto, 273
transfer of land to, 262
in Vancouver, 277
Ministry of Trade and Industry (Italy),
110
Ministry of Transport (MOT) (Canada)
authority of, 242
and citizen participation, 214
and citizen protest, 88, 198, 204,
205, 207
and compensation, 165–166
consultants employed by, 262
and decision making, 93, 107*t*, 109,
110
displacement by, 118

in experts' conflict, 147
forecasts by, 78, 87, 88, 90, 91, 138
goals of, 59, 123
inconsistency of, 232
and inter-agency conflict, 115
land taking by, 55, 167–168
and Malton expansion, 272
and Montreal development, 14, 114
and public hearings, 116
responsibility of, 11, 263, 273
role of, 108
in site selection conflict, 54
studies by, 277, 278
in Toronto expropriation, 169, 274
Toronto requirements, study for,
    272
transfer of land by, 262
use of experts by, 135, 137,
    141–142, 148
and Vancouver development, xxxvii,
    123, 255, 276, 277
in Vancouver expropriation, 167
Ministry of Transport, Property
    Services Branch (*see* Department
    of Public Works, Real Property
    Division)
Ministry of Transport and Civil
    Aviation (France)
and ADP, 108
in decision process, 107*t*
interviews in, 243
Ministry of Transport and Civil
    Aviation (Italy)
in decision process, 111*t*
forecasts by, 77, 87
and Malpensa rail link, 258
Minters Chapel, Tex., 164
Mirabel Airport, Montreal
criticisms of, 108
and Dorval Airport, 15, 16, 262, 263
and intra-city transfer, 118
map of, 15
size of, 8, 70
traffic at, 16, 120, 262
MM (Milan subway system) (*see*
    Metropolitan Milanese)
Montreal
airport system of, 14, 15, 22*t*
air travel forecasts for, 77–78, 79

air travel growth for, 47*t*
division of function in, 118
field work in, 246, 248
Montreal airport development, 11,
    14–16, 22*t*, 262–264 (*see also*
    Dorval Airport; Mirabel Airport;
    Ministry of Transportation; Ste.
    Scholastique, Quebec)
availability of land for, 116, 116*n*
citizen protest in, 174, 175, 186*t*,
    187, 191*t*, 197 (*see also* Centre
    d'information et d'animation
    communautaire)
and compensation, 166, 171*t*,
    172–173, 264
cost of, 70
decision process in, 106, 107*t*
economic projection for, 94
and expansion instead of
    construction, 51
expropriation for, 161*t*, 166–167,
    172–173, 264
and forecasting, 90, 93
and inconsistent treatment, 232
"Kingston Plan" for, 148–149, 272
lack of economic growth from, xlii,
    235
land acquisition in, 70, 159, 174,
    175
lessons from, 232
outcomes in, 101, 106, 107*t*, 108,
    117, 144
and overconstruction, 231
and public hearings, 116
rational planning in, 101
role of experts in, 119, 137, 144
as steppingstone to other projects,
    119
and Toronto airports, 118
and Vancouver compensation
    precedent, 210
Morris County, New Jersey
as New York airport site, 16, 265
opposition in, 183, 187, 196, 199
political threat from, 202
veto on, 209
Moses, Robert, ix, xiv–xvii, xviii, xx
MOT (*see* Ministry of Transport,
    Canada)

MSUA (*see* Ministry of State for
    Urban Affairs, Canada)
MTA (*see* Metropolitan Transportation
    Authority, New York)

Nachmias, David, 102, 129*n*
Narita Airport, Tokyo, 235
National Academy of Sciences (U.S.),
    265, 266, 267
National Agency for Reconstruction
    (Italy), 111*t*
National Airport, Washington, 231
National Organization to Insure a
    Sound-Controlled Environment
    (NOISE), 195
Nelkin, Dorothy, 34*n*, 151*n*, 178*n*,
    220*n*
Nelson, Joan, 35*n*, 36*n*, 216
Nelson, Richard, xxi
Nespor, Stefano, 260
de Neufville, Richard, 120
Neustadt, Richard, 104
New Airport Now (NAN) (Toronto),
    186*t*, 191*t*, 195*t*, 273
Newark Airport, N.J., 16, 17, 266
Newburgh, New York, 164, 266
    citizen protest in, 183, 194
    political threat from, 202
New Jersey
    and airport development, 54, 90,
        202, 205, 209, 265
    and MTA, 112
    studies for, 267
    in support of protest, 196
New York, City of
    airport system of, 118
    air travel forecasts for, 74*t*, 75*t*, 78,
        79, 81
    air travel growth for, 47*t*
    field work in, 246, 248
New York, State of
    and airport development, 90
    in conflict with New Jersey, 208
    lawsuit against, 165
    legislature picketed, 199–200
    and MTA, 266
    in site selection conflict, 54
    and Stewart Airport, 164, 265
    studies for, 267

New York airport development, 11,
    16, 22*t*, 265–268 (*see also*
    Metropolitan Transportation
    Authority; Port Authority of New
    York and New Jersey; New
    Jersey; New York, State of)
    and adequacy of facilities, 119
    citizen protest in, 164, 186*t*, 187,
        191*t*, 197, 205, 217, 267 (*see also*
        Hudson River Valley Council;
        Jersey Jetport Site Association)
    and compensation, 165, 171*t*, 268
    conflict in, 115
    decision process in, 107*t*
    expropriation for, 161*t*, 164–165,
        176*n*, 268
    and JFK Airport, 174, 266
    land-taking strategy in, 172–173, 174
    outcomes for, 57, 101, 107*t*
    site for, 16, 116, 265 (*see also*
        Morris County, New Jersey;
        Stewart Airport)
Nie, Norman H., 216
Noise
    from aircraft, 84, 93–94
    from Paris Aerotrain, 144
Noise Abatement League (*see* Greater
    Vancouver Citizens Committee for
    Noise Abatement)
North American Aviation, 87
North Central Texas Council of
    Governments, 242
North West Essex and East Herts
    Preservation Association
    (NWEEHPA) (London), 186*t*, 191,
    191*t*, 193*t*, 195*t*, 207, 208, 256
Nuthampstead, U.K., 204, 255

"Office to Help Airport Neighbors,"
    Aeroport de Paris, 163
O'Hare Airport, Chicago, 231
Olmsted, Frederick Law, ix, xi–xiv, xx
Ontario, Canada
    decision process in, 107*t*
    in federal decision making, 109, 110,
        116
    as Quebec rival, 91
    response to protest by, 198
    in site selection conflict, 54

Ontario Department of Treasury and
  Economics, 87, 274
Orange County, N.Y., 112, 165, 268
Orangeville, Ontario, 188
Orly Airport, Paris, 18
  capacity of, 118n
  and Charles de Gaulle Airport, 92,
    93, 269, 270
  citizen protest, 174
  division of traffic in, 118
  and inconsistency, 232
  and urban development, xlii
  virtues of, xl
Ottawa (Canada), 246, 262
Outcomes, of airport development
  and citizen opposition, 207–209
  and conflict, 109–112, 114, 226
  and control, 105–106, 108, 114, 226
  in Dallas–Fort Worth, 106, 107t,
    108
  explanation of, 101–102, 115–122,
    225–226
  failures and faults, 108, 119–120,
    125, 226
  in London, 107t, 112
  in Milan, 107t, 110
  in Montreal, 101, 106, 107t, 108,
    144
  in New York, 57, 101, 107t
  in Paris, 101, 106, 107t, 108
  and rational planning, 106
  and technocrats, 136
  in Toronto, 57, 101, 107t, 109, 117n
  in Vancouver, 57 101, 107t,
    109–110, 117n, 276
  variations in, 101

Page, William, 68
Painter, Martin, 127n, 128n
Parco del Ticino (Italy), 111t, 244
Paris
  air travel forecasts for, 77, 77t
  air travel growth for, 47t
  interviews in, 246, 248
Paris, District of, 269
Paris airport development, 10, 18, 22t,
    269–271 (*see also* Aeroport de
    Paris; Le Bourget Airport; Charles
    de Gaulle Airport; Orly Airport)

access planning for, 120
citizen protest in, 160, 186t, 191t,
    196 (*see also* Comite de defense
    des riverains de Roissy)
compensation in, xli, 160–162, 171t,
    173, 232, 271
conflict in, 235
decision process in, 106, 107t
expropriation in, 160, 161t,
    162–163, 178, 270–271
and forecasting, 91, 92, 93–94
and inconsistency of treatment, 232
land acquisition for, 55, 173, 175
lessons from, 232
and noise tax, 163, 184n, 207
outcomes in, 101, 106, 107t, 108
and overconstruction, 231
planning for, 144
rationale for, 269
site selection in, 53, 54, 116, 116n
    (*see also* Plains of France)
time required for, 70
Paris-Nord, 92, 269 (*see also* Charles
    de Gaulle Airport)
Parkin and Associates, 272
Parkin Plan, 273
Peak, G. Wayne, 216
Pennock, J. Roland, 178n, 179n
Pennsylvania Central Railroad, 165
People or Planes (POP) (Toronto), 146,
    186t, 191, 191t, 192, 193t, 194,
    195t, 196, 198, 199, 200, 201,
    204, 206, 207, 208, 209, 273
People over Welfare (POW) (Toronto),
    189
Peters, Guy, 104
Piccolo Teatro, Milan, as protest site,
    258
Pickering Township (Canada)
  agricultural value of, 204
  airport sentiment in, 201
  expropriation in, 118, 169
  as new Toronto airport site, 19, 88,
    272, 273, 274
Pickersgill, Jack, 167, 274
Pickering Impact Study, 138
Plains of France
  availability of land in, 116, 116n
  price for land in, 160

as site of Charles de Gaulle Airport, 18

Planning (*see also* Decision making; Rational planning), xxxvii–xxxviii, 168

Policy process (*see* Decision making)

Political culture, 24, 217, 218 (*see also* Citizen protest; Political values)

Political science (*see also* Methodology, of this book)
  comparative politics, 25–26, 28–29
  cross-case comparison in, 28–29
  cross-national study in, 42–43, 232
  institutional approach, 25–26
  limitations of traditional approaches, 29
  political sociology, 25

Political values
  and decision making, 42, 62
  as determining political choice, 1, 3, 21–23, 24–25, 33

Politicians, 182, 184 (*see also* Bureaucrats; Democracy; Institutions)

Port Authority of New York and New Jersey
  aviation forecasts by, 73, 79, 81, 83n, 87, 90
  basis of authority, xviii–xix
  and citizen participation, 234
  and citizen protest, 201, 205
  and conflict, 115
  in decision process, 107t, 112
  and economic aims, 59, 61
  in expropriation, 164
  and fourth N.Y. airport, 16, 90, 265
  officials interviewed in, 242
  responsibility of, 266
  and site selection, 53, 54
  vs. state government, 197
  and Stewart Airport, 116
  studies by, 265, 267
  technocrats in, 134
  use of experts by, 135, 142

Porter, John, 30

Port of London Authority, 256

Powell, G. Bingham, 34n, 35n

Private property, taking of (*see* Expropriation; Land acquisition)

Problem definition, in airport development, 46, 49

Protest (*see* Citizen protest)

Public Inquiry of Stansted (*see* Chelmsford Inquiry, London)

Public interest
  in airport development, 61
  and business mentality, 123, 225, 238
  and client preferences, 143
  constituencies, 212
  criteria for, xlv
  and technology, xliv, 24

Public protest (*see* Citizen protest)

Public works, viii–xix

Pulling, Robert W., 96n, 97n

Quebec
  decision process in, 107t
  and expropriation, 178
  on Eastern Ontario airport, 148–149
  in federal decision making, 109, 110, 116
  and "Kingston Plan," 148–149
  as Ontario rival, 91
  opposition funding by, 194
  promises to, 94, 120
  in site selection conflict, 54

Rational planning (*see also* Airport development; Decision making)
  in airport development, 105, 225, 226
  assumptions in, 125
  and business mentality, 122–123, 125–126, 225, 226
  and citizen protest, 122
  and conflict, 102–104, 106, 226, 238
  and coordination, 103–104
  definition of, 102
  and different outcomes, 101–102
  experts as performing, 113
  and institutions, 226
  and liberal democracy, 238
  narrow focus of, 113, 122
  treatment of, in this book, xliii

RATP (Regie Autonome de Transports Parisiens—Paris Metro), xl, 120, 122, 243, 269, 270

Regional Plan Association (New York), 72, 267
Reynolds, John, 277
Richmond, British Columbia, 168, 201, 277
Rockefeller, Nelson, 16, 112, 164, 265, 266
Roissy-en-France
  airport construction at, 44
  citizen protest in, 187, 194, 206, 217, 270
  ease of development in, 54
  expropriation in, 162–163
  noise at, 94
Roper, Elmo, 215
Rosenbloom, David H., 102, 126*n*, 129*n*
Roskill, Justice, 254
Roskill Commission
  and citizen protest, 188, 198, 200, 209
  and cost-benefit analysis, 123, 138, 139
  experts' bias in, 138
  forecasts by, 76
  as independent board, 256
  as opposition forum, 201
  report of, 254, 255
  sites listed by, 13
  and social costs, 54
  study by, 256
  and use of expertise, 148
Rousseau, Jean-Jacques, 236, 237
Rush, Howard, 68

Ste. Scholastique, Quebec (*see also* Montreal airport development)
  citizen opposition in, 187, 205, 217, 262 (*see also* Centre d'information et d'animation communautaire, Montreal)
  compensation to, 207
  expropriation in, 166, 262
  as new airport site, 16, 263
Sani, Giacomo, 218
Schilling, Warner, 103
SEA (*see* Societa Esercizi Aeroportuali)
Sea Island, British Columbia
  airport expansion on, 274

bridge built to, xl
  expropriation on, 118, 159, 167, 168, 169, 178
  and Vancouver International Airport, xxxvii, 21
Sea Island Ratepayers Association (SIRA) (Vancouver)
  in land acquisition agreement, 275
  in protest, 277
  and Vancouver land taking, 167–168
Sectoral approach, in policy analysis, 25–28
  and cost-benefit analysis, 27
  and environmental issues, 27
  and externalities, 26–27, 35*n*
  faults of, 27–28
Seelye Stevenson, Value and Knecht, 267
Senior Council for Public Works (Italy), 111*t*
Sheppey, Isle of, 256
Sheppey Group (London), 142, 186*t*, 188, 191*t*, 193*t*, 195*t*
Shonfield, Andrew, xxi
Sierra Club, in support of citizen protest, 195
Simon, Herbert, 102
Single-interest groups (*see also* Citizen action groups)
  as citizen opposition, 181, 185
  and democracy, 219
  impact of, xliv–xlv
  lack of study on, 185
  membership of, 185–187
  treatment of, in this book, xliii
Site selection
  and citizen protest, 173
  and consumer demand, 52
  and economic growth, 52
  factors in, 51–52
  irregularities in, 53
  secrecy in, 52–53
  and social costs, 54
  and technical expertise, 175
  variability in, 52
  weighing of factors in, 52, 53–54
Smith, Adam, 236
S.N.C.F. (*see* Société Nationale des Chemins de Fer)

Societa Esercizi Aeroportuali (SEA)
and access to Milan airport, xl
and ADP, 138, 143
and citizen protest, 205
and compensation, 171
in decision process, 107t, 110, 111t
difficulties of, 209
and forecasting, 81, 87, 92, 94, 143
inconsistency of, 232
land taking by, 170, 258, 259
objectives of, 59, 123
in opposition to Bergamo airport, 259
role of experts in, 134, 135–136,
142–143, 148
studies by, 205, 260
Societa per la Matematica e
l'Economica Applicate (SOMEA),
260
Société Nationale des Chemins de Fer
(SNCF) (France), xl, 120, 243,
269, 272
Société de Recherche Economique et
Sociologie en Agriculture, 162
Society for Aircraft Noise Abatement
(SANA) (Toronto), 186t, 188, 191t,
192, 193t, 195t, 204, 273
Solberg Airport, N.J., 188
SOMEA (see Societa per la
Matematica e l'Economica
Applicate)
Somma Lombardo, Italy, 170, 217,
258, 260
Southwest Marine Drive, Vancouver,
169
SST, 84
Stansted, England
citizen protest in, 183, 187, 207
and cost considerations, 116
development of, 255
as London airport site, 123, 254
study on, 256
State Park of Ticino (see Parco del
Ticino, Italy)
Stead, Gordon, 277
Stewart, Walter, 36n, 104
Stewart Airport
acquisition by New York State, 164,
265

and citizen protest, 197, 208, 268
(see also Hudson River Valley
Council; Stop the Jetport Action
Committee)
consultants on, 119
continued plans for, 123
and courts, 267
development of, 266
displacement for, 118
as fourth N.Y. airport, 16
land taking for, 116, 159
map of, 17
STOL-craft, 84
Stop the Jetport Action Committee
(SJAC) (New York), 186t, 188,
191t, 193t, 195t, 200
Structural functionalism, 25–26, 33
Suleiman, Ezra, 103
Sullivan, Thomas, 252
Supreme Council for Public Works
(see Consiglio Superiore dei
Lavori Pubblicci, Italy)

TAAP (see Toronto Area Airports
Project)
Tarrant County, Tex., 163, 242, 252
Taylor, Rupert, 142
Technical Institute for Beetroot
(France), 160
Technical Office for Land Evaluations,
Province of Varese (see Ufficio
Tecnico Erariale, Italy)
Technocracy
and bureaucracy, 125
and democracy, xliii, 126, 228,
237–239
and democratic rights, 181–182
and equity, 211–213
Technocrats (see also Experts)
in airport development, 132
vs. bureaucrats, 132–133
and citizen protest, 132, 142
and compensation, 175
conflict among, 146–147
and data limitations, 139–140
definition, 132
and decision making, 131–132,
145–146

disciplinary biases of, 138–139
impact of, 136, 145–147
and inter-agency conflict, 139
as public-works decision makers, xix
rise of, 131
as servants, 132, 141
and site selection, 175
treatment of, in this book, xliii
varieties of, 132, 134
Technological determinism, 42
Technological imperative
assessment of, 56–62
vs. business mentality, 60–62
and cross-national similarities,
45–46, 49
definition, 42
and decision making, 45
objections to, 42, 124
and political decision making, 42
treatment of, in this book, xliii
and varied outcomes, 57, 62
Technology
and airport development, 124, 229
and aviation forecasting, 84
and business mentality, xliv
and citizen participation, 3–4
comparative analysis of, 5
and democratic rights, xliv
as determining political choices, 23,
24–25, 33, 57
government promotion of, 41, 43–44
in international airports, 43
in plan of this book, xliii, 4, 5–6, 29
and politics, xliv
and public interest, 24
questioning of, 45
Teterboro Airport, N.J., 267
Tempelhof Airport, Berlin, xlii
Tennessee Valley Authority, 210
Texas, 106, 197, 242
TGV (high speed rail system), 229
Third World, and airport
development, 9, 144, 235
Thurleigh, U.K., 204, 255
Tippets-Abbett-McCarthy-Stratton
(TAMS), 137, 152, 253
Tobin, Austin, 265
de Tocqueville, Alexis, 217

Toronto
airport map of, 19
air travel congestion in, 118
air travel forecasts for, 72, 78, 80t
air travel growth of, 47t
field work in, 246, 248
Toronto airport development, 11, 19,
21, 22t, 272–274 (*see also* Malton
Airport; Ministry of Transport;
Toronto Area Airports Project)
and adequacy of facilities, 119
citizen protest in, 91, 165, 174, 175,
186t, 187, 191t, 197, 198 (*see also*
Metropolitan Toronto Airport
Review Committee; New Airport
Now; People or Planes; Society
for Aircraft Noise Abatement)
compensation in, 169–170, 171t,
172, 207
conflict in, 115
decision making in, 107t, 110
and economic aims, 61
and expansion instead of
construction, 51
experts' conflict in, 146
expropriation in, 161t, 169–170, 177
and Expropriation Act, 166
and forecasting, 87, 90, 142
and inconsistency of treatment, 232
and "Kingston Plan," 148, 272
land acquisition in, 118, 159, 172,
175, 274
and "minimum international
airport," 147
vs. Mirabel, 120
outcomes of, 57, 101, 104, 107t,
109, 117n
and Parkin Plan, 19, 272, 273
and public hearings, 116
site for, 19, 116, 123, 272, 273, 274
(*see also* Pickering Township)
use of experts for, 137, 144, 146,
148
and Vancouver compensation
precedent, 210
Toronto Area Airports Project (TAAP),
93, 273, 274
Trans-Plan, Inc., 267

Transport Canada (*see* Ministry of
    Transport, Canada)
Troop, Peter, 275
"Troop Formula," 168, 169, 275
Tyhurst, James, 190, 277

Ufficio Tecnico Erariale (UTE) (Italy)
    as determining compensation,
        158–159, 171
    in decision process, 111*t*
    in land taking, 173
    in property evaluation, 258
Ulam, Adam, 33*n*, 36*n*
Uniform Relocation Assistance and
    Real Property Acquisition Policies
    Act (U.S.), 176
United Kingdom
    airport control in, 56, 242
    citizen advisory committees in, 199
    citizen participation in, 218
    consulting industry in, 135
    control of airports in, 10–11
    cost-benefit analysis in, 139
    decision process in, 107*t*
    forecasting in, 91
    political culture in, 217
    protest channels in, 198
    role of experts in, 31
United Kingdom, Ministry of Aviation
    (*see* Ministry of Aviation (U.K.))
United Research, Inc., 88
United States
    air traffic growth in, 85–86
    airport responsibility in, 56
    citizen advisory committees in, 199
    citizen protest in, 160, 187
    and compensation, 232
    conflict reduction in, 235
    consulting industry in, 135
    coordination in, 104
    expropriation in, 161*t*, 177
    law and property in, 176
    political culture in, 217
    role of experts in, 31
United States Air Force, 164, 266
University Consortium for Research on
    North America, 248

Urban encroachment, on airports, xlii,
    50
UTE (*see* Ufficio Tecnico Erariale)

Vallée de Montmorency, France, 94
Vancouver
    air travel forecasts for, 78, 88
    air travel growth for, 47*t*, 80*t*
    field work in, 244, 246, 248
    sale of airport by, 274
    study by, 277
Vancouver airport development,
        xxxvii–xxxviii, 11, 21, 22*t*,
        274–278 (*see also* Airport Planning
        Committee; Ministry of Transport)
    and adequacy of facilities, 119
    citizen participation in, 214
    citizen protest of, 88, 165, 175,
        186*t*, 187, 191*t*, 197, 198 (*see also*
        Community Forum; Greater
        Vancouver Citizens Committee for
        Noise Abatement; Sea Island
        Ratepayers Association)
    compensation for land, 171*n*, 173,
        210
    conflict in, 115
    decision process in, 107*t*, 110
    delay in, 109
    as expansion over construction, 51
    expropriation in, 159, 161*t*,
        167–169, 177, 274
    and Expropriation Act, 166
    and forecasting, 91, 92, 141–142
    and inconsistency of treatment, 232
    land acquisition for, 172–175, 278
    Master Plan for, 276
    outcomes for, 57, 101, 107*t*,
        109–110, 117*n*, 276
    planning conflicts of, xxxvii–xxxviii
    as policy issue, 169
    provincial government role, 116
    rationale for, 276
    site selection, 21, 116, 123, 274, 276
        (*see also* Sea Island)
    and social impact study, 140
Vancouver International Airport
    aviation forecasts for, 80*t*

map of, 20
traffic at, 276
and urban development, xlii
Vancouver International Airport
    Planning Committee (*see* Airport
    Planning Committee, Vancouver)
Varese, Province of, Italy
    and airport access, 260
    noise study for, 136, 138, 143, 260
    and property evaluation, 258
    SEA in conflict with, 209
    as SEA shareholder, 259
Verba, Sidney, 24, 216, 217, 218
Veterans Land Administration (VLA)
    (Canada), xxxvii, 274
Vietnam War, 211
Volpe International Terminal (*see*
    Logan Airport, Boston)

Walther, H. O., 142
Webb and Knapp, 278
Welland Canal, 137

Western European Airports
    Association, 232
White paper, on proposed London
    airport (1967)
    and citizen opposition, 208–209
    forecasts in, 76, 81
    repudiation of, 254
Wildavsky, Aaron, 127n
Wilensky, Harold, xxi
Wilson, Malcolm, 265
Wing Airport Resistance Association
    (WARA) (United Kingdom), 186t,
    189, 191t, 192, 193t, 195t, 204,
    207, 209, 256
Winner, Langdon, 33n, 42
Wood, Derrick, 190, 199, 256
Woodward, Julian L., 215
World Wildlife Federation, 195, 244,
    260

Ziegler, L. Harmon, 215
Zupan, Jeffrey M., 96n, 98n